A MODERN HISTORY

OF

SOMALIA

Nation and State in the Horn of Africa

I. M. LEWIS

LONGMAN

LONGMAN GROUP LIMITED
LONDON AND NEW YORK

Associated companies, branches and
representatives throughout the world

First published 1980

ISBN 0 582 64657.X

Lewis, Ioan Myrddin
  A modern history of Somalia. – Revised ed.
  1. Somalia – History
  I. Title II. Modern history of Somaliland
  from nation to state
  967'.73   DT401   79–40569

Set in Monotype Garamond
Printed in Hong Kong by
Wilture Enterprises (International) Ltd

Acknowledgement
Chapters 1 to 8 of this book were first published
as *The Modern History of Somaliland, from Nation to State,*
I. M. Lewis, Weidenfeld and Nicolson, London, 1965.
The cover photograph shows a Somali student teaching
a nomad to write Somali in the new Latin script during the
Rural Development Campaign of 1974 (courtesy of Ministry
of Information, Somali Democratic Republic).

CONTENTS

Preface   iv

Chapter

   I The Physical and Social Setting   1

  II Before Partition   18

 III The Imperial Partition: 1860–97   40

 IV The Dervish Fight for Freedom: 1900–20   63

  V Somali Unification: The Italian East African
     Empire   92

 VI The Restoration of Colonial Frontiers: 1940–50   116

VII From Trusteeship to Independence: 1950–60   139

VIII The Problems of Independence   166

 IX The Somali Revolution: 1969–76   205

  X Nationalism, Ethnicity and Revolution in the
     Horn of Africa   226

Maps   253

Notes   256

Index   273

PREFACE

THIS STUDY OF Somali nationalism in the Horn of Africa traces the unfolding of a process rare in the recent history of the continent – the transformation (albeit still incomplete) of a traditional African nation into a modern state. This phenomenon is rendered all the more striking by its juxtaposition with a rival tradition of political sovereignty in neighbouring Ethiopia, a state built on conquest and comprising many different nations, peoples and tribes. Although in pre-colonial Africa, both nation-states (like Somalia) and pluralist, multi-national states (like Ethiopia) were equally common, European colonization and decolonization altered decisively the balance in favour of the latter type. Today, with the exception of the Somali Democratic Republic, Botswana and Lesotho, sub-Saharan Africa's traditional nations and tribes are not autonomous, but encapsulated in multi-national states formed haphazardly and without regard to ethnic boundaries in the European partition of the continent. Indeed, the 'map of Africa' today is virtually identical with that under European colonization at the turn of century. It is this prevailing cultural heterogeneity, with the growth of ethnic friction and conflict since independence, which makes African states so fragile and so vehemently attached to the territorial frontiers which alone establish their identity. If this accounts for what amounts to a kind of frontier-fetishism, it also explains the pervasive preoccupation with 'nation-building', the very understandable struggle to achieve a culturally homogeneous unity which would transform these colonial artefacts into viable nation-states. This aspiration is not, as some theorists of nationalism claim, a mere imitation of European nationalism – nineteenth-century or otherwise – but rather harks back to the pre-colonial era when Africa consisted of a mixture of authentic nation-states (like Buganda) and of multi-national states (like Ethiopia). The contemporary prevalence of the latter pluralist type, reminiscent in many respects of the Habsburg empire, should not be allowed to distort our vision of the past and its connexion with the present.

The growth of modern Somali nationalism which is our primary concern here, and its conflict with Ethiopian (or Amhara) nationalism, has to be seen against this wider background if its special features are to be fully understood. Here the contrast with Ethiopia is critical. Despite its ancient Christian legacy, its Semitic languages and its long-standing if intermittent connexions with Europe, Ethiopia is essentially a traditional, pluralist African conquest state. It owes its exalted status in African eyes to a unique, if fortuitous, combination of virtues. Having defeated a European army (the Italians at Adowa in 1896), it not only survived the scramble for Africa but gained from it, participating directly in the partition of Somali and other territory, almost as an equal partner. Its biblical connexions, as Marcus Garvey appreciated and contemporary Rastafarians commemorate, made Ethiopia a potent symbol of Black Power. This image was enhanced rather than diminished by the sympathy which Ethiopia attracted as a consequence of Mussolini's ill-starred attempt to create an Italian East African empire on the eve of the Second World War. The career, remarkable by any standards, of Haile Selassie, Ethiopia's last and most famous Emperor, greatly consolidated and magnified this unique legacy. As well as this brilliant endowment, Ethiopia enjoyed the additional advantage of embodying in traditional African form the Habsburg style of state which colonization and decolonization left as the dominant strain in the continent.

If Ethiopia thus entered the modern African stage with all the attributes necessary for playing a leading role, it could not readily dispense with the expansionist dynamic enshrined in its traditional political structure. This rivalled and challenged the expansionist principle patently present in the constitution of the neighbouring Somali Republic. The creator of modern Ethiopia, Emperor Menelik, had in the nineteenth century participated directly with Britain, France and Italy in the dismemberment of the Somali nation and its division into five colonial territories. The formation in 1960 of a Somali state, based on the principle of self-determination (here in effect Somali-determination) applied to the former British and Italian Somali territories, established a state which was inherently incomplete. It left outside the goal of Somali nationalist aspirations the remaining three Somali communities then under foreign rule in the French territory of Jibuti, in Harar Province of Ethiopia (mainly the Ogaden), and in the northern province of Kenya (then still British). Other African nationalists in their Habsburg-style states sought to transform their fragile tribal mosaics into cohesive nations. For the Somalis, in contrast, the problem was – through self-determination for the three remaining Somali colonies – to extend the frontiers of the state to embrace the whole nation, a process with familiar parallels in Europe. In traditional African terms, as we have emphasized, this aspiration was as legitimate as that enshrined in the formation of pluralist states.

However, as our study attempts to demonstrate, the juxtaposition in the Horn of Africa of two expansionist states (Ethiopia and the Somali Republic) based on the two contrasting principles of state formation inevitably creates a fundamental structural conflict of interests and aspirations which is more deeply grounded and refractory than the routine 'border problems' that plague inter-state relations in Africa. With the achievement of independence from European rule, the principle of self-determination which was formerly so stridently voiced by African nationalists has receded into the background (except in relation to those last bastions of European power in Rhodesia and South Africa), to be replaced by the principle of the inviolability of Africa's frontiers. Thus, partly no doubt because of Ethiopia's special status, and partly because their own states are of the pluralist, territorially-bounded type, African leaders have shown little inclination to see the Somali dispute as a self-determination issue meriting serious attention and sympathy. This is understandable and, as I have suggested, reflects the fortuitous bias in favour of tribally heterogeneous states produced by the colonial experience. The strains this model imposes in Zaire, in Ethiopia, in Nigeria and numerous other cases are increasingly evident. It seems probable, moreover, that the powerful currents of ethnicity and local level nationalism which are today so prominent in Europe and America are likely to encourage rather than discourage parallel movements in Africa. Whether this is a good or a bad thing is debatable and certainly outside the scope of this book. It seems, however, inevitable that if Africa is to overcome its systemic instabilities, concessions may have to be made to its ethnic problems – whether through devolution or some other process. Certainly the acute problem posed by the antagonism between Ethiopian and Somali irredentism in the Horn of Africa will not disappear by being ignored. This is not a matter that can be satisfactorily resolved by short-term military expedients. What is needed is a radical political solution based on a full and accurate appreciation of the unique features of this intractable issue. If this book can contribute in any way towards this outcome, it will have more than served its purpose.

My more specific aim is to provide a sociologically and anthropologically informed history of the Somali people. In contrast to many other cases where political aspirations inspire cultural cohesion and nationalism is invoked as a means rather than an end, here I argue cultural nationalism has in contrast become increasingly politicized. But if the history of Somali nationalism is the major focus of this book, I have also tried to explore a number of subsidiary questions. In this unusual case of multiple colonization (by Britain, France, Ethiopia and Italy), I have given some attention to the different, and often conflicting, interests and policies of the colonial powers, and to the contrasts which can be seen between the various systems of rule established by them. I have also sought to elucidate the circumstances of the holy war waged by Sayyid Muhammad 'Abdille Hassan against the colonizers between 1900 and 1920. Here I have made considerable use of unpublished traditional source material and have tried to indicate something of the complex interplay of personalities, clan attachments and religious rivalries which forms the essential background to any full comprehension of Sayyid Muhammad's aims and achievements.

This brings me to the problem of sources. Although there is a considerable, indeed formidable, body of detailed writing on Somali linguistics, ethnography and sociology, and in Italian particularly an extensive general literature, history remains poorly served. With a very few honourable exceptions, there is scarcely a detailed study of any period, and few works which show insight into the cultural complexities of internal history. So it was in 1965 when the first edition of this book was published. In this revised edition, to which I have added two new chapters

PREFACE

covering the period up to 1978, it is a pleasure to record the
remarkable growth of an indigenous school of Somali history
spearheaded by the brilliant self-taught historian, Sheikh Jama
Umar 'Ise, whose splendid volumes on Sayyid Muhammad
'Abdille Hassan are, by any standards, models of scholarship. *

I have limited chapter notes and references to a minimum,
seeking only to document or dilate upon a few important points,
and to call attention to some of the more useful sources. Many of
the works cited contain lists of other relevant publications.
Fuller bibliographies are contained in my *Peoples of the Horn of
Africa*, London, 1969, pp. 177–89 and my review of research
trends in the *Journal of Semitic Studies*, 1964, Vol. IX, No. 1, pp.
122–34.

My use of both written and oral material is largely conditioned
by my social anthropological field research in Somalia in 1955–7,
in 1962, 1964 and 1974 – not to mention briefer visits in the
intervening years. My original research in what was then the
British Somaliland Protectorate was supported by the Colonial
Science Research Council, then by the Carnegie Trust and in 1974
by the British Academy. I owe an inestimable debt to all these
bodies and to a succession of Somali governments, Somali
officials and friends whose generosity far exceeds my capacity to
repay it adequately. I have been studying Somali culture and
society for twenty-five years and, in the anthropological tradition,
have participated in (to some limited extent at least) as well as
observed historical developments in this period. While visiting
the Somali Democratic Republic in 1974, as a guest of the Somali
National Academy and the Ministry of Higher Education, I was
delighted to find, quite by chance, a group of Somali teachers
engaged in the preparation of textbooks in the new Somali script,
translating passages from the earlier version of this book. I hope
that this new, enlarged volume may prove equally useful.

I.M.L.   *London, 1978*

*See also Dr. Ali Abdirahman Hersi's recent Ph. D. thesis ('The Arab Factor
in Somali History', University of California, Los Angeles, 1977). This bold
work, whose publication is eagerly awaited, is especially important for its
extensive use of newly discovered or previously neglected Arabic sources.

viii

Buuggan waxa aan u hibaynayaa dadka Soomaaliyeed, kuwa taariikhdooda sameeya iyo kuwa qoraba, aniga oo galladcelin uga dhigayaa sidii wacnayd ee ay iigu soo dhaweeyeen dalkooda. Waxa kale oo aan ugu deeqayaa gabadhayda 'Joanna', loona yaqaan Dalmara oo ku dhalatay Soomaaliya, haatanna ku jirta raadraaca taariikhda Afrika.

CHAPTER I

THE PHYSICAL AND SOCIAL SETTING

The Land

WITH A POPULATION numbering perhaps four and a half million, the Somali-speaking people can scarcely be regarded as a large nation. Yet they form one of the largest single ethnic blocks in Africa, and though sparsely distributed on the ground, live in continuous occupation of a great expanse of territory covering almost 400,000 square miles in the north-east corner, or 'Horn', of the continent facing Arabia. From the region of the Awash Valley in the north-west, this often arid territory occupied by the Somali stretches round the periphery of the Ethiopian highlands and along the Gulf of Aden and Indian Ocean coasts down to the Tana River in northern Kenya. This region forms a well-defined geographical and ethnic unit which Somalis see as a natural base for a sovereign state, although today it is split up into four separate parts. In the ex-French Republic of Jibuti, which became independent in 1977, Somalis make up about half the local population (c. 200,000 in 350,000); in the adjoining country of Ethiopia (mainly in Harar and Bale Provinces) they number probably almost one million; in the Somali Republic itself their strength is approximately 3,250,000;[1] and finally, in the North-Eastern Region of Kenya,[2] they number about 250,000. Outside this region, other Somali are settled as traders and merchants in many of the towns and ports of East Africa (e.g. in Nairobi); in Aden, in whose history they played an important role; and throughout Saudi Arabia and the Gulf States. Farther afield, the roving existence which life at sea affords has led to the establishment of small and fluctuating immigrant Somali communities in such diverse European ports as Marseilles, Naples, London, and Cardiff.

In their dry savanna homeland, the Somali are essentially a

nation of pastoral nomads, forced by the exigencies of their demanding climate and environment to move with their flocks of sheep and goats and herds of camels and cattle in an endless quest for water and pasturage. The northern coastal plains (Guban, from *gub* to burn) which extend from the lava-strewn deserts of the Republic of Jibuti along the Gulf of Aden shore to Cape Guardafui are especially arid. Here the annual rainfall rarely exceeds three inches and is concentrated in the comparatively cool months from October to January. In the hot months between June and September, the Guban fully lives up to its name; and except for the urban populations of such ports as Jibuti (pop. 180,000), capital of this territory, and Berbera (pop. 60,000) in the Somali Republic, at this season is generally deserted by the nomadic tribesmen for the cooler and greener hills which rise behind it. Despite its often torrid heat and low rainfall, however, the run-off from the mountains behind ensures that water is usually easily obtainable only a few feet below the Guban's characteristically sandy soil. With these water resources, and the sometimes surprisingly generous pastures which spring up after the autumn rains, this region provides the winter quarters for the most northerly Somali clans.

The Golis and Ogo mountains, with their magnificent and often dangerously precipitous escarpments, which rise behind the coast dominate the whole physical structure of the region. This range achieves a height of almost 8,000 feet at points to the east; and, in the west where it joins the Ethiopian Highlands, rises as high as 9,000 feet near the ancient Muslim city of Harar (pop. 60,000). To the south, the mountains descend into a great tilting plateau which has an average elevation of 3,000 feet in the centre, and embraces most of the Somali hinterland. On the hills and in the north of the plateau, which includes the important centre of Hargeisa (pop. 60,000), capital of the former British Somaliland Protectorate, the rainfall is sometimes as high as twenty inches, especially in the northwest where, between Hargeisa and Harar, sorghum is cultivated. Here water is generally abundant, and the perennial wells excavated often at great depth in the dry waddies provide the winter watering-places of many of the central clans of the north. To the south of Hargeisa, the northern plateau opens into that vast wilderness of thorn-bush and tall grasses known as the Haud. In northern Somali the name 'Haud' means simply 'south'; and the region, which contains no permanent water, is of indeterminate extent. The northern and eastern tips lie within the Somali Republic, while the western and southern portions (the latter merging with the Ogaden plains) form part of Harar Province of Ethiopia.

To the south of the Haud, the plateau inclines gradually from the west as it reaches out towards the south-eastern coast of the Indian Ocean. Here it is intersected by low-lying plains and valleys, lined with welcome vegetation, which are more widely spaced than in the precipitate north. The most important of these southerly valleys are those traversed by the Shebelle and Juba Rivers as they flow from their sources in the Ethiopian Highlands towards the coast. Both rivers contain water in all seasons and together make up the main river system of the whole Somali area north of the Tana.

The Shebelle or 'Leopard' River extends for some 1,250 miles but does not enter the sea; after crossing the southern part of the Ogaden it flows eastwards as far as Balad, twenty miles from the Indian Ocean coast, where it veers to the south to cover a further 170 miles before disappearing in a series of marshes and sand-flats close to Jelib on the Juba. Only with exceptionally heavy rains does the river join the Juba and thus succeed in reaching the sea. To the south of the Shebelle, the Juba River descends much more directly from the Ethiopian Highlands to the sea which it enters as a strong stream some 250 yards wide near the port of Kismayu (pop. 60,000). It is navigable by shallow draft vessels from its mouth to the rapids a few miles beyond Bardera, in which the German explorer von der Decken's steamship *Welf* perished in 1865. In contrast to the wide belts of scrub-bush and grassy plains, interspersed with lonely tall acacias, which cover so much of the country, these two rivers are lined in places by narrow lanes of attractive high forest. Here elephant and hippopotamus replace the multitude of antelope species and smaller game which are so abundant elsewhere.

In comparison with the north, the southern part of the Somali Republic between the Shebelle and Juba Rivers is relatively well-watered: and, indeed by local standards, so fecund as to constitute the richest arable zone in the whole of Somaliland. Here the principal crops are sorghum, Indian corn, sesame, beans, squashes and manioc; as well as fruits, and sugar-cane, which, however, are mainly cultivated in the plantations owned by large corporations. The chief export crop is the banana produced by a number of Italian and Somali companies on a quota system controlled by the Somali government. Outside this fertile southern zone between the rivers there are no comparable arable resources, although the north-west of the country now supplies a valuable sorghum harvest and grain production is expanding as well as date cultivation.

Despite this general division in physical features and productivity, both northern and southern Somaliland are subject to a similar cycle of seasons associated with the rotation of the N.E. and S.W. monsoons. Apart from a variety of minor local wet periods, the main rains fall twice yearly – between March and June, and between September and December – throughout the region. The dry seasons are similarly distributed: but while the hottest time of the year on the northern coast falls in the summer, the south is by contrast pleasantly cool at this period. In the volcanic wastes of the Jibuti Republic, this fairly regular cycle of seasons loses most of its coherence, and the weather is generally less predictable except in its torridity. Mogadishu (pop. 350,000), capital of the Somali Republic, and the other ports of the southern Indian Ocean coast have a climate which though often humid is pleasant in the cool season.

The People

Ethnically and culturally the Somali belong to the Hamitic ethnic group. Their closest kinsmen are the surrounding Hamitic (or as they are often called 'Cushitic') peoples of the Ethiopian lowlands, and Eritrea – the traditionally bellicose 'Afar (or Danakil),[3] the Oromo (Galla), Saho, and Beja. Their immediate neighbours to the north are the pastoral 'Afar with whom they share Jibuti and who extend into Eritrea and Ethiopia. To the west, in Ethiopia, the Somali are bounded by the cultivating and pastoral Oromo; and in the south by the Boran Galla of Kenya.

Although there is much variation amongst them, the physical features which immediately strike the eye and seem most generally characteristic of the Somali people as a whole, are their tall stature,

4

thin bone structure and decidedly long and narrow heads. Skin colour shows a wide range from a coppery brown to a dusky black. In their facial features particularly, the Somali also exhibit evidence of their long-standing relations with Arabia; and, in the south, amongst the Digil and Rahanweyn tribes, physical traces of their past contact with Oromo and Bantu peoples in this region. Traditionally, however, Somali set most store by their Arabian connexions and delight in vaunting those traditions which proclaim their descent from noble Arabian lineages and from the family of the Prophet. These claims, dismissed by Somali nationalists today as fanciful, are nevertheless part and parcel of the traditional and profound Somali attachment to Islam. They commemorate the many centuries of contacts between the Somali and Arabian coasts which have brought Islam and many other elements of Muslim Arab culture.

Thus, the Somali language[4] contains a considerable number of Arabic loan-words, and Arabic itself is sufficiently widely known to be regarded almost as a second language. Nevertheless, although unwritten until 1972,[5] Somali retained its distinctiveness as a separate and extremely vigorous tongue possessing an unusually rich oral literature. Within Somali, the widest dialect difference is between the speech of the northern pastoralists and of the Digil and Rahanweyn cultivators. These differ to much the same extent as Portuguese and Spanish. Yet, since many of its speakers are also familiar with standard Somali, the existence of this distinctive southern dialect does not alter the fact that, from the Jibuti Republic to Garissa on the Tana River in Kenya, standard Somali provides a single channel of communication and a common medium in which poems and songs compete for popularity. Poetry, it should be added, today as much as in the past, plays a vital part in Somali culture, and the extensive use of radio broadcasting has enhanced rather than diminished its significance. Often a poem is not merely the private voice of the author, but frequently the collective tongue of a pressure group, and propaganda either for peace or for war is more effectively spread through poetry than by any other means.[6]

The distinction between the speech of the Digil and Rahanweyn and their more nomadic countrymen to their north and south is one feature of the wider cultural, geographic, and historical primary division in the Somali nation between the 'Samale' or Somali proper and the Sab. The former make up the bulk of the nation, and their name (Samale) has come to include the Sab, perhaps in the same fashion as the word 'English' is applied by foreigners to all the inhabitants of the British Isles. This larger fraction of the Somali nation consists of four principal groups of clans or 'clan-families'. Descent in Somaliland is traced in the male line, and each of these units has a separate founding ancestor from whom, traditionally, its members trace their descent and take their collective name.

The Samale clan-families comprise the Dir, Isaq, Hawiye, and Darod, all of whom are primarily pastoral nomads and variously distributed throughout the land. The Dir clans ('Ise and Gadabursi) are mainly concentrated in the western part of the northern regions of the Somali Republic (the former British Somaliland), in the Jibuti Republic, and the east of Harar Province of Ethiopia: a smaller nucleus also occurs in the south in Merca District, and between Brava and the Juba River. The Isaq (who in conjunction with the Dir probably number almost three quarters of a million) live mainly in the centre of the northern regions of the Republic, but in their grazing movements extend also into the Ethiopian Haud. To their east, the Isaq mingle with the Dulbahante and Warsangeli divisions of the Darod who, with a strength of perhaps one and a half million, are the largest and most widely distributed of all the Somali clan-families. As well as the eastern part of the former British Somaliland Protectorate, the Darod occupy the Eastern, Nugal and Mudug Regions, most of the Haud and Ogaden; and finally, although interrupted by a large wedge of Hawiye in the centre of the Republic and the Digil and Rahanweyn between the rivers, extend eventually into the North-eastern Region of Kenya. The Hawiye, who boast probably more than half a million persons, live to the south of the Majerteyn Darod in Mudug, Hiran, and round Mogadishu. They extend some way across the Shebelle basin where they mingle with the Sab tribes, and also, like the Darod, are found again in strength in the northern part of Kenya.

With a total population of little more than half a million, the Sab tribes are less numerous, less widely distributed, and contain only the two major divisions already mentioned. Having a stronger

6

cultivating bias than any other Somali group, their habitat is primarily restricted to the fertile region between the two rivers where their pastoral and cultivating sections mingle not only with each other but also with pastoral nomads of the other Samale clans.

In addition to these divisions of the Somali nation whose distribution and relative strengths are vital to an understanding of both past and present events, there are a number of smaller ethnic communities which require to be mentioned. The most numerous (some 80,000 strong) are Somalized Bantu scattered in cultivating villages along the Shebelle and Juba Rivers and in pockets between them. These derive in part from earlier Bantu and Swahili-speaking groups, as well as from former slave populations freed by the suppression of slavery at the end of the nineteenth century. Although they still retain today much of their physical distinctiveness, socially these communities are becoming increasingly absorbed in the wider Somali society. The best-known groups are the Shidle, and Shabelle on the Shebelle River, and the Wa-Gosha (or Gosha) and Gobaweyn on the Juba. Less numerous but economically and politically more important is the immigrant Asian community (some 40,000 in the Republic, about 12,000 in the Jibuti Republic) which consists chiefly of Arabs (many of families domiciled on the coast for centuries) and a smaller number of Indians, Pakistanis, and Persians. Similarly largely occupied in trade and commerce and also in development and technical aid is the small European community, numbering about 5,000 in Somalia and 15,000 in the Republic of Jibuti. The few permanent European settlers live mainly as farmers and estate owners in the south of Somalia.

Mode of life and social institutions

Although the proportion of people who practise some form of cultivation is higher, probably not much more than an eighth of the total Somali population are sedentary cultivators, and these mainly the southern Digil and Rahanweyn tribes. Thus for the majority, in the arid conditions of the north, centre, and extreme south (Northern Kenya) of their country, nomadism is the prevailing economic response, and mode of livelihood and social institutions in general are tightly adjusted to the scant resources of an

7

unenviably harsh environment. In these regions, with their home-wells as a focus of distribution, the pastoralists move over many miles in the year, driving from pasturage to pasturage and water-point to water-point their flocks of sheep and goats and herds of camels, and, in some southern areas particularly, of cattle also.

Of this mixed patrimony, although the Somali pony remains the prestige beast *par excellence*, it is their camels which Somali most esteem. These are carefully bred for milk and for carriage. Milch camels provide milk for the pastoralist on which alone he often depends for his diet; burden camels, which are not normally rid-den except by the sick, transport his collapsible hut or tent and all his worldly possessions from place to place. Camel-hide is used to make sandals to protect his feet on the long treks across the coun-try. But these uses do not in themselves account for the way in which the pastoralists value their camels or, despite the long-standing and wide use of money as a currency, explain why it is primarily in the size and quality of his camels that a man's sub-stance is most tellingly measured. This striking bias in Somali cul-ture is best expressed briefly by saying that in their social as well as economic transactions the pastoralists operate on a camel standard. Thus the exchange of substantial gifts of livestock and other wealth which cements a marriage between a man and a woman and their respective kin is ideally, and often still in practice, conducted in the medium of camels.[7] It is also in camels that the value of a man's life and the subordinate position of women are expressed in material terms. Generally the blood-compensation due when a man is killed is rated at one hundred camels, while a woman's life is valued at half that figure. Lesser injuries too are similarly com-pounded in a standard tariff of damages expressed in different amounts of camels. Although in these traditional terms sheep and goats are regarded as a sort of small change, they evoke none of the interest and attention which men bestow on their camels and indeed are considered primarily as the concern of women.

This difference in attitudes is consistent with the fact that the milch camels and sheep and goats usually form two separate herd-ing units. A man's wife, or wives, and children move with the flocks which provide them with milk and the few burden camels necessary for the transport of their tents and effects. With their much greater powers of endurance and resistance to drought, a man's milch camels are herded by his unmarried brothers, sons and nephews, moving widely and rapidly about the country far from the sheep and goats which, in the dry seasons especially, have to cling closely to sources of water. Particularly in the dry seasons, when long and frequent treks back and forth between the pastures and wells are required, camel-herding is an arduous and exacting occupation and one well calculated to foster in the young camel boys all those traits of independence and resourcefulness which are so strongly delineated in the Somali character.

With this dual system of herding the nomads move about their country with their livestock in search of pasture and water, ordering their movements to conform as closely as possible to the distribution of these two necessities of life. Pasturage is regarded as a gift of God to man in general, or rather to Somalis, and is not considered to belong to specific groups. Generally, people and stock are most widely deployed after the rains when the grazing is fresh and green; while in the dry seasons they are forced to concentrate nearer the wells and make do with what grazing can be found in their proximity. Only the herds of milch camels with their attendants to some extent escape from this seasonal curtailment of movement, and even they must also be placed in areas where they can conveniently satisfy their less frequent but more substantial watering needs. Rights of access to water depend primarily upon its abundance and the ease with which it can be utilized. Only where water is not freely available, and where the expenditure of much labour and effort is required before it can be used, are exclusive rights asserted and maintained, if necessary, by force. And while in the general nomadic flux there is no rigid localization of pastoral groups and no appreciable development of ties to locality, the 'home-wells' regularly frequented in the dry seasons, and the trading settlements which spring up all over Somaliland wherever people congregate even temporarily round water, provide some check to a more random pattern of pastoral mobility.

Subject to the vagaries of the seasons and the very variable distribution of rain and grazing, there is some tendency for the clans, which are the largest effective political units with populations ranging from 10,000 to over 100,000 persons, to be vaguely associated with particular areas of pasturage. Clans are traditionally led by Sultans (in Somali: *Suldan, Boqar, Garad, Ugas,* etc.). This title, which evokes something of the pomp and splendour of Islamic states, ill accords with the actual position of Somali clan leaders, who are normally little more than convenient figureheads and lack any firmly institutionalized power. Indeed for the majority of northern Somali clans, the position of Sultan, though often hereditary, is hardly more than an honorific title dignifying a man whose effective power is often no greater, and sometimes less, than that of other clan elders. It is in fact the elders – and this in its broadest connotation includes all adult men – who control clan affairs. With a few special exceptions, a hierarchical pattern of authority is foreign to pastoral Somali society which in its customary processes of decision-making is democratic almost to the point of anarchy. It must at once be added, however, that this markedly unstratified traditional political system does recognize a subordinate category of people known as *sab* who fulfil such specialized and to the nomad degrading tasks as hunting, leather- and metal-working, and haircutting. The *sab* who practise these occupations form a minute fraction of the total population and, traditionally, were separated from other Somali by restrictions on marriage and commensality. Today the enfranchisement of these Midgans, Tumals, and Yibirs, is far advanced and most of their traditional disabilities are disappearing.[8]

With the absence of institutionalized hierarchical authority, Somali pastoral groups are not held together by attachment to chiefs. This principle of government which is so important in so many other parts of Africa is here replaced by binding ties of patrilineal kinship. Somali political allegiances are determined by descent in the male line; and, whatever their precise historical content, it is their lineage genealogies which direct the lines of political alliance and division. Although Somalis sometimes compare the functions of their genealogies to a person's address in Europe, to understand their true significance it has to be realized that far more is at stake here than mere pride of pedigree. These genealogies define the basic political and legal status of the individual in Somali society at large and assign him a specific place in the social system.

While descent in the male line (*tol*) is thus the traditional basis of Somali social organization, it does not act alone but in conjunction with a form of political contract (*her*). It is this second, and scarcely less vital principle which is used to evoke and give precise definition to the diffuse ties of descent. As recorded in the genealogies which children learn by heart, descent presents the individual with a wide range of kinsmen amongst whom he selects friends and foes according to the context of his interests. Thus, sometimes he acts in the capacity of a member of his clan-family, sometimes as a member of a constituent clan, and sometimes as a member of one of the large number of lineages into which his clan is divided internally. But, within this series of diffuse attachments, his most binding and most frequently mobilized loyalty is to his '*diya*-paying group'. This unit, with a fighting strength of from a few hundred to a few thousand men, consists of close kinsmen united by a specific contractual alliance whose terms stipulate that they should pay and receive blood-compensation (Arabic, *diya*) in concert. An injury done by or to any member of the group implicates all those who are a party to its treaty. Thus if a man of one group is killed by a man of another, the first group will collectively claim the damages due from the second. At the same time, within any group a high degree of co-operation and mutual collaboration traditionally prevails.

To grasp the significance of this political and legal entity – whose members do not necessarily camp or move together in the pastures – but which is nevertheless the most clearly defined political unit in pastoral society, it must be appreciated that the nomadic Somali are a warlike people, driven by the poverty of their resources to intense competition for access to water and grazing.[9] Even under modern administration self-help still retains much force as the most effective sanction for redressing wrongs and adjusting political and legal issues between groups. Hence, with the difficulty under present conditions of adequately policing much of the country, the security of the individual pastoralist's person and property depends ultimately upon his membership of a *diya*-paying group. At the same time, the existence of this well-defined social group does not preclude the formation of wider kinship alliances as occasion demands. Thus, within a clan, *diya*-paying group opposes *diya*-paying group; but when the clan is attacked by an external enemy, its various sections unite in common cause to protect their interests. Beyond the clan, the widest kinship ties are those which unite kindred clans as members of the same clan-family. In the traditional social system, however, the six clan-families into which the Somali nation is divided (the Dir, Isaq, Hawiye and Darod; and the Digil and Rahanweyn) are generally too large, too widely scattered, and too unwieldy to act as effective corporate political units. But in the modern situation of party political competition, such extended kinship links acquired new vitality and significance.

Cultivation

In the better watered reaches of the western part of the Northern Regions of the Somali Republic and in Harar Province of Ethiopia, where sorghum millet is grown over an extensive area, this pastoral regime has undergone a number of modifications. Here within the past two or three generations, following the example of the neighbouring Oromo farmers, Somali pastoralists have turned to plough cultivation, and stable agricultural villages have replaced the nomads' temporary encampments. With a growing sense of attachment to territory, ties of neighbourhood are beginning to be acknowledged, which, although no formal change in the traditional political system has yet taken place, constitute a novel principle of grouping. This is evident in the organization on a basis of co-residence, as much as of kinship, of such local agricultural activities as harvesting and the excavation and maintenance of the ponds on which these cultivating settlements depend for their water supplies. With this development goes also a change in the bias of livestock husbandry: here cattle largely replace camels, and oxen are trained to the plough. The transition, however, is by no means absolute for many farmers are either transhumant, or, although themselves sedentary, maintain herds of camels which are sent out to graze in the charge of younger kinsmen. Farmers indeed frequently invest profits from the sale of sorghum in camels; and apart from these distinctions there is little difference in culture or social organization between the pastoral and cultivating sections of a clan.

The influence of agriculture in modifying the traditional pattern of life is taken a stage further amongst the Digil and Rahanweyn cultivators, of the south of the Republic. Here the tilling of the soil, in which a hand hoe is used, has a tradition going back several centuries, and the innovating influence of agriculture has been strengthened and reinforced by such additional factors as the great admixture of peoples and cultures which has taken place in this region. For, besides a small core of the descendants of people of original Digil stock, the Sab represent an amalgam of many different elements of which the most disparate are perhaps those deriving from Bantu and Oromo sources. And despite the fact that the great bulk of the Rahanweyn are today people of northern nomadic provenance, representatives of almost every northern Somali clan being found amongst them, many traits of the old mixed Digil and Rahanweyn culture have survived and are now those characteristic of this group as a whole. Thus it is the Digil-Rahanweyn dialect of Somali, and not that of the majority of more recent settlers, which is often spoken here; although many people speak both this and northern Somali. Similarly, and equally distinctive, however unimportant it may sound, while amongst the northern nomads tea is the universal dish appropriate to every social occasion and in the austere nomadic life synonymous with feasting, amongst the Digil and Rahanweyn the corresponding delicacy consists of green coffee beans cooked in ghee. As the coffee beans are eaten, and passed from guest to guest in wooden dishes, the scalding ghee in which they have been cooked is rubbed over the arms and hair and snuffed up the nostrils with a characteristic and inimitable gesture of satisfaction and pleasure.

More significant for the present purpose, however, is the fact that in contrast to northern nomadic society, there is greater social stratification amongst the Sab. In general three classes of land-holders are recognized: putative descendants of the original groups, long-standing accretions, and finally, recently adopted clients. Those of the first category in every Digil and Rahanweyn clan possess the most secure rights to arable land and play a dominant part in ritual. Those in the other categories, and especially in the last, traditionally enjoy less secure possession of land. Membership in any clan is acquired by a client undertaking to accept all the obligations, including that of solidarity in the blood feud, binding his protectors. Only so long as these duties are fulfilled can a client traditionally continue to cultivate the land which he has been allocated by his hosts. At the same time, as might be anticipated, the institution of chieftainship is more developed, and the traditional lineage structure of the north is not so marked. In some cases, indeed, loyalties based on common residence and common land-holding are more important politically than those defined by kinship. Thus many of the names of clans and sub-sections in this area refer directly to territory and denote what are essentially territorial aggregations. Etymologically, the name 'Rahanweyn' itself means simply 'large crowd'. Finally, while often in the past Galla and Bantu serfs (now almost completely assimilated) provided some of the labour for cultivation and house construction, these and other activities for which collective enterprise is necessary are today entrusted to work-parties of young men recruited on a basis of residence rather than kinship.

Thus the division between the Sab and Samale, which is the widest cleavage in the Somali nation, depends not only on the different economic interests of the two groups but also upon their cultural divergencies. Traditionally these distinctions are entrenched ·by the nomad's assumption of proud superiority and contempt for his southern countrymen, and the latter's corresponding resentment and isolation. Yet despite this, the gulf between the two communities is not so wide as might at first appear, or as insuperable as each sometimes likes to suggest. As has been said, many of the Sab are in reality of northern pastoral origin; many again speak both dialects of Somali. Moreover there is much that draws the two groups together economically. Many of the southern cultivators not only have pastoral clients, but are also sometimes clients to pastoralists. Nomads moving across the territory of cultivators frequently exchange their milk in the dry seasons for the right to pasture their herds on the farmers' fields. Similar transactions also regulate the use of water-holes by both parties. In addition the Sab trade much of their grain with the nomads: and many of those pastoralists whose grazing movements impinge on this fertile area have adopted, or are adopting, cultivation, despite their traditional scorn for agriculture, just as in the north-west, where it seems to be profitable, nomads are turning to the plough. Finally, the Swahili riverine communities are also similarly involved in this increasingly ramified network of ties of mutual advantage between pastoralist and farmer.

This sense of a commonality of interests, over and above the cultural and historical features which divide the two halves of the nation, is traditionally represented in the national genealogy in which ultimately every Somali group finds a place. Here Sab and Samale are represented as brothers of common descent from a line of ancestors which eventually links the Somali as a whole to Arabia and proclaims their single origin. The distinction between the cultivating life of the Sab clans, and the pastoral nomadism of the Samale, is fittingly explained by a number of picturesque legends and anecdotes in terms of the different characters attributed to their respective founding ancestors.

Religion and society

Despite the prevalence of war, feud, and fighting, particularly amongst the nomads, not all men are warriors. Those who devote their lives to religion and in some sense practise as men of God are known as *wadads* or sheikhs, and thus distinguished from the remainder and majority of men who, whatever secular calling they follow, fall into the category of warriors (*waranleh*, 'spear-bearers'). This general division still retains validity despite the proliferation of occupations available today. Men of religion, or sheikhs – to use the Arabic title which is usually applied to the more learned among them – fulfil such important tasks as teaching the young the Quran and the elements of the faith, solemnizing marriage and ruling according to the Shariah in matrimonial disputes and inheritance, assessing damages for injury, and generally directing the religious life of the community in which they live. Essentially their rôle is to mediate between men; and, through the Prophet, between man and God – with the help of the many local saints to whom Somali look for support in the preferment of their pleas for divine aid and succour. Ideally, whatever their *diya*-paying and clan obligations, men of religion are assumed to stand outside secular rivalry and conflict, although in practice in the circumstances of Somali life this expectation is rarely if ever fully sustained. What is significant here, however, is that in contrast to the position in so many other Muslim countries, Somali sheikhs are not normally political leaders and only in exceptional circumstances assume political power.

Although the settled conditions and more hierarchical political organization of the southern cultivating Somali might seem to afford more purchase to the theocratic ordinances of Islam, it would be very mistaken to imagine that Islam rests lightly upon the pastoralists. For if in some respects the circumstances of southern cultivating society conform more closely to the theocratic Muslim pattern elsewhere, there is no distinction between the two communities in their observance of the five 'pillars' of their faith – the profession of belief in God and the Prophet, the daily prayers, fasting, alms-giving, and pilgrimage. Nor, certainly, are the nomads any less pious or devout than the cultivators. The true position is rather that each community has adopted Islam in slightly different ways corresponding to differences in traditional social organization.[10] Thus, for example, while in the north many lineage ancestors have been accommodated in Islam as saints, in the south where lineage organization is less strong and important, these are replaced by a multitude of purely local figures who have no significance as founders of kinship groups. Hence, notwithstanding these regional variations, for the Somali as a whole, it is not too much to say that in many important respects Islam has become one of the mainsprings of Somali culture; and to nomad and cultivator alike the profession of the faith has the force almost of an initiation rite into their society.

Thus while the Somali draw many of their distinctive characteristics, especially their strong egalitarianism, their political acumen and opportunism, and their fierce traditional pride and contempt for other nations from their own traditional culture, they also owe much to Islam. And it is typical of their mutual dependence upon these two founts of their culture that the highly pragmatic view of life which nomadism seems to foster is tempered by a deep and, as it must seem to some, fatalistic trust in the power of God and His Prophet. Above all, Islam adds depth and coherence to those common elements of traditional culture which, over and above their many sectional divisions, unite Somalis and provide the basis for their strong national consciousness. Although the Somali did not traditionally form a unitary state, it is this heritage of cultural nationalism which, strengthened by Islam, lies behind Somali nationalism today.

The features of Somali culture and society which have been

briefly touched on here are important for the understanding of what follows. The modern as well as the ancient history of Somalia* cannot be properly understood or appreciated, save in the most superficial terms, unless the progress of events is viewed against this very particular social background. Only in relation to the unremitting struggle for survival in a hostile environment, where men are engaged in a seemingly unending cycle of alliance and counter-alliance, is it possible to interpret both the past and present reaction of the Somali to local and external events. Modern developments have wrought great changes. But, in the absence of far-reaching urbanization, it is only quite recently (since the mid-1960s) that radical or extensive changes have begun to erode the traditional fabric of society. The interplay between these and traditional forces is examined in the final chapters of this book.

*Throughout this book, unless otherwise indicated, the terms 'Somalia' and 'Somaliland' are used interchangeably to denote the territory occupied by the Somali-speaking people.

CHAPTER II

BEFORE PARTITION

UNTIL THE late nineteenth century the history of the eastern Horn of Africa is dominated by the protracted Somali expansion from the north, and the rise and decline of Muslim emporia along the coast. To a certain extent each of these two themes has its own particular history, but at no time over the centuries was one entirely independent of the other. The gradual enlargement of their territory by the Somali was not achieved by movements in the hinterland only, nor were events on the coast without their effect in the interior. About the tenth century, however, when our brief account opens, the pressure of events ran from the coast towards the hinterland. But by the mid-nineteenth century, a state approaching equilibrium had been attained between the outward pressures of movements in the interior and the inward trend from the coast: if anything, indeed, the balance was tipped in favour of the hinterland which had come to exert a dominant political influence over the coastal settlements. For the history of the coast documentary evidence from various sources is available, at least in some periods; but for events in the hinterland the historian has to rely much more heavily upon the testimony of oral tradition. Fortunately, oral records are on the whole sufficiently abundant and consistent in their essentials, to enable the broad outlines of the Somali dispersal to be traced with what is probably a considerable degree of accuracy. Certainly the evidence at present available leaves no doubt that the gradual expansion over the last ten centuries of the Hamitic Somali from the shores of the Gulf of Aden to the plains of northern Kenya is one of the most sustained, and in its effects, far-reaching movements of population in the history of North-East Africa.

This was not a migration into an entirely empty land. It in-

18

volved considerable displacements of other populations, and the Somali sphere was only extended by dint of continuous war and boodshed. Those who were mainly involved, other than the Somali, were the ethnically related Oromo peoples – or some of them – and a mixed negroid or Bantu population which, prior to the incursions of the Hamitic Galla and Somali, appears to have possessed part of the south of what is today the Somali Republic.

This people known to the early Arab geographers as the Zanj, and apparently mainly concentrated in the fertile land between the two rivers, seems to have consisted of two principal elements. The major part was made up of Bantu cultivators living as sedentaries along the banks of the Shebelle and Juba and in fertile pockets between them. They figure in Oromo and Somali tradition, particularly in the folk history of those Digil and Rahanweyn clans who entered this area from the north and settled amongst the Zanj as a kind of aristocracy. Something of their life and social organization is preserved also in a late Arabic compilation known as the 'Book of the Zanj'.[1] These sources are supplemented by more tangible evidence. Remnants, partly Swahili-speaking, reinforced by ex-slaves from the south and from Zanzibar, survive today in five distinct communities along the Shebelle River and in two on the Juba. Others again are found near Baidoa in the hinterland between the rivers, and also in Brava district in whose ancient capital a Swahili dialect, Chimbalazi, is spoken to this day.

The second component of this pre-Hamitic population, apparently much less numerous than the riverine cultivators, was a hunting and fishing people living a precarious nomadic existence. Their present-day descendants, much affected by Hamitic influence, survive in a few scattered groups in Jubaland and in the south of the Republic where they are generally known as Ribi (or Wa-Ribi) and as Boni (or Wa-Boni). Their mode of life and their physical appearance invite comparison with the Bushmen of other areas of Africa, but their precise ethnic affiliation is still obscure. Politically and economically they seem to have been attached in small groups to the Bantu sedentaries, and still today small hunting communities of this stock are found living under the tutelage of more powerful Bantu groups in the south.

By about the tenth century it seems that these two peoples, who are not necessarily the autochthonous inhabitants of the area, did not extend north of the Shebelle, and were in contact with the Oromo tribes, who, in turn, were already under pressure from the expanding Somali in the north-east corner of the Horn. This distribution gleaned from oral tradition is supported by the descriptions of the early Arab geographers who refer to the Hamitic peoples (the Galla and Somali) of the north and centre by the classical name 'Berberi', and distinguish them in physical features and culture from the Zanj to their south.

The coastal settlements

Before tracing the sustained surge southwards which displaced most of this Zanj population, and led eventually to the present distribution of peoples in the Horn of Africa and indirectly in part to those in Ethiopia, it is necessary to consider first the early phases of Arab settlement along the coast. This is essential since Arab colonization introduced a more diversified technology, and a more centralized system of government, which, however restricted its influence, undoubtedly made itself felt even in nomadic areas. Finally and most important of all, the new immigration brought Islam, the unifying force which played so significant a part in the sixteenth-century conquest of Abyssinia, and which remains the living faith of the Somali and of many of the peoples of present-day Ethiopia. At the same time, indirectly if not always directly, the absorption of Arab settlers seems to have given an impetus to, or to have precipitated, the movements of expansion of the Somali and Oromo.

There is little doubt that Arabian penetration along the northern and eastern Somali coasts is of great antiquity. It probably antedates the Islamic period; and certainly shortly after the *hegira* Muslim Arabs and Persians were developing a string of coastal settlements in Somaliland. From their condition today, from traditional sources, and from such documentary evidence as is available, it is clear that in these towns Arab and Persian merchants and prosyletizers settled usually as local aristocracies, bringing the faith, marrying local women, and eventually merging with the local inhabitants to form a mixed Somali-Arab culture and society. This new culture representing varying degrees of mixing and blending at different periods, and by no means uniform throughout the coastal ports, is the Somali counterpart to the more extensive Swahili society of the East African coast to the south.

Typical of these centres of Arab influence in northern Somaliland are the ancient ports of Zeila and Berbera. Zeila first appears in the record of the Arab geographers at the end of the ninth century when it is mentioned by Al-Ya'qubi, and later writers describe it in increasing detail. Berbera, which conserves the name given in classical times to the northern coast as a whole, is probably of similar antiquity, but its history is much more obscure: it is first mentioned by the Arab geographers in the thirteenth century. Thereafter, beyond the fact that during the period of Portuguese domination in the Red Sea the town was sacked in 1518 by Saldanha, little is known of its history until the eighteenth and nineteenth centuries. Similar obscurity surrounds most of the history of the ancient port of Mait, on the eastern coast in Erigavo District, and one of the principal centres of early Somali expansion.

Thus at present, of the northern ports as a whole, most is known of Zeila. This town was politically the most important of the Arab settlements in the north and owed its economic prosperity, at times considerable, to its geographical position as one of the chief ports of the Abyssinian hinterland in the trade with Arabia and the Orient. Through Zeila local Somali produce, consisting chiefly of hides and skins, precious gums, ghee, and ostrich feathers, and slaves and ivory from the Abyssinian highlands, were exported: and cloth, dates, iron, weapons, and chinaware and pottery imported. Politically, Zeila was originally the centre of the Muslim emirate of Adal, part of the state of Ifat, which lay in the plateau region of eastern Shoa. From the time at which the port enters Islamic history, it had apparently a mixed Arab, Somali, and Danakil ('Afar) population. In the course of time, no one knows exactly when, these three separate elements to some extent fused to form a distinctive Zeila culture and Zeila dialect which was a blend of Arabic, Somali, and 'Afar. No doubt other minor ethnic elements were also represented; Persians and Indians seem to have settled in the port at an early period, but the main elements in the Zeila culture were Arab, Somali, and 'Afar.

While these northern coastal centres were developing, Arab settlers were opening, or consolidating, a similar series of ports in the south. Of these the most important were Mogadishu, the present capital of the Republic, Brava, and Merca – all commercial towns largely dependent for their prosperity upon the entrepôt trade between Abyssinia, Arabia, and the markets of the East. The evidence of the Arab geographers and local inscriptions and documents indicate that by the first half of the tenth century Arab and Persian colonizers had established themselves at Mogadishu in considerable numbers, some years prior to the foundation of Kilwa on the East African Coast. Similar sources suggest that Merca and Brava are of comparable antiquity. Thus, in both the north and south, by the tenth century a ring of coastal emporia had been created, largely as a result of Arab enterprise, and through these ports Islam and Arab trade had gained a foothold which, consolidated and strengthened in succeeding centuries, was to become the foundation for Muslim expansion in North East Africa.

The first wave of Somali expansion

About the tenth century while these developments were proceeding on the coast, some areas of southern Somaliland were still occupied by the Zanj, while the land in the centre and north was occupied first by various Oromo tribes and then by the Somali. From Somali oral tradition and other local evidence it seems that Galla communities occupied part of northern Somaliland prior to the Somali, and that about the tenth century, the Dir Somali, universally regarded as the oldest Somali stock, were already in possession of much of the northern coastal strip and exerting pressure on the Oromo to their south.

But the first major impetus to Somali migration which tradition records is the arrival from Arabia of Sheikh Isma 'il Jabarti about the tenth or eleventh century and the expansion of his descendants, the Darod clans, from their early seat in the north-east corner of Somaliland. This cannot be dated with certainty, but the period suggested here accords well with the sequence of subsequent events. It was followed perhaps some two centuries later by the arrival from Arabia of Sheikh Isaq, founder of the Isaq Somali, who settled to the west of the Darod at Mait where his domed tomb stands today, and who like his predecessor Darod, married with the local Dir Somali. While present evidence, or to be more precise, its lack, suggests that much of the very detailed tradition which surrounds these two patriarchs is legend, it appears likely that it should be interpreted as reflecting the growth and expansion of the Darod and Isaq clans about this time. For while Darod and Isaq themselves may be legendary figures, there is no doubt about the authenticity of the movements of their descendants.

On this interpretation, by the twelfth century the Dir and Darod, and later the Isaq, were pressing upon their Oromo neighbours and the great series of movements which finally disestablished the latter may be said to have begun. Folk tradition today offers little information as to the causes of this movement. It would not be unreasonable to conjecture, however, that mounting population pressure, augmented by continued Arab immigration, and perhaps exacerbated by a series of severe droughts, prompted a general Somali movement in search of new pastures. And this was no doubt furthered by the messianic and militant fervour of early Islam.

If the motives which inspired this great movement of population are still a matter of conjecture, its general direction is fortunately well-established. The traditions of migration indicate that in their gradual and by no means co-ordinated movement towards the south the Somali followed two main routes: they descended from the north down the valley of the Shebelle and its tributaries, or along the line of coastal wells on the Indian Ocean littoral. These vital water-lines were traversed by group after group as the Somali as a whole moved forward.

As the Darod and Isaq grew in numbers and territory, the Dir vacated the north-eastern region of Somaliland, striking off westwards and to the south. In the west, the powerful 'Ise and Gadabursi clans pushed gradually, and not without many set-backs, into what is today Harar Province of Ethiopia and the Jibuti Republic, leaving the graves of their ancestors several hundred miles behind them in the Erigavo District. To anticipate for a moment; it seems that by the sixteenth and seventeenth centuries these movements by the Dir, Darod, and Isaq, had proceeded to the point where the two last groups of clans had taken over much of northern Somaliland and the Ogaden region of Ethiopia. Thus, probably by the close of the seventeenth century, the clans of northern Somaliland had assumed approximately their present distribution, although the gradual drift of population from the north still continued.

In step with these Somali movements in the north, the Oromo were increasingly thrust westwards and southwards and ultimately into Ethiopia, where, however, their main invasion did not take place until the sixteenth century.[2] As the Galla withdrew, not without fierce resistance, the Bantu Zanj were in turn driven farther south. At the same time, the Somali were maintaining their pressure and, in the early stages of their expansion, some groups managed to infiltrate through the main mass of the Galla. In this way, by as early as the thirteenth century, some sections of the Hawiye had established themselves close to the Arab settlement of Merca. The occupation of this region by the Hawiye at this time is recorded by the geographer Ibn Sa'id, and this is the earliest known mention of any Somali group.[3] Local tradition throws further light on the position and suggests that these Hawiye intruders had already been preceded by other Somali groups including several sections of the Digil. These earlier pioneers had apparently settled for a time on the Shebelle River, and had then crossed the river to move towards the coast. Thus, in the thirteenth century, the position apparently was that the coastal region between Itala and Merca was occupied by the Hawiye Somali: farther south and towards the interior lay the Digil; and finally to the west the Oromo were still dominant.

In this general area local tradition has most to say of the Ajuran, a clan tracing descent from a noble Arabian patriarch on the same pattern as the Darod and Isaq, but related maternally to the Hawiye. Under a hereditary dynasty, the Ajuran consolidated their position as the masters of the fertile reaches of the lower Shebelle basin and established a commercial connexion with the port of Mogadishu where some of their own clansmen were also settled. The fortunes of this Ajuran Sultanate thus appear to have been closely linked with those of Mogadishu, and the Ajuran reached the summit of their power in the late fifteenth or early sixteenth century when Mogadishu was ruled by the Muzaffar dynasty,[4] an aristocracy related to the Ajuran if not actually of Ajuran stock. Later, the two centres declined about the same time; but this is again to anticipate.

The holy wars against Abyssinia

Before pursuing these Somali migrations, we must refer briefly to the prolonged struggle further inland between the expanding Abyssinian Kingdom and the loose congeries of Islamic states including Ifat, Dawaro, Bale and Hadiya, lying to the south-east of the Christian Amhara Highlands. Here our reconstruction of events from oral tradition is supplemented by written records from both Christian and Muslim sources. These show that by the thirteenth century the Muslim state of Ifat which included Adal and the port of Zeila was ruled by the Walashma', a dynasty then claiming Arab origins. Early in the fourteenth century, Haq ad-Din, Sultan of Ifat, turned the sporadic and disjointed forays of his predecessors into a full-scale war of aggression, and apparently for the first time, couched his call to arms in the form of a religious war against the Abyssinian 'infidels'. At first the Muslims were successful. Christian territory was invaded, churches razed, and Christians forced to apostasize at the point of the sword. In 1415, however, the Muslims were routed and the ruler of Ifat, Sa'd ad-Din, pursued and eventually killed in his last stronghold on the island off the coast of Zeila which to this day bears his name. From this period the Arab chroniclers refer to Adal as the 'Land of Sa'd ad-Din'. This crushing defeat, and Sa'd ad-Din's martyrdom, for his death soon came to be regarded in this light, took place in the reign of the Abyssinian Negus Yeshaq (1414–29) and it is in the songs celebrating his victories over the Muslims that the name 'Somali' is first recorded.

The Abyssinian victories and the temporary occupation of Zeila itself dealt a severe blow to the Muslim cause: Sa'd ad-Din's sons fled to Arabia where they found refuge with the King of Yemen. Yet they were able to return after a few years; and the Walashma' dynasty then assumed the title of Kings of Adal, and moved their capital to Dakkar, to the east of Harar, farther from the threat of Abyssinian attack. After almost a hundred years of tranquillity Adal had recovered sufficiently for a new onslaught against the Christians, and in Imam Ahmad Ibrahim al-Ghazi (or 'Gran') (1506–43), the Muslims had at last found the charismatic leadership they sought. The origins of Ahmad Gran, 'the left-handed' as he was known to Muslims and Christians alike, are appropriately obscure.[5] But under his leadership resounding victories were won. Equipped with cannons imported through Zeila, his armies penetrated eventually into the heart of Abyssinia after a series of savage battles which are still vividly recalled today.

Somali contingents played a notable part in the *Imam*'s victories and Shihab ad-Din, the Muslim chronicler of the period writing between 1540 and 1560, mentions them frequently.[6] Most prominent were the Darod clans of the Harti faction who were now in possession of the ancient port of Mait in the east, and expanding westwards and southwards from this centre. This Darod support was reinforced by ties of marriage, for the *Imam* was related by marriage to one of the Darod leaders. The Isaq Somali are not mentioned by name, but one branch of them appear to have participated in the *Imam*'s campaigns; and some Dir groups were also involved. Yet the bulk of Gran's Somali forces were drawn from the Darod clansmen, one of whose leaders was his namesake and often confused with the *Imam* himself. It was probably about this period too, that the Majerteyn Darod clan developed their sultanate which came to control much of the coast of north-east Somalia and whose later history consequently belongs to that of the coastal settlements generally.

The effective participation of these pastoral Somali nomads, renowned 'cutters of roads' in the words of the Muslim chronicler, indicates the greatness of the powers of leadership – spiritual as well as temporal – of the *Imam*. For the northern Somali have never had strongly developed hierarchical government and were certainly not accustomed to joining together in common cause on so wide a front. Few indeed are the occasions in Somali history when so many disparate and mutually hostile clans have combined together with such great effect, however ephemeral their unity.

As might readily have been anticipated, this extraordinary outburst of Muslim enterprise was not long sustained. Both sides invoked foreign aid; the Abyssinians turning to the Portuguese now at the height of their power in the Red Sea, while the Muslims sought support from the Turks. After some further successes, *Imam* Ahmad unwisely dismissed his Turkish contingents and in 1542 was routed near Lake Tana by Galawdewos, the reigning Emperor of Abyssinia. The *Imam* was killed and Galawdewos's victory marked the turning point in the fortunes of Abyssinia.

Although the Muslims, with Harar as their new headquarters, continued the struggle, they were unsuccessful, and the glorious victories of the *Imam* were never repeated. Both sides had now to contend with a new menace in the form of the massive Oromo invasion from the south-west. In these circumstances Adal declined rapidly, and from Harar the capital was transferred in 1577 to the oasis of Aussa in the scorching Danakil deserts where it was hoped to be secure from further Abyssinian attack. Here, however, it was regularly harried by the Galla invaders who by this time had swept through Abyssinia; and it was ultimately overthrown by the local nomadic Danakil ('Afar), its ancient dynasty disappearing towards the end of the seventeenth century.

Adal's confines have thus a shifting and fluid history, and although Somali played so striking a part in the sixteenth-century conquest of Abyssinia, it is not yet clear to what extent they formed part of this Muslim state at other periods. Since, however, in addition to Zeila, Berbera, and Mait, at least twenty other Muslim towns flourished in the fifteenth and sixteenth centuries in the Somali hinterland, it seems that at this time at any rate the Muslim state must have exerted some influence on the Somali of these regions.[7]

The aftermath of the holy wars with Abyssinia

Ahmad Gran's campaigns had at least two major effects on the history of Abyssinia and the Horn. First, Ahmad's appeal to the Turks led to the Turkish occupation in 1557 of Massawa and Arkiko in what is now Eritrea. And although the initial Turkish attempt to extend their authority into Abyssinia was defeated to the extent that in 1633 the Turkish garrison was withdrawn from Massawa, and a local Beja chieftain installed as Ottoman representative, Turkish pretensions to the coast lingered on to become extremely important again in the nineteenth century. Secondly, and more immediately, Ahmad's campaigns seem to some extent to have prepared the ground for the great Galla invasion from the south-west which followed his death. The Oromo in conquering hordes thrust far up into northern Abyssinia where they became an equal scourge to Muslims and Christians alike. This new factor, the subsequent recovery of Abyssinia, and

the decline of Adal appear to have effectively closed the gateway
to further Somali expansion in the west, thus causing the Somali
to press increasingly upon their southern Galla neighbours and
hence sustaining, and even reinforcing the latter's massive invasion of Abyssinia.

By this time some Darod and Dir groups had apparently installed
themselves in the Harar–Jigjiga region. And in the south, as the
Oromo withdrew on one front to attack on another, northern
Somali settlers gathered in increasing numbers. New groups of
Hawiye immigrants fought their way to the Shebelle and began to
challenge the authority of the Ajuran, eventually overwhelming
them. The city of Mogadishu was also invested and the ancient
Muzaffar dynasty overthrown. Both documentary and oral evidence place these events early in the seventeenth century.[8] After
their defeat the Ajuran and their allies the Madanle – to whom so
many striking wells and stone works are attributed – were harried
south eventually into what is today the North-Eastern Region of
Kenya where they appear to have been amongst the earliest
recorded inhabitants. Here they were joined later by the Boran
and Warday Galla who established a local ascendancy which was
only finally overcome by the massive wave of Somali migration in
the nineteenth century. But this is to anticipate.

About the time of the overthrow of the Muzaffar dynasty in
Mogadishu, it appears, again from local tradition, that much of
the zone between the Shebelle and Juba rivers, including Bur
Hacaba, was still mainly in Galla hands. Thus the situation was
now that, from the coast about Mogadishu westwards towards the
hinterland, the country was occupied first by the Hawiye, then by
the Galla, and finally by the Rahanweyn Somali.[9] Farther north, in
Majerteynia, a strongly entrenched party of Galla at Galkayu were
finally dislodged about the middle of the century.

In the following decades the Rahanweyn continued their pressure and, probably about the end of the seventeenth century, succeeded after hard fighting in driving the remaining Galla from
their stronghold at Bur Hacaba. These Galla withdrew westwards,
eventually crossing the Juba and moving on to its right bank.
This, of course, increased the pressure upon the Zanj whose
traditional capital, Shungwaya, was at this time in the Juba region.
Thus by the turn of the century, the Oromo, whose strength must

have been very greatly reduced by their massive drive into Abyssinia, had lost to the Somali all their former territory in Somaliland to the north of the Juba River. Of their former presence, however, they left behind firm evidence in the many minority groups of Oromo origin which are found today in various degrees of absorption amongst the Rahanweyn and Digil Somali of the Shebelle and Juba regions.

Finally, groups of Dir Somali whose displacement from the east and centre of northern Somaliland must by now have been almost complete, reached the south. Their most important representatives here are the Bimal who, encountering the Digil, fought and overcame them, and eventually established themselves near Merca where they are today. Thus by the eighteenth century southern Somaliland as far south as the Juba River had assumed more or less its present ethnic complexion.

But the main Somali advance did not long halt at the Juba. Darod from the north and Ogaden continued to push south, often against the fierce resistance of those who had preceded them.[10] Eventually these new northern invaders reached the Shebelle, and began to press heavily upon the Digil of the region early in the nineteenth century. Their progress was arrested, however, by the Rahanweyn, from about 1840 onwards under the strong leadership of the Geledi clan based on the Shebelle. This opposition forced these new Darod immigrants to move up to the Juba and brought them into contact with the Galla on the right bank of the river. Although so much of their territory had been lost in Somaliland, the Galla were still tenaciously clinging to what land was left to them, and from their centre at Afmadu, launched occasional raids across the river into what was now Somali territory. Their power in this region was thus by no means yet broken; and from time to time their raiding parties menaced the Somali religious centre at Bardera, founded in 1820 on the middle reaches of the Juba. Thus the new Darod invaders encountered a formidable neighbour whom, for the present, it was more expedient to appease than to provoke. Hence having gained their protection, parties of Darod clansmen crossed the river as clients and allies of the Oromo. The trans-Juban Oromo seem to have welcomed this new support and to have turned it to advantage in their relations with the turbulent Akamba and Masai to their west.

As time passed, the Darod movement continued and further Darod clansmen entered the area, sought alliance with the Galla, and crossed the river to join their kinsmen. Thus the strength of the Darod immigrants under Oromo protection gradually increased. This situation of uneasy Darod–Galla alliance, however, continued for some time and is that described by the French explorer Charles Guillain when he visited the southern Somali coast in 1847. Much the same position is recorded also by the ill-fated German traveller, von der Decken, who, in 1865, made history by sailing up the Juba River in his shallow-draught steamship *Welf*, only to founder in the rapids above Bardera.[11] It was apparently in this same year that a severe epidemic of smallpox amongst the Galla provided the opportunity for which their Darod neighbours had obviously been waiting. Almost immediately, the Darod fell upon their Galla hosts on all sides and inflicted very heavy losses. The few Oromo who survived fled to the south; and, by the turn of the century, most of the southern Galla had been cleared from the area, retaining footholds only at Wajir and Buna. A new factor now made itself felt in the form of desperate Ethiopian raids into the Ogaden and down the Juba. This, with further waves of new Somali immigrants – some of whom had sailed down the coast by dhow – maintained and even increased the Somali pressure. Indeed, by 1909, parties of Darod immigrants had pressed as far south as the Tana River with livestock estimated to number as many as fifty thousand beasts.

By 1912, when administrative and military posts were opened by the British in this turbulent northern part of the East African Protectorate, the situation was still fluid. The Darod were still on the move and were now seeking to dominate completely the whole region from Buna in the west, through Wajir, to the Tana in the south-east. Many of those non-Hamitic WaBoni hunters who had survived the tides of migration and battle had now become the serfs of the Darod, and most of the Warday Galla who remained had to be moved across the Tana River to prevent their extinction by the Somali. A good number, however, chose to stay with their former Darod subjects as clients, thus completely reversing the earlier position when the Oromo had been masters of Jubaland. To the west, the once powerful Ajuran, who after their defeat in the seventeenth century had been so ignominiously harried southwards, had now lost much of their cohesion and were rapidly being infiltrated by other Somali. Finally, the southern Boran Galla were being thrust north-west by the continued Darod pressure.

By 1919, feeling between the Darod and those Warday Galla who had been moved across the Tana River reached such a pitch that it was again necessary for the British authorities to intervene. The consequence was an undertaking by both sides, known as the Somali–Orma (Galla) agreement, which allowed the Galla who remained with the Darod on the left bank to choose finally between accepting the formal position of serfs, or of moving across the river to join their free kinsmen. Those who decided to cross the Tana were obliged to leave behind them with their Somali patrons half the cattle which they had acquired during their bondage. Under these conditions it is perhaps not surprising that few of the Warday Galla moved.

Some twelve years later, further unrest broke out among the Galla subjects of the Darod, and a rumour began to circulate that the Somali were about to disregard the 1919 agreement. Whether on this account, or for other reasons, about eight hundred Oromo dependents with ten times as many head of livestock made a forlorn bid for freedom, trekking towards the Tana River at the very height of the dry season. The result was disastrous; nearly half their number perished, and the few who survived were ignominiously returned to the left bank of the river. In 1936, the agreement ended and the government of Kenya tacitly recognized that, except for those on the right bank of the Tana, the Warday Galla with whom the Somali had so long been struggling had been finally assimilated. Of the Oromo who had once occupied so much of this territory, only the Boran and Gabbra remained.

Thus ended the great series of migrations which, over a space of some nine hundred years, had brought the Somali from their northern deserts into the more fertile regions of the centre and south and finally into the semi-desert plains of northern Kenya. These movements had far-reaching social repercussions. Through contact with the Oromo and the absorption of those Galla who remained behind, and with an added leaven from the earlier Bantu communities, the Digil and Rahanweyn tribes emerged with their distinctive characteristics. From the Bantu they adopted cultivation, and from the Galla temporarily adapted their system of age-grades to their expanding military needs. In much the same way, the Darod who later crossed the Juba briefly assumed the Galla warrior age-grade system, and like the Rahanweyn, later discarded it.

At every stage in their expansion the tactics employed by the Somali were based upon their traditional evaluation of political power in terms of military strength. While at various times and places, small family groups and lineages, the spear-heads of the greater clan migrations, accepted the protection of their numerically dominant Oromo hosts, as soon as they were sufficiently strong they overthrew their patrons and made them their subjects. Wherever by force of numbers and arms they could, the Somali triumphed. Both sides seem to have relied on similar weapons, mainly spear and leather shield sometimes reinforced perhaps with bow and arrow. The Somali may, however, have enjoyed superiority in the use of a few matchlock guns, although it is doubtful if this was very significant. Probably, more significantly, their warriors were sometimes mounted on horseback, a technique which the Oromo later adopted and used to good effect in their massive migration into Abyssinia. Yet it was probably above all their overwhelming numerical superiority, and the dynamism which their movement acquired, which enabled the Somali to conquer so much territory at the expense of the Oromo. This and other considerations suggest that those Galla whom the Somali smote and put to flight – mainly Akishu, Raitu, and Arussi in the north, and Warday and Boran in the south – did not represent the main mass of the Oromo nation,[12] but were rather sparsely distributed outlying groups far from their traditional homelands in the south-east of Ethiopia. Finally, in considering the character of the Somali expansion, it should be remembered that this was not a concerted operation under a single direction: it was a disjointed series of clan and lineage movements in which there were many cross-currents of migration as group jostled group in the search for new pastures. Nor does this sequence of Somali and Oromo movement exclude the possibility that the ultimate origins of both peoples may be traced to the same area on the upper reaches of the Juba river.

New European interest in the coast

While this great upheaval was taking place, with the exception for a time of Adal in the north and of states such as those of the Ajuran and Geledi in the south, it was only on the coast that any degree of centralized government was established and maintained, however irregularly, over long periods of time. It is now necessary to revert to this theme and to examine the final fortunes of the coastal centres before the partition of the Somali region.

Afrer the decline of the Adal state, Zeila retained its commercial position as the main outlet for the ancient caravan routes from the hinterland, particularly those descending from the Abyssinian highlands through Harar, although in the sixteenth century trade was severely disrupted for a time by the Oromo invasions. In the following century Zeila, and apparently to some extent Berbera also, fell under the authority of the Sharifs of Mukha and both ports were thus nominally incorporated in the Ottoman Empire. And this was still the position when Sir Richard Burton visited the coast in 1854 in the course of his celebrated expedition to Harar which, in contrast to Zeila, was still an independent Muslim principality.

Zeila's governor was now a Somali, Haji Shirmarke 'Ali Salih (of the Habar Yunis clan), who had begun his remarkable career as the captain of a training dhow. Having acquired wealth and reputation, the Haji obtained the office of governor about 1840 from the hereditary holder Sayyid Muhammad al-Barr, representative of the Ottoman Pasha of Western Arabia. His success was also apparently facilitated by the gratitude which he had earned from the British government of Bombay for protecting the lives of the crew of the *Mary Ann*, a British brig attacked and plundered by the local Somali at Berbera in 1825. Notwithstanding Haji 'Ali's intervention, this incident had led the British to blockade the coast regularly until 1833, when £6,000 in compensation had been recovered from the Somali. In the meantime, in 1827, a commercial treaty had been signed between the British East Africa Company and the local Habar Awal clan.

In 1854, Burton records that Haji Shirmarke, tall and, despite his sixty-odd years, strong and active, had not forgotten the military exploits of his youth and contemplated the conquest of

Berbera and Harar. He lived modestly, however, in an indifferent mud and wattle *'arish*, and not in one of the grander double-storeyed stone houses of the town. His 'secretary' was a Swahili slave; and although he was himself illiterate, his eldest son Muhammad, married to an Arab woman, had been educated at Mukha and proved to be something of a scholar. The town, Burton found, Haji 'Ali governed with a light hand, and the aid of a tough Hadrami soldier and forty mercenaries from Hadramaut, Mukha, and Aden, all armed with matchlock and sword. The Kadi administering Islamic law was at this time a Hawiye Somali whose predecessors, from about 1670, had been Sayyids from Arabia.

The dimensions of Zeila Burton compares to Suez, sufficient to hold a few thousand inhabitants, and provided with six mosques, a dozen large white-washed stone houses, and two hundred or more thatched mud-and-wattle huts. The ancient wall of coral rubble and mud defending the town was no longer fortified with guns, and in many places had become dilapidated. Drinking water had to be fetched from wells four miles from the town. Yet trade was thriving: to the north caravans plied the Danakil country, while to the west the lands of the 'Ise and Gadabursi clans were traversed as far as Harar, and beyond Harar to the Gurage country in Abyssinia. The main exports were slaves, ivory, hides, horns, ghee, and gums. On the coast itself Arab divers were active collecting sponge cones. And provisions were cheap.

Burton soon found that this orderly town life at Zeila did not extend far beyond the gates of the city. The nomadic clans, through whose pastures Burton and his companions passed on their way towards Harar, recognized no political dependence upon Zeila. Indeed raids and skirmishes occurred under the very walls of the city.

While in 1855 Zeila thus continued the coastal tradition of instituted authority under a Somali governor, although its political influence was a mere shadow of what it had once been, at Berbera the position was very different. Here Burton found that the process of nomadic encroachment had gone much further and the town was in fact no longer politically distinct from its nomadic hinterland. In February 1855, when Burton, having successfully completed his exploration of Harar, entered Berbera he discovered that the Habar Awal clan were in possession, but divided as to which of their sections should control the port. At the same time, the Habar Yunis clan was also advancing claims to the lucrative trade which the town commanded.

Before this, and prior to the British settlement at Aden in 1839, the Ayyal Yunis and Ayyal Ahmed lineages of the Habar Awal clan had held Berbera and jointly managed its trade, sharing in the profits on all commercial transactions as 'protectors' (*abans*) of foreign merchants from Arabia and India. When under the stimulus of developments at Aden the port's prosperity markedly increased, the numerically dominant Ayyal Yunis drove out their rival kinsmen and declared themselves commercial masters of Berbera. This led to a feud in which each side sought outside help; the defeated Ayyal Ahmad turned to Haji Shirmarke 'Ali and his Habar Yunis clansmen for support. With this backing, they were then able to re-establish themselves and to expel the Ayyal Yunis who moved to the small roadstead of Bulhar, some miles to the west of Berbera. By 1846, however, the menace of other clans had led the two rival Ayyal lineages to compose their differences and Haji 'Ali's services had been dispensed with: he had been 'British Agent' at Berbera in 1842.

This struggle and earlier vicissitudes had left their mark on Berbera, for while the bare ground for about a mile on either side was strewn with broken glass and pottery, the debris of former generations, the area of the town actually inhabited, 'a wretched clump of dirty mud-huts', occupied only a fraction of the ancient contours. And the old aqueduct from the wells at Dubar eight miles to the south-east had long ceased to bring sweet water to the town.

Having formed this unfavourable impression of Berbera, Burton and his companions left the Somali coast for Aden which they reached on 9 February, 1855. April of the same year, however, saw Burton back again at Berbera as the leader of a new expedition, with the object of exploring the Ogaden hinterland. In the two months in which he had been absent the appearance of the port had greatly changed. It was now filled with bustle and activity: 'The emporium of East Africa was at the time of my landing in a state of confusion. But a day before, the great Harar caravan, numbering three thousand souls, and as many cattle, had entered for the purpose of laying in the usual eight months supplies, and purchase, barter, and exchange were transacted in most hurried and unbusiness-like manner. All day, and during the greater part of the night, the town rang with the voices of buyer and seller: to specify no other articles of traffic, 500 slaves of both sexes were in the market. Long lines of laden and unladen camels were to be seen pacing the glaring yellow shore: . . . . . . already small parties of travellers had broken ground for their return journey: and the foul heap of mat hovels, to which this celebrated mart had been reduced, was steadily shrinking in dimensions.'[13]

Burton and his companions were not allowed long to contemplate this scene. On 19 April, 1855, in the early hours of the morning, several hundred Somali spearmen launched a savage attack upon Burton's camp. In the ensuing mêlée, Lt Stroyan was killed, and Lt Speke (later to gain fame for his explorations of the Nile source) severely wounded: Burton himself received a spear-thrust in the mouth. Yet despite the numerical superiority of their assailants, Burton and his companions managed to escape to Aden, and the expedition was abandoned: Burton never returned to Somaliland. He is still remembered, however, with a mixture of amusement and admiration as 'Haji 'Abdallah', the guise he assumed for his journey to Harar, and as one who regularly led the prayers in the mosques, and could hold his own with any sheikh.

The British authorities at Aden reacted promptly to the incident in the manner of the times. Two vessels of the India command were dispatched to blockade the coast until Stroyan's murderer and Speke's attacker were surrendered to justice. The following year the elders of the Habar Awal clan announced that Stroyan's assailant had been executed by his own kin and offered 15,000 dollars as compensation. Then in November, a treaty was signed with the Habar Awal in favour of British commerce at Berbera and to provide for the eventual appointment of a British Resident. Much the same series of events had followed the plunder of the brig *Mary Anne* off Berbera in 1825 when Shirmarke 'Ali had intervened. Now, however, the link between Aden and the northern Somali coast had been strengthened and the basis laid for future British activity. Conditions on this remote coastline were no longer a matter of indifference to the Imperial Powers.

Meanwhile the southern Somali coast had similarly become exposed to new foreign interests. Here, in contrast to Zeila with its long tradition of far-flung connexions between Abyssinia and Arabia, the local ports had generally a narrower sphere of influence. Events in the Christian kingdom of Abyssinia hardly impinged upon them, and the chief external factors affecting their fortunes were the political situation in the Indian Ocean and that in their Somali hinterland.

Thus Mogadishu, which in the tenth century consisted of a loose federation of Arab and Persian families, had by the thirteenth become a sultanate ruled by the Fakhr ad-Din dynasty. Three centuries later these rulers were supplanted by the Muzaffar Sultans and the town had become closely connected with the related Ajuran Sultanate in the interior. In this period Mogadishu was attacked but not occupied by the Portuguese. The true conquerors of the ancient city were those new Hawiye Somali settlers who defeated the Ajuran and brought the downfall of the Muzaffar dynasty in the early seventeenth century. By this time Mogadishu had split into two rival quarters, Hamarweyn, and Shangani in which the new invaders were established.

At this time the rise of Omani influence in the Indian Ocean introduced an important new factor into the situation; and by the close of the seventeenth century Mogadishu, with the other East African ports, had come under the protection of Oman. In 1814, however, the governor of Mombasa declared his town independent and sought British support from Bombay. After a delay of nine years, Captain Owen's fleet arrived off the East African coast and in 1824, Owen established his famous but short-lived 'Protectorate'. Mombasa'a rebellious example now affected the people of Mogadishu, and in 1825 Owen obligingly visited the port offering British protection against the anticipated Omani reprisal. This was refused, but at the port of Brava to the south of Mogadishu, Owen was more successful.

In the following year the situation changed radically, and with the refusal of Owen's government to ratify his protectorate, British intervention disappeared as suddenly and almost as inexplicably as it had come. The rebellious towns of East Africa were now left to face their Omani overlords alone. In 1828, Mogadishu was bombarded and compelled to capitulate. But when, shortly after, the Muscat state was divided, Mogadishu and her sister ports of the southern, or 'Benadir',[14] Somali coast passed under the jurisdiction of the Sultan of Zanzibar.

Meanwhile, beyond the Benadir Coast to the north, the Majerteyn Sultanate had apprently retained its independence from outside interests. In 1839, however, for an annual allowance of 360 dollars, the Sultan signed a treaty at Aden with the British, guaranteeing to protect the lives and property of ships wrecked off his coast. By this time the Sultanate was also in contact with Oman, though not it seems formally under Omani jurisdiction.

These various centres along the coast were visited by the French explorer, Charles Guillain, captain of the brig *Ducouedic*, between 1846 and 1848. As a whole the Benadir ports, Guillain found, acknowledged both the authority of the Sultan of Zanzibar and that of the Somali Geledi clan in the hinterland who, as masters of the Shebelle, were now at the height of their power. And while the Sultan of Zanzibar was no doubt potentially more powerful, because better armed, than his Geledi colleague, it was easier for the latter to give direct effect to his authority. Thus it was typical of the delicate distribution of power between the two Sultans that, when in 1870 the Sultan of Zanzibar wished to build a fortress for his representative at Mogadishu, this required the consent and assistance of the Geledi.

At the·time of Guillain's sojourn, however, although the ancient cotton-weaving industry was still profitable,[15] Mogadishu was largely in ruins. A recent scourge of plague and famine had reduced its population to a mere 5,000; and Hamarweyn and Shangani, the two quarters of the city, were at variance and each under a separate leader. The Sultan of the Geledi had in 1842 been invited to mediate and his action then had led to an uneasy truce between the two factions. By contrast, the Sultan of Zanzibar's authority over the town was slight and hardly more than nominal. In 1843, a Somali had been appointed as governor by the Sultan of Zanzibar and furnished with two soldiers to collect the taxes; but after a short time this official had relinquished his office, and now at the time of Guillain's visit, the only Zanzibari representative was an old Arab with an Indian assistant as tax collector.

The governor for the Benadir coast as a whole was stationed at Brava which, compared with Mogadishu, impressed Guillain with its prosperity. This city of 5,000 souls, while acknowledging the overlordship of Zanzibar, was effectively led by two personages, one a Somali, and the other an Arab who spoke some English. Finally, between Brava and Mogadishu, at Merca, the Somali intrusion was complete and this port was led by a member of the local Bimal clan; here the only Zanzibar representative was an aged customs official. Recently the town had been devastated by the Sultan of the Geledi in the course of strife between his clan and the Bimal, and the citizens of Brava were now preparing to counter-attack: in this situation Guillain wisely decided not to prolong his visit.

Thus by the middle of the nineteenth century, the southern Benadir coast as a whole recognized the suzerainty of Zanzibar, although the Sultan's power was vague and uncertain compared with the direct influence exerted by the Geledi who dominated the hinterland. Yet the Geledi did not generally dispute Zanzibar's position, and the two Sultans were friends rather than rivals maintaining between them a delicate balance of control over the Benadir. Farther to the south the Sultan of Zanzibar's writ ran more directly, so that, for example, when in 1868 after the rout of the Galla Warday, new Darod reinforcements arrived to swell the further Darod thrust south, and came from the north by sea to Kismayu, they sought and obtained the Sultan's authority.

To the north beyond the Benadir ports, the Majerteyn Sultanate, while having connexions with Oman, remained politically independent. Zeila, and less definitely Berbera, however, were still formally part of the Turkish Empire, though both were now heavily involved in trade with the British at Aden, and in the case of Berbera linked with Britain by commercial treaties.

Thus by the middle of the nineteenth century the Somali coast was no longer isolated, and locally it was now rather the nomads of the hinterland who controlled the ports than the other way about. To a large extent the coastal and hinterland traditions had merged, and the centre of political pressure had swung from the coast to the interior. The new external links between the coast and the outside world, however, served in the following decades of the nineteenth century to pave the way for a new colonial impact in which the pressure, initially at least, was again mainly from the coast towards the hinterland.

CHAPTER III

THE IMPERIAL PARTITION: 1860-97

The first phase of Imperial Partition

IN THE YEARS following the middle of the nineteenth century, Somalia was rapidly drawn into the theatre of colonial competittion between Britain, France, and Italy. On the African continent itself, Egypt was also involved; and later Abyssinia, expanding and consolidating her realm in this period. By 1897 the partition of Somaliland was virtually complete; and though subsequent adjustments occurred, the frontiers of the new Somali territories had been defined, at least theoretically. Such gaps as remained in the division were later adjusted in subsequent colonial consolidation. Only the frontiers remained to be demarcated, a practical step which turned out to be infinitely more difficult than could have been envisaged in 1897.

Britain's interest in the Somali area stemmed from her possession of Aden which had been acquired by force in 1839 as a station on the short route to India. With its poverty in local resources, the Aden garrison was almost entirely dependent upon northern Somaliland for supplies of meat. There was also a considerable Somali community at Aden, many of whom found employment with the new rulers there. The Aden authorities and the Bombay government were thus directly concerned that orderly conditions should prevail on the Somali coast, and more especially that the feeder caravan routes from the interior, and the ports of Berbera and Zeila, should function freely. But although travellers like Burton and local officials at Aden might advocate a definite British occupation of the Somali coast, their plans fell on deaf ears in Westminster. The British government was only interested in Somaliland's meat supply as a necessary ancillary to the garrisoning of Aden. Only if this were seriously threatened would any occupation of the Somali coast be justified. This attitude on the part of Whitehall towards the Somali coast, given different emphasis by different administrations in England, was still the guiding policy when events had driven Britain to establish a Somaliland Protectorate in 1887. This evaluation is also reflected in the character of the Anglo-Somali treaties of protection. It figures strongly in the negotiation of the 1897 treaty with Ethiopia, and it later bred a tradition of parsimony and neglect which dominated British action in her Somali Protectorate throughout most of its life. Yet although Britain's utilitarian interest in her Protectorate was always limited and secondary, this did not deter the government from using her holdings in Somaliland as a convenient counter in bargaining for bigger stakes with Ethiopia in 1897.

The other powers who began to display interest in the Red Sea coast had more definite and more directly imperial ambitions. In this region Britain's main rival was, first, France. In 1859 the French consular agent at Aden obtained the cession of the Danakil port of Obock. Three years later a treaty was drawn up by which France purchased the port outright from the 'Afar and the French flag was hoisted. But it was not until 1881, eleven years after the opening of the Suez canal, that France took advantage of her lonely stake at Obock and the Franco-Ethiopian trading company was installed there. In the interval, Italy had replaced France in claiming Red Sea territory, while Britain's Liberal ministers were far from pressing imperial claims. Empowered by the Italian Foreign Minister to select a place on the Red Sea coast for an Italian settlement, Giuseppe Sapeto, a former missionary in Ethiopia, in 1869 obtained an interest in the port of Assab on the Eritrean coast. In the following year, Assab was bought outright from the local 'Afar by an Italian shipping company which proposed to run services through the Suez canal and Red Sea to India. Britain did nothing to contest these Italian gains.

Meanwhile, however, no doubt prompted by this foreign interest, Egypt revived Turkey's ancient claims to the Red Sea coast. By 1866 Turkey had transferred the Red Sea ports of Suakin and Massawa to the government of the Khedive Isma'il, and the latter claimed that this new jurisdiction also embraced the Somali coast.[1] In the following year the governor of the Sudan visited the Red Sea ports and also Tajura, Zeila, and Berbera, seeking declarations of fealty from the local leaders. In 1869 an Egyptian vessel visited Berbera, and in the following year Muhammad Jamal Bey was sent to the Somali coast to raise the Egyptian flag at Bulhar and Berbera.

The Egyptian occupation provoked immediate British protests. While not herself seeking to occupy Somali territory, in the interests of the safety of the Aden garrison's meat supplies, Britain did not wish to see any other power established on the opposite side of the Gulf of Aden. Indeed to this end emissaries had already been sent from Aden to intrigue amongst the Somali against Egypt, and in 1869 British agents had successfully frustrated the cession of harbourage to France by one of the eastern Somali clans. The India Office accordingly urged that measures should be taken to preserve Somali independence from Egypt. But the home government refused to sanction any military action, although resistance to Egyptian claims to the coast east of Zeila was maintained through diplomatic channels from 1870 to 1874. During this period the area under effective Egyptian jurisdiction rapidly expanded. In Eritrea, Annesley Bay was occupied in 1873 and Keren in 1874, and the allegiance of the local peoples there and on the Somali coast won. Between 1874 and 1876 this forward policy was continued; Abyssinia was attacked and expeditions sent to the Somali coast south of Cape Guardafui, although no effective dominion was established there. As events turned out, the Abyssinian ventures failed, but the Egyptians succeeded in expanding behind Zeila and established a garrison in the ancient commercial city of Harar.

By this time, faced by other less predictable rivals, Britain had come to regard the Egyptian occupation as more in keeping with her interests than hostile to them. Accordingly, in 1877 a convention was signed with the Khedive by which Britain recognized Egyptian jurisdiction as far south as Ras Hafun. This arrangement Lord Salisbury described as 'our only security against other European powers obtaining a footing opposite Aden'. The convention included the precautionary provision that 'no part of the Somali coast . . . should be ceded on any pretext whatever to a foreign power', a stipulation which was later to be written into Britain's treaties of protection with Somali clans.

The Egyptians, it seems, had little difficulty in establishing their authority over the ports of Zeila, Bulhar, and Berbera, though their influence over the nomads of the interior was more limited. At this time the Somali had no firearms, and had to depend for their security upon the traditional spear and dagger. In addition, despite their sense of cultural identity, they did not constitute a single political unit. Foreign aggression thus encountered not a nation-state, but a congeries of disunited and often hostile clans which themselves were regularly divided by bitter internecine feuds. The Egyptians consequently experienced no united opposition, although they had serious difficulties with individual clans and lineages throughout their brief rule of the coast (1870–84).

At Zeila ruled Abu Bakr Pasha, a local 'Afar, who had been Turkish governor of the town before the arrival of the Egyptians, having earlier supplanted his Somali predecessor Haji 'Ali Shirmarke. Abu Bakr was actively engaged in the slave trade, still considerable at this time, and was regarded by the British at Aden as favourable to the interests of their French rivals. The governor at Berbera was an Egyptian, 'Abd ar-Rahman Bey, whose rule, according to the vigilant Aden authorities, was oppressive and unjust: certainly it aroused the hostility of his Somali subjects. And despite the community of religion between the Egyptian colonizers and their Somali subjects, at both Zeila and Berbera there were the inevitable difficulties with the nomadic clans of the interior. The new administration sought to manage the appointment of Somali clan Sultans, and in order to secure some degree of control over the smaller clan segments appointed headmen (Akils) to represent them. These Egyptian candidates were not always acceptable. In 1883, there was trouble with the Gadabursi clan over the recognition of their leader, *Ugas* Nur, who was eventually sent to Egypt, where, if tradition is accurate, he was fêted by the Khedive and presented with a gift of firearms. Other similar incidents occurred.

Yet, however distasteful their régime to the eyes of the British at Aden, the Egyptians did succeed in creating tangible evidence of their presence on the Somali coast. This was especially the case in the field of public works where much was achieved by corvée labour. The port facilities of both Zeila and Berbera were greatly improved; piers and lighthouses were erected; and at Berbera the ancient Dubar aqueduct was restored to supply fresh water to the town. The Egyptians also naturally encouraged Islam and several new mosques were built during their tenure of the coast. Whatever its merits or demerits, however, the Egyptian régime was abruptly terminated by the Mahdi's revolt in the Sudan which necessitated a concentration of Egyptian resources and a drastic curtailment of outlying responsibilities in Eritrea, Harar, and the Somali coast: or, at least, so it seemed to Britain. The consequent Egyptian evacuation of Harar, Zeila, and Berbera took place in 1884 and immediately raised again the question of how these areas were to be administered to the advantage of Britain.

Meanwhile France and Italy had also been active. Recent French acquisitions in Madagascar and China, and the collapse of the Anglo-French condominium in Egypt gave France an impetus to establish a base on the Red Sea route which was now a vital link in her overseas communications. The time had come to rescue Obock from the oblivion of its moribund trading company, and to create an efficient coaling station. This was all the more necessary since, in the climate of acute Anglo-French rivalry of the period, the British authorities at Aden now refused to allow French transports to coal at the port. Léonce Lagarde, who laid the foundations of the French *Côte des Somalis*, and who played so prominent a part in the expansion of French influence in Ethiopia and N.E. Africa, was nominated governor of Obock in June 1884.

In the same period Italian influence at Assab, owned still by the Raffaele Rubattino shipping company, was consolidated and extended. At first the British reaction to these Italian moves was hostile; but by 1882 when under British pressure Italy had agreed to recognize Egyptian sovereignty to the north and south of her settlement, the Italian government felt sufficiently confident of its position to claim Assab openly and the port was bought from the company. Notwithstanding continued misgivings in some quarters as to Italy's ambitions, the British government began to move towards the position of viewing Italian involvement as a convenient counterpoise to French expansion which was regarded as infinitely more threatening. The British Liberal government was by now in any case prepared to take more effective measures to safeguard the use of the Suez canal. By July 1882 British troops had occupied Suez, Ismailia, and Port Said. Yet the possibility still remained that the Mahdists would obtain control of the eastern Sudan and the port of Suakin. In an atmosphere of rumours of a French bid for the Eritrean port of Massawa after the withdrawal of the Egyptian garrison in 1885, Britain encouraged Italy to slip in and made the necessary juridical arrangements with the Turks. By February 1885 Italy had proclaimed her protectorate on the Eritrean coast from Assab to Massawa.

This establishment of the Italian colony of Eritrea well to the north of the farthest extension of the Somali area did not of course give Italy a stake amongst the Somali. But the further thrust of Italian expansion inland soon led to encroachments within Abyssinia and to the treaty of Ucciali signed between the two countries in 1889, a treaty which in the eyes of Italy established an Italian protectorate over Abyssinia. The same year saw Italy's first direct acquisition of Somali interests, and Italian influence established on the littoral to the north-east and south-east of Abyssinia. By the treaty of Ucciali itself, moreover, Italy became directly concerned in the partition of the Somali nation.

The establishment of the British and French Protectorates

If from the British point of view Italy seemed to provide a suitable replacement to Egypt in Eritrea, the same solution was not applicable at Harar or on the Somali coast opposite Aden. The problem of the future status of these areas was complicated; no one friendly or fully acceptable to Britain seemed to want them.[2] The Egyptians were not prepared to conduct the evacuation of their garrisons themselves; Turkey showed no willingness to resume control of Tajura and Zeila; and the local clans of the Somali coast, who of course were not consulted, were manifestly incapable of maintaining their independence and guaranteeing permanent peace and order at Berbera.

It seemed also likely that the Egyptian withdrawal itself would provoke disorder. Major Hunter, Assistant Resident at Aden and Consul for the Somali coast since 1881, reported that the sudden evacuation of the Egyptian garrison from Harar would be likely to lead to a struggle between the Somali and Oromo and that the retreating Egyptian forces would almost certainly be attacked by 'Ise and Gadabursi Somali clansmen on the road to Zeila. Harar itself would be open to attack and would present an attractive target for the growing ambitions of King Menelik of Shoa. On the Somali coast the news from the Sudan was causing restlessness amongst the Somali at Berbera. Apart from the growing menace of the French at Obock, affairs at Zeila, however, were, momentarily at any rate, more placid. Yet the general effect of the Egyptian withdrawal was likely to be disruptive and to promote unrest.

In these circumstances it was reluctantly decided that direct British action was needed to ensure the safety of the trade-routes and to safeguard the Aden garrison's meat supplies. A British mission led by Admiral Hewitt was dispatched to Abyssinia in 1884 to secure King John's co-operation in the evacuation of the Egyptians from Harar. And after an Italian ironclad had visited Berbera and staged a somewhat equivocal incident at Zeila, Major Hunter was authorized to make the necessary arrangements with the local Somali clans for a British occupation. Tired of the Egyptian rule, and perhaps already sensing the expansionist moves of Abyssinia and of other foreign powers which they were soon to experience so much more forcibly, the Somali clans seem to have readily consented to British protection. By the end of the year formal treaties, replacing the earlier Anglo-Somali trade agreements, had been signed with the 'Ise, Gadabursi, Habar Garhajis,[3] Habar Awal, and Habar Tol Ja'lo clans.

These new Anglo-Somali treaties were presumably regarded by their Somali signatories as contractual alliances of the same sort as those used so extensively in internal Somali clan politics. Certainly little was ostensibly conceded to Britain. The preamble to each clan treaty explained that its purpose was, from the Somali side: 'for the maintenance of our independence, the preservation of order, and other good and sufficient reasons'. The preambles to some of the treaties also alluded to the new situation created by the Egyptian withdrawal, stating that, 'Whereas the garrisons of His Highness the Khedive are about to be withdrawn from Berbera and Bulhar, and the Somali coast generally, we, the undersigned Elders of the . . . tribe, are desirous of entering into an Agreement with the British Government for the maintenance of our independence, the preservation of order, and other good and sufficient reasons.' Nor did the clans concerned expressly cede their land to Britain; they merely pledged themselves 'never to cede, sell, mortgage, or otherwise give for occupation, save to the British Government, any portion of the territory presently inhabited by them or being under their control'.

The Somali clansmen did, however, grant to the British Government the right to appoint British Agents to reside on the Somali coast. A further supplementary treaty was signed with each of the five clans in 1886 which referred to the desire of each side for 'maintaining and strengthening the relations of peace and friendship existing between them', and which announced that the British government undertook to extend to the clansmen concerned and to their territories 'the gracious favour and protection of Her Majesty the Queen-Empress'. A further clause obliged each clan not to enter into relations with any foreign power except with the knowledge and consent of Britain.[4]

Once these arrangements were completed the way was clear. But despite the enthusiasm of the Aden officials who had been preparing for an occupation of the Somali coast for some time, and who had especially trained a party of about forty members of the Aden police, instructions were issued that the occupation was to be as unobtrusive as possible: there was to be no attempt to extend British control inland. By the end of 1884 three British 'Vice-Consuls' were established on the Somali coast. One was stationed at Berbera with an assistant at Bulhar; and another at Zeila, where a joint condominium had temporarily been agreed to with Turkey, and Abu Bakr Pasha, the 'Afar official, was still nominally governor of the port. These Vice-Consuls worked under the direct authority of the British Resident at Aden. They were given explicit directions that their duties were those of British agents in a native state: they were to keep the peace, but not to assume powers beyond this. No grandiose schemes were to be entertained; expenditure was to be limited to a minimum, and was to be provided by the local port revenues. All this was fully in accordance with Britain's secondary interest in the Somali coast as a source of provisions for Aden.

L. Prendergast Walsh, undoubtedly one of the most flamboyant of the Vice-Consuls in this period, describes his administration at Berbera as 'parental'.[5] Under Walsh, building material which was scarce in the town was obtained by issuing camel drivers with a rope sling by means of which they were to bring two boulders into Berbera whenever they came in from the interior. Before entering the town, the nomads of the hinterland were encouraged to deposit their weapons at the police station and an ingenious procedure was devised to discourage violence. If two men were caught fighting, they were separated and deprived of their arms. They were then obliged to dig a grave. When this was completed to the satisfaction of the police, their arms were returned and they were urged to resume their dispute on the understanding that the victor would bury his adversary. Walsh found that under these conditions the most bellicose of warriors preferred to forget their differences, at least temporarily: the whole story was then broadcast in the town by the town crier.

With such methods as these and the aid of a small force of about a hundred Somali Coast Police armed with rifles, order was maintained quite effectively at Berbera and Bulhar. The safety of trade with the interior was ensured by the activities of an irregular force of armed caravan guards paid by the merchants whose caravans they escorted. And at Berbera the Ayyal Yunis, and at Bulhar the Ayyal Ahmad were still the officially recognized agents for all foreign traders: they exercised a monopoly in the organization of caravan trade with the interior.

Farther inland the maintenance of order sometimes required punitive expeditions organized with the aid of supplementary forces from Aden. Here the normal conditions of periodical raiding and looting between clans and upon caravans were aggravated by popular sympathy for the Mahdi's cause in the Sudan. This was furthered by the activities of local agents of the Senusi Muslim Order and by Mahdist emissaries: fortunately for the British, however, these were often at loggerheads and thus did not make the immediate impact they might otherwise have done. Early in 1885, however, the Zeila police who had been taken over from the Egyptians mutinied; but serious trouble was averted by the intervention of the Indian Infantry who had been stationed at Zeila to cover the Egyptian withdrawal from Harar. A minor riot followed at Berbera. To counteract the effects of religious propaganda, a pro-British sheikh was unobtrusively appointed as the official Muslim judge in place of two 'self-styled' Kadis who were both Arabs and extremely anti-British.

While this modest but surprisingly effective administration was being established, the Egyptian garrison withdrew from Harar without serious incident in 1885 and 'Abdallah Muhammad, a Harari, was left as governor of the city with a British adviser. At the same time, the French were active at Obock: and their rivalry with the British, especially through their intrigues at Zeila conducted by the enterprising French Consul with the support of the Danakil governor, had become acute. Here the position of the local British officials was complicated by their government's reluctance to come to a decision on the future status of Zeila.

Under the inspiration of the forceful Lagarde, the French station had been extended to the northern shore of the Gulf of Tajura after the departure of the Egyptians. Early in 1885 the French asserted that their dominion extended beyond Tajura to close on Jibuti, and Britain replied with a counter notification of her Somali Protectorate from Berbera to a point within the sphere claimed by France. Having gained a treaty of perpetual friendship (which included an unambiguous and total cession of land to France) with the 'Ise of Ambado and Jibuti, France answered by extending her claim to the latter port.

This wrangle, conducted without regard for the interests of the local inhabitants, now looked as though it might lead to open conflict; and indeed by the end of 1885 Britain was preparing to resist an expected French landing at Zeila. Instead, however, of a decision by force, both sides now agreed to negotiate. The result was an Anglo-French agreement of 1888 which defined the boundaries of the two protectorates as between Zeila and Jibuti: four years later the latter port became the official capital of the French colony. The effect of this new arrangement was, of course, to divide the 'Ise with whom both France and Britain had treaties of 'protection', the British treaties being designed to protect the 'independence' of the clan and giving Britain no outright claim to 'Ise territory.

The Italian sphere

The Italians, used conveniently as allies in the face of French opposition, were now in a position to extend their claims inland from their colony of Eritrea. The effect of this with the added menace of the Mahdia in the Sudan was, like the earlier Egyptian invasions, to give a further impetus to Abyssinian unity. To counter the growing Abyssinian resistance to their expansion, the Italians sought to play off King Menelik of Shoa against John of Tigre who held the title of King of Kings. Italy supported Menelik and armed and encouraged him to contest John's title. The two leaders, however, concluded a dynastic alliance, agreeing to a division of their anticipated conquests, and John accepted that on his death Menelik should take the title of Emperor. In 1887, after the ardent Muslim ruler of Harar, 'Abdallah Muhammad, had conveniently caused his soldiers to massacre a party of Italian explorers, Menelik seized the city and appointed his cousin Ras Makonnen as governor. In a message to the British at Aden, Menelik made it clear that he regarded 'Abdallah Muhammad as a latter-day successor to the sixteenth-century Muslim conqueror Ahmad Gran, and that 'Abdallah's defeat, like Gran's, was a vindication of Christian sovereignty.

Meanwhile King John was engaged in keeping both the Mahdists and the Italians at bay. After what amounted to an Italian victory, although an indecisive one, in 1888, John was killed in the following year on the battlefield of Metemma against the Dervishes; and the Italians succeeded in making the treaty of Ucciali with Menelik who had now assumed John's title. The Italian version of this treaty was interpreted as making Abyssinia an Italian protectorate, but Menelik claimed that the Amharic version did not oblige him to conduct all his external relations through Italy. This inconsistency, however, was not to come to light until later. For the moment, the Italians, who had gained formal recognition of their sovereignty over Eritrea, felt confident of their position and made arms and ammunition freely available to Menelik: loan capital was also granted, and in 1890 Italy sponsored Abyssinian membership of the Brussels General Act which empowered her as a Christian state to import munitions legally. French merchants had already long been engaged in the lucrative arms trade with the Abyssinian rulers, having paid little attention to an Anglo-French convention of 1886 prohibiting the import of arms. France's ally, Russia, which vied with Italy to make Ethiopia her protectorate, likewise poured arms and military advisers into the country. This influx of war material which on the Italian reading of the Ucciali treaty accorded with Italian interests, was in succeeding years to be applied to the consolidation of Menelik's realm, and finally enabled the Emperor to assert his country's independence. In the process, Somali clans which hitherto had lain outside the ancient Abyssinian hegemony were incorporated in the new Ethiopian empire.

In the year in which the ambiguous treaty of Ucciali was concluded, Italy established direct claims to the Somali coast on the Indian Ocean to the east of the British sphere. In February, a treaty was concluded between Vincenzo Filonardi, the Italian Consul at Zanzibar, and Yusuf 'Ali, the Majerteyn Sultan of Obbia,[6] by which the latter placed his country and his possessions under the 'protection and government' of Italy in return for an annuity of 1,800 tallers. Two months later, a similar convention was signed with Yusuf 'Ali's kinsman 'Isman, the hereditary Sultan of the Majerteyn clan at Alula. And at the end of the year (1889) Italy rounded off these new Somali acquisitions when the Imperial British East Africa Company sublet the southern Benadir ports which it held in lease from the Sultan of Zanzibar. The Somali territory to the south of the Juba remained within the British Company's domain, until 1895 when, after the suppression of the rebellion which the incompetence of its officials had provoked, the I.B.E.A.C. surrendered its charter, and the establishment of British colonial rule was proclaimed. Thus Jubaland, as the area was called, became for the time being part of the British East Africa Protectorate.

The Italian claim to the Benadir coastal strip, for this was all it was, was strengthened in 1892 when the Sultan of Zanzibar ceded the ports of Brava, Merca, Mogadishu, and Warsheikh directly to Italy for a term of twenty-five years, the annual rent being fixed at 160,000 rupees. The Italians were free to derive what profit they might from the coast and to administer it, but it still remained the property of the Sultan. In the interval,

Filonardi had deserted his consular post to form the commercial enterprise of V. Filonardi e Co., to which the Italian government entrusted the management of its Benadir holding. The first Italian station was opened in 1891 at Adale (called Itala by the Italians) where the local Somali leaders had signed a treaty of protection with Filonardi. Here the new rulers of the coast were represented by an Arab agent and a small garrison of twenty native soldiers. These were the modest beginnings of the colony which the Italians were to use forty-five years afterwards as their principal base for the conquest of Ethiopia.

While the Company thus assumed its functions on the Benadir coast, Italian explorers were also active. In 1891 Robecchi-Brichetti trekked from Mogadishu to Obbia, and thence crossed through the Ogaden to Berbera. In the same year Baudi di Vesme and Candeo crossed the Ogaden and in the process obtained requests for Italian protection from elders of the Ogaden clan. At the end of the following year, Prince Ruspoli set out from Berbera to traverse much the same area, but from the opposite direction. When he reached Bardera on the Juba in April 1893, he concluded a treaty of protection with the Somali of that region. These Italian pioneers were not the first Europeans to visit all the regions included in their explorations: in 1883 a party of Englishmen had reached the Shebelle from Berbera despite difficulties with the Aden authorities; and between 1886 and 1892 the Swayne brothers had surveyed much of the country between the northern coast and the Shebelle River. But unlike their Italian colleagues, these British explorers did not enter into protectorate agreements with the clansmen they encountered.

More orthodox conventions were established with the Filonardi Company as it began to extend its jurisdiction. The coastal Somali, however, did not always welcome the new rulers. In October 1893, at Merca, as Filonardi and his companions were about to board the Italian warship on which they were travelling, having successfully signed a treaty with the leaders of the town, one of the party was attacked and mortally wounded. In reprisal, twelve Somali elders were taken prisoner and the city heavily bombarded. There were other occasions also when the Italian warships plying Eritrea, Aden, Zanzibar, and the Benadir ports found that such methods had a salutary effect and facilitated the Company's gradual expansion. But in 1896, after only three years of existence, the Company's slender financial resources proved inadequate and it was forced to wind up its affairs. By the end of the year, in addition to Itala, six other stations had been opened: two, Giumbo and Warsheikh, were like Itala mere outposts with no Italian official; but at Brava, Merca, Mogadishu, and Lugh there were now Italian Residents in command.

The collapse of Filonardi's Company followed the resounding Italian rout at the battle of Adowa which decisively shattered Italy's ambiguous claim to a protectorate over Ethiopia. Italy managed, however, to retain her Eritrean colony, and despite the furore at home which greeted the news of Menelik's victory, she still clung optimistically to her new Somali possessions. Indeed, with the help of the small flotilla of warships stationed in the Red Sea and Indian Ocean, preparations were being made to defend the Benadir against a possible Ethiopian attack. And attempts were also being made to extend Italian influence inland. In November 1896, without waiting for the consent of the Sultan of the Geledi, a party led by Cecchi, the Italian Consul at Zanzibar, set off to reconnoitre the left bank of the Shebelle River. The expedition ended disastrously at Lafole where its members were ambushed by Somali clansmen, only three of the seventeen Italians escaping with their lives.

This set-back did not, however, deter the Italian government which interpreted the situation as calling for an intensification of the work of 'pacification'. Consequently, until a new company could be found to assume the burden of administering the Benadir, Giorgio Sorrentino, commander of the cruiser Elba, was appointed as Special Commissioner to restore order, and more native troops were hurriedly shipped to the coast from Massawa. By November 1897, Sorrentino's reprisals for the incident at Lafole had convinced the Sultan of the Geledi of the wisdom of accepting the new colonizers and the Special Commissioner's mission was complete. Six months later, despite the continued lack of enthusiasm in Italy for further colonial adventures, the 'Benadir Company' was ready to take over where Filonardi had left off. Like its predecessor, however, this new organization soon found that it had neither the means nor the resources to conduct the undertaking profitably, and succumbed in 1905 when the Italian government at last realized that if anything was to be made of the Benadir, it would have to assume direct responsibility.

The acquisition by Italy of her two northern Somali protectorates and her lease of the southern Benadir ports, although she was at first hardly in a position to assert her authority, naturally raised the question of how the frontiers between these and Britain's Somaliland Protectorate should be drawn. The issue was in fact much wider than this for it also included the more important question of how much territory Italy had gained as protector of Abyssinia, on her interpretation of the Ucciali treaty which Britain accepted but France contested. Interest was focused mainly on Harar and Zeila. France sought to divert the lucrative trade from Harar to the ports of her new colony. Britain endeavoured, within the scope of her limited interests on the Somali coast, to keep the trade flowing along the ancient caravan route to Zeila in her Protectorate. Italy, in her turn, regarded Harar as part of her Abyssinian protectorate and coveted Zeila, the natural outlet of Harar's trade.

Italian interest in the Harar–Zeila area was emphasized as early as 1890 when the Italian government expressed concern about the possible consequences at Harar of a punitive expedition in the British Protectorate against the 'Ise clan. In September of this year, Menelik wrote to the King of Italy pointing out that the Amharic version of the Ucciali treaty allowed him to make use of the Italian government in his relations with foreign powers but did not compel him to do so. The Italian government replied by dispatching Count Antonelli to take the matter up with the Emperor. Another object of Antonelli's visit was to induce Menelik to address a circular letter to the powers defining the ancient boundaries of Abyssinia. This remarkable document was dispatched and received in 1891: in Somaliland it claimed 'the Province of Ogaden, the Habar Awal, the Gadabursi, and the 'Ise' (the last three Somali peoples being clans with whom Britain, and in the case of the 'Ise, France also, had treaties of protection). The letter also contained the challenging declaration: 'Ethiopia has been for fourteen centuries a Christian island in a sea of pagans. If Powers at a distance come forward to partition Africa between them, I do not intend to be an indifferent spectator.'

Nevertheless, it was as protector of Abyssinia that Italy entered into negotiations with Great Britain over their respective boundaries. In March of 1891 an Anglo-Italian protocol was signed which defined the boundary between East Africa and Italian Somaliland, and the Italian government proceeded to press for a further delimitation between her and Britain's Somali territories. At the time Britain was not as anxious as Italy to settle this matter and consequently embarked upon delaying tactics. However, in May 1894 a protocol was signed defining the respective spheres of influence.

By this time Menelik had succeeded in giving some colour to his claims over Somali clans advanced in his circular letter of 1891. The conquest of Harar in 1887 had been followed by the subjugation of the turbulent local Oromo peoples. These achievements encouraged the Abyssinians to turn their attention towards their Somali neighbours. From Harar, Ras Makonnen's forces began foraging not only amongst the 'Ise, Gadabursi, and Habar Awal clans, but also to the east and south-east amongst the Somali of the Haud and Ogaden. This placed the British Protectorate authorities in an awkward position, especially after a small Abyssinian force had opened a post in 1891 at Biyo Kaboba on the British side of the Protectorate's western border. Italy insisted that all negotiations with Abyssinia should proceed through her, and Britain accepted this position protesting vainly to the Italians as incident followed incident. Although the clans concerned turned to the Protectorate authorities for support, nothing effective was done, despite the fact that the Abyssinian pressure could easily have been countered with little cost in arms. The possibility of arming the Somali to protect themselves was raised, and inevitably dismissed.

This unwillingness to honour fully the terms of the Anglo-Somali protectorate treaties, however distasteful to the local British authorities, was of course consistent with the official British attitude towards the Somali coast. The effect was to strengthen Abyssinia's hand, and Italy's as Abyssinia's protector, although there was now growing British scepticism as to Italy's real influence with Menelik.[7]

The negotiations which led to the 1894 Anglo-Italian Protocol discussed a possible surrender of the 'Ise and Gadabursi clans along with the port of Zeila to the Italians in exchange for Italian concessions in their northern Somali protectorates. In the event, however, this course was not followed, and the decision eventually agreed to, amounted to a recognition that the Ogaden lay within the Italian sphere,[8] and the Haud in the British. Three years later Britain was severely to curtail her newly defined rights in the Haud.

The treaties of 1897 with Ethiopia

The Italian defeat at Adowa in 1896 completely destroyed the Italian claim to a protectorate over Abyssinia: the irksome treaty of Ucciali had served Menelik well. The Christian state of Ethiopia to which Menelik's genius had contributed so much, had now become a sovereign power whose position and aspirations had to be taken seriously if European imperial interests were to prosper. This France had long appreciated and had already reaped the fruits of conciliation. Britain, however, remained unconvinced until the Italian débâcle at Adowa drove the point home. Then events in the Sudan, and increasing Ethiopian encroachments in Somaliland, made it imperative for the British government to treat directly with the real masters of the hinterland. Accordingly in 1897, Rennell Rodd, the First Secretary in the British Agency in Cairo, was instructed to go to Addis Ababa to settle these and other wider issues with the Emperor.

By this time, as has been seen, the 'Ise and Gadabursi clans were divided between Britain, France, and Ethiopia in their affiliation. Some of the 'Ise were under French 'protection', some under British, and others, further to the interior, open to the *de facto* influence of Ras Makonnen at Harar. The Gadabursi were similarly divided between the British and Ethiopians; their clan-head, *Ugas* Nur, paid an annual fee of 100 sheep to Ras Makonnen on the understanding that his clansmen would not otherwise be disturbed. He received gifts and drew a salary from both the Ethiopians and the British. In the centre of northern Somaliland, the Isaq clans, which in the course of their grazing movements in the Haud encounter the Ogaden clan, were experiencing periodical Ethiopian raids. Some of the Habar Awal clan had been threatened with attack unless they offered tribute. Even the religious centre at Hargeisa was regularly menaced.

To the south, Ethiopian raiding parties had penetrated as far down the Juba River as Lugh. Here the head of the local Somali clan had requested protection from the Sultan of Zanzibar and had been provided with ten muzzle-loaders which enabled him to maintain his position for a time. About 1893, however, his village was overrun by an Ethiopian attack and he sought help from the Italians on the coast. The pioneers Bottego and Ugo Ferrandi reached Lugh in 1895 and occupied the town after beating off an Ethiopian attack. Bottego then continued his trek towards Lakè Rudolf and Shoa where he was killed, while Ferrandi stayed to administer the Company's new station at Lugh, later known as Lugh Ferrandi. In 1896 a further Ethiopian attack was successfully repulsed.

Thus, with Russian officers attached to their forces,[9] the Ethiopians had continued their forward thrust and enlarged their sphere of influence since 1894. Now, not merely in the north, but over most of their western periphery, the Somali clansmen were experiencing Ethiopian pressure, which though for the most part irregular and spasmodic in its application nevertheless produced a considerable effect. And caught between the conflicting ambitions of the Ethiopians on the hinterland, and the French, British, and Italians, on the coast, individual Somali clans and lineages sought to profit from this rivalry by playing one side off against another. The effect of this was to weaken the general position of the Somali and to encourage the entrenchment of foreign interests.

In the north, the 1894 Anglo-Italian delimitation of territory, which had not been communicated to Menelik, had not in any way improved the growing tension between the Protectorate authorities and Ras Makonnen at Harar. With the increasing Ethiopian pressure, matters indeed had worsened, and by the beginning of 1897 were moving towards a climax. Ras Makonnen refused to allow the British Protectorate administration to act against the 'Ise over an incident which had occurred on territory which he claimed belonged to Ethiopia, and he reinforced his point with a threat to assert Ethiopian authority by force. The British Resident at Aden, who had been trying to settle the dispute with Makonnen, was instructed by his government to refrain from further communications with Harar, since the whole issue of the Protectorate's frontiers would be dealt with by the Rodd mission to Menelik.

In a statement in the House of Commons, the Rodd mission was described as being sent to Ethiopia: 'to assure King Menelik of our friendly intentions, to endeavour to promote amicable political and commercial relations, and to settle certain questions which had arisen between the British authorities on the Somali Coast and the Abyssinian governor of Harar'. Although the wider aims of the Mission were to reassure Menelik as to Britain's interests in the context of Anglo-French rivalry on the Nile, and to secure at least Ethiopian neutrality in the war against the Khalifa in the Sudan, the settlement of the British Protectorate's frontiers was described as one of the principal objects of the negotiations. However, the actual terms in which the Protectorate's frontiers were to be defined and the concessions which might have to be made were of relatively minor importance if Rodd could succeed in establishing friendly relations with Ethiopia. Britain was not prepared to defend the 1894 frontiers if this would entail any considerable expenditure: indeed the possibility of abandoning the Somaliland Protectorate altogether had already been raised. The Aden authorities, however, had insisted that this drastic course was impossible, and so the problem remained of retaining the Protectorate in a form sufficient to satisfy Aden's requirements in meat imports but within boundaries acceptable to Menelik.

Several French missions had already preceded the British Mission to Addis Ababa, but Menelik received Rodd hospitably. And Rodd was impressed by the Emperor, of whom he records somewhat patronizingly, that he ended 'by feeling a great respect for the strong man of Ethiopia, who made a genuine effort to understand the position and overcome his mistrust of his own inexperience'.[10] Menelik's conduct of the negotiations, however, suggest that he required little tutelage in diplomacy. Although Rodd succeeded in getting Menelik to pledge himself to prevent the passage of arms to the Mahdists whom he declared the enemies of Ethiopia, subsequent events show that the Emperor continued to conduct clandestine negotiations with the Dervishes.

No agreement was reached on the definition of Ethiopian boundaries in the Sudan. And the price Rodd had to pay was considerable. Britain authorized the transit of arms and ammunition for the Emperor's use, and waived customs duties at Zeila on goods destined for the use of the Ethiopian state. On the other hand, the ancient caravan route between Harar and Zeila which was already threatened by the proposed railway from French Somaliland, was to remain open to the commerce of both nations, and in Ethiopia itself Britain was to be accorded most favoured nation treatment in trade and commerce. However striking these trade arrangements may have seemed at the time, in practice they amounted to little; French commerce was already strongly entrenched in Ethiopia, and the Jibuti railway soon completely eclipsed Zeila's trade.

The discussion of the Protectorate's frontiers proved exceedingly difficult. The Emperor advanced claims for a reconstitution of the 'ancient frontiers' of Ethiopia and referred to his circular letter of 1891, a document of which Rodd disclaimed knowledge. At first Menelik pressed for the inclusion of the British Protectorate within his empire, but he eventually yielded ground and agreed to Rodd's proposal that the actual definition of the Protectorate's boundaries should be left for settlement to Rodd and Ras Makonnen at Harar: Article II of the Treaty provided that the frontiers thus decided should be attached to the treaty as an annex. A prior annex agreed to at Addis Ababa, foreshadowed the concessions that Rodd was to make at Harar. This stipulated that such Somali clansmen who, as a result of any adjustment of boundaries might eventually become Ethiopian subjects, were to be well treated and assured of 'orderly government'.

The discussion of boundaries with Ras Makonnen at Harar was again tedious and difficult. But in the end a compromise was reached by which, while abandoning her claim to some 67,000 square miles of land in the Haud, Britain was able to retain Hargeisa and part of the hinterland within her Protectorate. This represented a considerable concession to the Ethiopian claims which, though not in 1897 supported by any firm Ethiopian occupation on Somali soil beyond Jigjiga,[11] could not be challenged without the use of force, a course which Rodd rightly understood his government would not countenance.

It is important to emphasize that the terms of the agreement were carefully drawn up to yield Ethiopian recognition of the new boundaries of the British Protectorate. The lost lands in the Haud which were excised from the Protectorate were not, however, ceded to Ethiopia; nor did the agreement bind Britain to recognize Ethiopian sovereignty over the territory which had been relinquished.[12] This one-sided recognition was indeed already implied in the wording of the annex to the treaty which Menelik had accepted at Addis Ababa guaranteeing orderly government and equitable treatment to those Somali who might, in the future, become Ethiopian subjects. Moreover, the adroit form of words adopted by Rodd, is consistent with the terms of the original Anglo-Somali treaties of protection which it will be recalled did not, in fact, cede Somali territory to Britain. The treaty also – and this was essential – did not in any way compromise the Italian claims agreed to between Britain and Italy in 1894.

The eventual effect, of course, clearly envisaged by Rodd and his government of this unilateral withdrawal or curtailment of protection by Britain, was to place the Somali clansmen concerned in a position in which they would not be able to maintain their independence from Ethiopia. It was merely a matter of time before Ethiopia followed up her spasmodic thrusts and transformed her infiltration among the Somali into a definite occupation. This contingency was clearly provided for in the third annex to the treaty which stipulated that the clans on each side of the new British Protectorate frontier should have access to the grazing areas and 'nearer wells' both within and outside the British sphere; during such migratory movements they were to be under the jurisdiction of the appropriate territorial authority. However, Rodd and the other British officials concerned thought that the Ethiopians would be slow to take advantage of what they had in effect already gained; it was considered that in practice things would continue much as they were with the Haud remaining as a sort of buffer zone used by the British clans only temporarily for grazing. The effects of the gradual adoption of agriculture by the western Somali clans were not envisaged, for this process had hardly yet started. A more serious objection which might more reasonably have been anticipated was the effect of the centuries' old trend of population movement away from the highly eroded north towards the centre and Haud. This gradual drift of population was to bring increasing numbers of British protected Somali into what was now effectively the Ethiopian sphere.

These and other more immediate objections to the effects of the treaty were, however, of only local importance, and although there were protests in England as well as misgivings amongst the local Somali Coast administrators, these carried little weight in the face of the imperatives of imperial strategy. From this wider point of view, given Britain's secondary interest in Somaliland and her refusal to undertake any financial commitment there which went beyond the purpose for which the Protectorate had been created, Rodd had in reality merely yielded to the inevitable. A notable attempt had at least been made to secure Ethiopian goodwill, and Ethiopian recognition had been obtained for the British Somaliland Protectorate within frontiers which were still consistent with the requirements of the trade to Aden. That this had been achieved at the price of unilaterally abandoning protectorate treaties with Somali clansmen, was, of course, unfortunate, but whatever misgivings Rodd himself may have had were reassured when an interview with Lord Salisbury revealed that the Foreign Minister was 'not much preoccupied by Abyssinian encroachments in Somaliland'.[13]

Nevertheless, the Government of Bombay which was directly responsible through Aden for administering the territory was not entirely satisfied and prophesied that trouble with the Somali, who had not been consulted and knew nothing of the treaty, would be likely to follow. Any additional expenditure which might thereby be incurred should not, Bombay urged, fall upon its exchequer. The point was taken, and the Foreign Office, which had been responsible for the treaty, assumed responsibility for the Protectorate in the following year, in time to bear the burden of the first phase of the twenty years rebellion which broke out two years later.

Thus 1897 saw the definition of the British Somali sphere in relation to Ethiopia. But it was not until 1934, when an Anglo-Ethiopian boundary commission attempted to demarcate the boundary, that British-protected Somali became aware of what had happened, and expressed their sense of outrage in disturbances which cost one of the commissioners his life. This long period of ignorance, far from indicating acquiescence, was facilitated by the many years which elapsed before Ethiopia established any semblance of effective administrative control in the Haud and Ogaden.

Yet 1897 remains the crucial year in the imperial history of the

Horn of Africa; and the boundary agreements made then have left a legacy of indeterminacy and confusion which still plagues the relations between Ethiopia and the Somali Republic. Nor was it only the British who unilaterally abrogated some of their protectorate obligations towards Somali. The Lagarde mission to Menelik, which had preceded Rodd's, had also discussed boundary questions and reduced the extent of the *Côte des Somalis* to the satisfaction of the Emperor. In return, commercial guarantees were obtained which included agreement on the construction of the proposed railway from Jibuti, the new capital of the *Côte*, to the Ethiopian hinterland: the effect of this was to make French Somaliland the official outlet for Ethiopia's trade.

Farther to the south, though as yet only weakly established, Italy was determined to cling to her new Somali interests and forced, after her defeat at Adowa, to reach a boundary settlement acceptable to Ethiopia. This was negotiated by Major Nerazzini who had earlier conducted with Menelik the negotiations for the Italo-Ethiopian peace treaty.[14] And although in that treaty Menelik described himself as 'Emperor of Ethiopia and of the Galla countries', making no reference to his pretensions in Somaliland, Italy was forced to reduce her claims to the Ogaden which Britain had accepted in the Anglo-Italian Protocol of 1894. In fact, the Italian sphere was defined vaguely as lying within an area up to 180 miles from the coast and running from the boundary of the British Protectorate to the Juba River, north of Bardera. At the time, when the Italian position was so weak, this hasty division of spheres of interest may have seemed advantageous to both parties; certainly in later years it fostered the growth of a tradition of uncertainty and conflict which led to the Walwal incident and Italo-Ethiopian war, and is still unresolved.

Nevertheless, for the time being at least, France, Britain, and Italy, had now pruned their Somali possessions to dimensions acceptable to Ethiopia, and the stage was set for the march of local events. For the next twenty-three years these were dominated by the religious war against the Christian 'infidels' led by Sheikh Muhammad 'Abdille Hassan in which Somali, who for the most part had so far seemed to accept those new imperial developments of which they had knowledge, fiercely strove to regain their lost independence.

CHAPTER IV

THE DERVISH FIGHT FOR FREEDOM: 1900-20

The Growth of Muslim brotherhoods

BEFORE FOLLOWING Sayyid Muhammad 'Abdille Hassan's remarkable struggle to free his country from foreign domination, it is necessary to pause for a moment to review the social and religious context in which this patriotic movement arose. Islam in Somaliland has long been associated with the brotherhoods or *tariqas* (literally, 'the Way') which express the Sufi, or mystical view of the Muslim faith, a view which, since it exalts the charismatic powers of saints, is particularly well adapted to the Somali clan system in which clan ancestors readily become transposed into Muslim saints. So well developed indeed had these religious organizations become in the nineteenth century, that the Somali profession of the faith was now synonymous with membership of, or more frequently, nominal attachment to a Sufi brotherhood. The esoteric content of Sufism, however, was not strongly developed locally, although each religious Order had (and has) a distinctive liturgy for its adherents to follow in their worship of God. Despite their common aim of promoting religious as opposed to secular values, the relations between different Orders are characterized by rivalry centring on the respective religious merits and mystical powers of intercession of their founders. Generally, the Orders have a loose hierarchical organization, and many, though not all, Somali Sheikhs and men of religion occupy positions of religious authority within the Order which they follow.

More significantly, notwithstanding their own rivalries, in their membership and following the brotherhoods cut across clan and tribal loyalties, seeking to substitute the status of brother in religion for that of clansman, so that men who are divided by clan affiliation may share common adherence to the same religious Order. In this way, by their very nature, the Muslim Orders contribute to national unity through Islam and seek to overcome the sectional rivalries which separate men in their secular activities. However, given the circumstances of Somali life and society in which, lacking any large centralized political units, the only security was provided by small bands of kinsmen, the loyalties of kin and clan remained paramount. Thus the transcendental appeal to unity through Islam which the Orders preached, although it found a response in the cultural nationalism of the Somali, remained only a potential force overridden by the more restricted political realities of everyday life. Indeed it was only realized, and then only partially, in a few religious communities and teaching centres established usually in those regions where the brethren could support themselves by cultivation and cattle-rearing. Elsewhere, the Orders merely provided, as for the most part they still do today, a congregational basis for worship; and in all large settlements of population each brotherhood has usually its own mosque.

Historically, the first Order to be introduced into Somaliland was the Qadiriya, the oldest Order in Islam, founded in Baghdad where its originator Sayyid 'Abd al-Qadir al-Jilani died in A.D. 1166. It is not yet certain when the Qadiriya came to Somaliland, but by the nineteenth century it was strongly established and had split into two powerful local branches, one associated with the name of Sheikh 'Abd ar-Rahman Seyla'i who died in the Ogaden in 1883, and the other with that of Sheikh Uways Muhammad who was assassinated in 1909. The former branch held sway in the north, in the British Protectorate and the Ogaden; while the latter was entrenched in the Benadir and south of Somalia. The other main Order of importance locally is the Ahmadiya, founded at Mecca in Arabia, by Sayyid Ahmad ibn Idris al-Fasi (1760–1837). This modern reformist movement with its sudsidiary branches had, by the end of the nineteenth century come to rival that of the longer established Qadiriya.[1]

Between them, these two Orders had by 1900 a score of permanent community settlements scattered throughout Somaliland, but concentrated mainly in the fertile regions between the

Juba and Shebelle rivers. At this time, one of the most important centres in the north was Sheikh Maddar's (1825–1917) large Qadiriya settlement at Hargeisa amongst the Habar Awal clan containing representatives of most of the Isaq clans. This was a haven of peace in a turbulent area, strategically placed at the intersection of the caravan routes leading from the coast to the Ogaden.[2] Other Qadiriya settlements were established in the Ogaden itself, while others again lay farther south in Somalia. Ahmadiya centres were similarly widely distributed; and, outside these local settlements, almost the entire Somali population was divided in religious affiliation between the two Orders.

Competition between the two brotherhoods was considerably increased when the militant Salihiya branch of the Ahmadiya Order, founded at Mecca by Sayyid Muhammad Salih (1853–1917), was introduced into Somaliland towards the end of the nineteenth century. It was to this reformist and puritanical movement that the Somali Sheikh Muhammad 'Abdille Hassan belonged, and under its banner he developed the campaign to free his country of 'infidel' dominion.

The rise of Sayyid Muhammad 'Abdille Hassan

Muhammad 'Abdille Hassan, according to his family's records,[3] was born on 7 April, 1864, at a small watering-place between Wudwud and Bohotle in the Dulbahante country of the eastern part of the British Somaliland Protectorate. His grandfather, Sheikh Hassan Nur, of the Ogaden clan, had left his homeland to settle amongst the Dulbahante in 1826 and had married there. At the early age of seven, Muhammad began to learn the Quran under a local teacher, and by the age of ten, when his grandfather died, could read the Quran and became his teacher's assistant. Some five years later, having decided to dedicate his life to religion, he set up as a teacher on his own account, and by the early age of nineteen had won the title of 'sheikh' for his learning and piety.

About this time Sheikh Muhammad left his home to travel widely in search of learning, visiting, as was customary, such local seats of Islam as Harar, and Mogadishu – where a tree, in whose shade he is said to have prayed regularly, is remembered to this day: he also travelled as far afield as the Sudan and Nairobi.

Some nine years or so passed thus, devoted to learning and teaching. About 1891 he returned to his home amongst his mother's people, the Dulbahante, and there married a woman of his own clan, the Ogaden. Three years later, in company with thirteen other sheikhs and friends, Sheikh Muhammad set out to go on pilgrimage to Mecca and spent about a year in Arabia, visiting also – it is said – the Hejaz and Palestine. At Mecca, Sheikh Muhammad met Sayyid Muhammad Salih and fell under the spell of his teaching. Consequently having joined the Salihiya Order, the Sheikh returned to Somaliland to preach its message, and settled for a time at Berbera where he married his second wife. Here with messianic zeal he taught and preached, denouncing smoking, the chewing of the stimulant Kat plant,[4] and generally condemning all excessive indulgence and luxury and exhorting his countrymen to return to the strict path of Muslim devotion.

Sheikh Muhammad's activities and his enthusiasm for the new Salihiya Order attracted considerable attention in this port where the majority were staunch adherents of the older Qadiriya brotherhood. Tradition records that about 1897 a colloquy of sheikhs and religious leaders was held to discuss Sheikh Muhammad's theological position and to examine his aims. The meeting took place in the house of one of the leading notables of Berbera. Amongst those present were Sheikh Muhammad's former teacher, Sheikh 'Abdille Arusi, and Sheikh Maddar, head of the Qadiriya community at Hargeisa. Sheikh Maddar, it is recorded, opened the proceedings by asking Sheikh Muhammad the name of the Order which he followed. Sheikh Muhammad replied, apparently, by remarking that it was laid down in Islam that for each generation God had provided one pre-eminent saint (the *quth al-zaman*), and that for his generation this was his master Sayyid Muhammad Salih whose 'Way' he was teaching. Sheikh Maddar agreed that it was the orthodox teaching that each generation had its great saint of Islam, but reminded Sheikh Muhammad that whoever he followed, and whatever he preached, God would judge him according to the strict ordinances of the Divine Law. This, of course, was a warning not to transgress the law of Islam, and came from one renowned for his piety and strict devotion.

Other members of the assembly then called upon Sheikh Muhammad to prove the power of his new Order with a sign,

Sheikh 'Abdille Arusi, remarking, it is said, that he marvelled at the strength of the town's foundations which had prevented Berbera from being turned upside down. To this veiled comment on his lack of immediate success in gaining adherents, Sheikh Muhammad replied that indeed the town was blessed in possessing strong religious foundations. However, Sheikh Muhammad urged that whereas formerly he had followed Sheikh 'Abdille Arusi, now he exhorted his teacher to follow him and share the blessings of the new Order.

Not long after this very characteristic Somali inquisition which had made clear to the leaders of the established Qadiriya the revolutionary character of Sheikh Muhammad 'Abdille's message, the Sheikh came into contact with the French Roman Catholic mission which had opened a station in the north of the Protectorate in 1891. This was originally at Berbera, but had now moved to Daimole, inland on the road towards Sheikh. The story goes that Sheikh Muhammad met a boy at the mission school and asked him his name. To his amazement and wrath, the boy replied 'John 'Abdillahi'. Another account relates that the Sheikh met a party of boys from the mission who when asked what clan they belonged to – the stock Somali inquiry to elicit someone's identity, replied 'the clan of the Fathers' (in Somali, *reer faddar*), thus apparently denying their Somali identity (many of the boys were actually orphans).

However apocryphal these accounts may sound to modern ears, in Somali terms they are highly credible, and without doubt they commemorate encounters with the mission which served to confirm Sheikh Muhammad's belief that Christian colonization sought to destroy the Muslim faith of his people. This fired his patriotism and he intensified his efforts to win support for the Salihiya, preaching in the mosques and streets that his country was in danger, and urging his compatriots to remove the English 'infidels' and their missionaries. He also inveighed against the practice of drinking alcohol which the foreigners had introduced. At first there was considerable resistance to his call, especially on the part of the Qadiriya who resented Sheikh Muhammad's messianic claims for the Salihiya, and his implication that their Order – whose founder had died so long ago – was no longer endowed with spiritual life and vigour. At the same time, under

67

the new and very modest British rule of the coast, commerce was flourishing (some 70,000 head of sheep were being exported annually to Aden) and many of the traders and merchants of Berbera consequently were too content with their prosperity and too intent on improving it further to listen to Sheikh Muhammad's uncompromising message.

In these circumstances in 1898 Sheikh Muhammad 'Abdille withdrew to his maternal home amongst the Dulbahante who, un-like the Isaq and Dir clans in the west and centre of the Pro-tectorate, had no treaty with the British, and there built a mosque with a Salihiya teaching centre. He also travelled widely amongst the pastoralists preaching his cause and warning his countrymen that the Christian missionaries would destroy their religion. At the same time, he acquired a wide reputation as a peace-maker in inter-clan strife and his remarkable gifts as a poet began to be recognized thus further enhancing his fame. He also began to gather weapons – mainly spears and bows and arrows at this time – and collected donations of livestock and money to support his campaign.

In 1899, a small party of the Administration's tribal constabulary – known as Illalos (from the Somali, *Illaali* to watch over) visited the sheikh and one of them surrendered his rifle for, it is said, four camels. On their return to Berbera, the Illalos reported, perhaps mendaciously, that Sheikh Muhammad had stolen a rifle and the Consul sent a curt letter requesting its return. Sheikh Muhammad replied equally curtly, with what amounted to a declaration of defiance. Shortly after this equivocal incident, the Sheikh held a large assembly amongst the Dulbahante calling upon men from every section of the clan to join him in his crusade against the infidels. With little vested interest in Berbera's trade, and hardly any direct experience of the British coast administration, the Dulbahante had less qualms than the rich Isaq merchants of the coast and many flocked to join Sheikh Muhammad. These recruits to what was rapidly assuming the character of a military crusade were issued with white turbans and a Muslim rosary.

Rumours were now circulating that Sheikh Muhammad was collecting arms and men and preparing to lead an expedition into Ethiopia. A decade previously, English explorers and travellers traversing the Ogaden had noted how the increasingly far-flung and gratuitously savage raids of Ethiopian military parties from Harar were provoking strong resentment and creating a situation in which a number of leading Somali sheikhs in the area were exhorting their congregations to mount a holy war against the encroaching 'infidels'.[5] That Sheikh Muhammad should now seek to marshal these currents of patriotic fervour and give this aim effective leadership seemed likely. In April 1899, he was officially reported to have at his command a force of some 3,000 men. In August, the news was that he was soliciting the Isaq Habar Tol Ja'lo and Habar Yunis clans for support. To forward this aim, Sheikh Muhammad succeeded in making peace between these two clans and his maternal kinsmen, the Dulbahante. And with this achieved, a great assembly was held at Burao amongst the Habar Yunis and Habar Tol Ja'lo. Here with a force estimated to number 5,000 at his command, Sheikh Muhammad formally declared a holy war against the Christian colonizers – particularly against the British and Ethiopians. Most of the Burao assembly supported the Sheikh's call to arms, but the Sultan of the Habar Yunis was not enthusiastic. Sheikh Muhammad, however, such was the popular support for his movement at this time, managed to persuade the Habar Yunis to depose their clan-head appointing in his stead one more favourable to the cause. Some dramatic act was now called for and this was supplied by a raid on two religious settlements of a small branch of the Ahmadiya Order which displayed little enthusiasm for Sheikh Muhammad's *jihad*. This caused some consternation, and an onslaught upon Berbera itself was reported to be imminent.

Administrative reports claimed that Sheikh Muhammad had now assumed the title of 'Mahdi'. But although widespread public awareness of earlier events in the Sudan, and sympathy for their co-religionists there, was certainly a contributory factor in the rise of Sheikh Muhammad's campaign, there is no independent evidence that he ever in fact claimed this title. Indeed, according to all reliable Somali sources, and the evidence of his letters and poems, he called himself 'Sayyid' by which title, or more simply as Ina 'Abdille Hassan (the Somali equivalent of the Arabic *ibn* 'Abdille) he is universally remembered throughout Somaliland today. His followers, in turn, soon became known everywhere in the country simply as 'The Dervishes', the term 'dervish' being applied in

Somaliland generally to the adherents of the Salihiya Order.

On 1 September, 1899, the British Consul-General for the coast received a letter from the Sayyid accusing the British of oppressing Islam and denouncing those who obeyed or co-operated with the Administration as liars and slanderers. The letter also contained the challenge: 'Now choose for yourselves. If you want war, we accept it; but if you want peace, pay the fine.'[6] The Consul-General replied by proclaiming Sayyid Muhammad a rebel, and urged his government in London to prepare an expedition against the Dervishes. Thus the opening moves in the long-drawn out conflict were completed with the official denunciation as a 'rebel' of one who, belonging to the Ogaden clan over which Ethiopia claimed but did not exercise sovereignty, and whose maternal kinsmen (the Dulbahante) amongst whom he lived had no treaty with England, was surely most doubtfully classed as a British subject.

The Holy War: the first campaigns

The scene was now set for the twenty-years Dervish struggle against the British, Ethiopian, and Italian colonizers who had so recently established themselves in Somali territory. After the Consul-General's proclamation, the Sayyid and his followers moved from Burao to collect – according to British reports by threats and violence – more supporters from the Habar Yunis clan. Towards the end of September, 1899, the Dervishes returned to the watering-place of Bohotle where some of the Dulbahante deserted them. About this time *Garad* 'Ali Farah, hereditary leader of one of the two main sections of the Dulbahante sent a letter of loyalty to the Consul-General at Berbera asking for help against the Dervishes. A similar message was also dispatched to *Boqor* 'Isman, the formidable hereditary leader of the powerful Majerteyn clan at Bender Qasim. This action, presumably, was taken in an effort by the Dulbahante leader to preserve his traditional authority. Whatever the reasons, the Sayyid's response when the news leaked out was characteristically prompt. A party of Dervishes was dispatched to assassinate the *Garad*, an action which turned out to be a miscalculation for it immediately provoked a further substantial withdrawal of Dulbahante support. Indeed, the reaction was so considerable that the Sayyid prudently withdrew to his own paternal kinsmen the Ogaden, where he married a daughter of one of the most prominent elders of the clan. This device of contracting political alliances by marriages was one which he was to employ frequently in the course of his campaign.

Although he was of Ogaden descent, however, his home had not previously been amongst them, and some members of the clan decided that they wished to have nothing to do with the Sayyid and plotted to kill him. But, as in subsequent attempts on his life, the news leaked out and Sayyid Muhammad confronted the ring-leaders and succeeded in rousing such public indignation against them that he was able to have them summarily executed. On this occasion these stern measures, in the current situation of Ethiopian menace, served not to alienate the Ogaden but to win him further support. Rifles and ammunition imported through the French port of Jibuti and the ports of the Majerteyn coast, were now reaching the Dervishes in quantity and this greatly increased their morale and prestige. With these resources, trading caravans traversing the Ogaden country were systematically looted by the Dervishes, and a hurriedly assembled Ethiopian expedition sent out to deal with the situation failed to locate the Dervishes and dissipated its energies in looting camels and other livestock indiscriminately. This, of course, only further inflamed Ogaden feelings against the Ethiopians, and Sayyid Muhammad found little difficulty in organizing a force some 6,000 strong which in March 1900 stormed the Ethiopian post at Jigjiga and recovered all the looted stock. This engagement the Ethiopians claimed as a victory; but in reality, although the Dervishes suffered heavy casualties and withdrew, they had achieved their object and established beyond doubt that they were a force to be reckoned with.

In contrast with the traditional position of men of religion in internal Somali affairs, Sayyid Muhammad had now become a political leader, a position which he was enabled to fulfil while still retaining his religious rôle in the circumstances of the wider conflict between Muslim Somali and Christian colonizers. He and his followers were now, moreover, in undisputed command of the Ogaden and to show their strength a force of about a thousand Dervish cavalry raided one of the Isaq clans in June carrying off 2,000 camels in loot. This daring attack, which took advantage of the long-standing conflict over grazing between the Isaq and Ogaden clans, caused consternation in the British Protectorate, and the protected clans withdrew from their summer grazing areas in and near the Ogaden to their northern winter quarters which soon became perilously overcrowded. The Protectorate authorities realized that immediate action had to be taken; for if the situation were allowed to continue, the Isaq clans concerned would be forced to choose between coming to terms with the Dervishes and starvation for their livestock and themselves.

In the circumstances, the Ethiopian Emperor Menelik proposed joint action and Lt-Colonel E. J. E. Swayne who with his brother (H. G. C. Swayne) had had considerable experience in the Protectorate was appointed to organize a British expeditionary force. The onset of the rains delayed preparations, but on 22 May, 1901, Swayne's force consisting of a Somali levy 1,500 strong with twenty-one officers of the British and Indian armies set out from Burao which at this time was still unadministered. The operations against Sayyid Muhammad, who was soon dubbed 'The Mad Mullah', had begun. Their course which, until the outbreak of the Great War in 1914, kept British war correspondents busy as well as providing an exciting field for adventurous British soldiers, has been fully recorded elsewhere[7] and need only be summarized here. Between 1900 and 1904 – with from time to time active Ethiopian support and Italian co-operation – four major expeditions were mounted. These though resisted bravely and brilliantly by the daring guerilla tactics of the Dervishes, who secured a number of notable victories (such as that at Gumburu Hill on 17 April, 1903, when 9 British officers and 189 men were killed), had by the close of 1904 so reduced the Dervish strength and morale that Sayyid Muhammad, who had evaded all attempts at capture, agreed to a peace.

He had now prudently withdrawn into the Italian Majerteyn protectorate, where there was no resident Italian administrative official, and which was controlled still from the Italian Consulate at Aden. The Sayyid stipulated four main conditions:

1 That he should have a fixed residence on Italian territory;
2 That he should govern his followers;

3 That he should enjoy religious liberty; and,

4 That he should have freedom to trade.

These conditions were accepted and a treaty was signed by the Sayyid and Cav. G. Pestalozza, the Italian Consul from Aden, at Illig on 5 March, 1905. Sayyid Muhammad had agreed to remain at peace with Italy, Britain, and Ethiopia, and to accept Italian protection – for what it was worth – being allocated a wedge of territory between the lands of the northern Majerteyn Sultanate, and the Sultanate of Obbia to the south. Although thus banished from the British Somaliland Protectorate, by agreement between the British and Italian governments, the Sayyid and his followers were granted grazing and watering rights for their livestock within the Protectorate up to the wells at Halin, Hudin, Togale, and Danod (the last of which, incidentally, lay outside British territory in the Ogaden).

This somewhat lame conclusion to the third and fourth British expeditions which together had cost some five and a half million pounds recognized that the Dervishes had not been completely eliminated, but assumed that they no longer constituted any serious threat. Or so at least it was convenient to think. And in the meantime, Sayyid Muhammad and his surviving adherents had been established as a kind of small theocratic state, sandwiched between the powerful northern Majerteyn under *Boqor* 'Isman, and the southern Majerteyn and Hawiye who recognized the Sultan of Obbia, Yusuf 'Ali Kenadid. Both these latter were under Italian protection, directed from the Italian Consulate at Aden, and subject to little direct control or interference except that provided by the periodical visits of Italian gunboats along the coast. To the west, between Sayyid Muhammad and his followers and the British 'friendly' clans subject to effective control from Berbera, the Dulbahante and Warsangeli provided a convenient if insecure buffer. At least the British could congratulate themselves on having transferred their stormy opponent to the custody of their allies the Italians, and both powers hastened to divest themselves of any responsibility for the Sayyid's actions towards the Ethiopians by a supplementary Anglo-Italian agreement of 19 March, 1907.[8]

While it is not difficult to understand British satisfaction, however guarded, at the conclusion of this arrangement, the Italian readiness to assume even such limited responsibilities as they had done for the Sayyid requires some explanation. It is possible that, even at this early date, the Dervishes were regarded hopefully as a potential aid to the extension of Italian interests into the Ethiopian sphere. But, probably of more significance, is the fact that Britain had in January 1905 enabled Italy to convert her lease of the Benadir coast from the Sultan of Zanzibar into an outright purchase conferring full rights of possession. In any event, the explanation given at the time to the Italian parliament by Tommaso Tittoni, the Minister responsible, was that the Illig agreement establishing peaceful relations between Italy and Sayyid Muhammad would greatly facilitate the extension of Italian authority in the Benadir. Events were soon to show how thoroughly mistaken this appreciation of the situation was.

From Illig to Taleh and defeat

The peace lasted until 1908,[9] Sayyid Muhammad ostensibly respecting the terms of the Illig agreement while using this period of respite to recoup his strength and influence. A widespread network of spies and agents were operating in the British Protectorate, seeking to undermine the loyalty of the clans and to attract them to the Dervish cause. At the same time, Sayyid Muhammad was pursuing a minor and rather desultory war against Yusuf 'Ali, the Sultan of Obbia who, though changeable and equivocal in his attachments, was during this period generally hostile to the Dervishes. Not so the Warsangeli clan within the British Protectorate on the eastern coast, who, under their spirited leader *Garad* Mahamud 'Ali Shirre (*d.* 1960), had now decided to throw in their lot with the Dervishes and in January 1908 fired on a British dhow as it was landing on their coast. This incident provoked a hostile exchange of letters with the Consul at Berbera and it was evident that the Dervishes would soon be on the march again.

Meanwhile, before the next round of battles, the British Administration was presented with a convenient opportunity of countering the formidable barrage of propaganda unleashed against it by the Sayyid, whose scathing poems, which spread like wildfire, constituted so formidable a weapon. Haji 'Abdallah Sheheri of the Habar Tol Ja'lo clan who had hitherto acted as the Sayyid's agent at Aden, and had played an important part in the negotiations with the Italian Consul Pestalozza leading to the Illig treaty, had gradually come to lose faith in the Dervish mission. He was thus readily persuaded by the Italian authorities to participate in a mission to Sayyid Muhammad Salih, the founder and head of the Salihiya Order, which obtained from this religious dignitary a letter referring to Muhammad 'Abdille Hassan's reported violations of Islamic law and threatening to repudiate him if he did not mend his ways. The contents of this somewhat mild denunciation were widely publicized by the British and Italians and the letter itself was delivered to the Sayyid at his headquarters in March, 1909.[10]

It appears likely that this manœuvre was jointly engineered by the British and Italian authorities, although there is little doubt also that Haji 'Abdallah Sheheri, like many other former adherents, now regarded the Dervishes as fanatics who paid scant attention to the ordinances of Islam or the rules of the Salihiya Order. Yet although this move undoubtedly had some effect, so great was the personal charismatic power of Sayyid Muhammad, and his reputation as a quite unique figure in Somali eyes so thoroughly established, that the damage to his position was by no means such as to seriously weaken his movement. The situation indeed called for more direct action.

But having already expended large sums of money totally out of proportion to their limited interest in the Somali coast, the British government decided that before any further military operations were undertaken a new appraisal of the whole situation was necessary. A fresh opinion, it was felt, was called for; and to supply this General Sir Reginald Wingate, Governor-General of the Sudan, was appointed to visit Somaliland to assess the situation and if possible to treat directly with Sayyid Muhammad. In this latter respect the Wingate mission was singularly unsuccessful, and having considered its report, which was never published, the British government decided to cut its losses and embark upon a new policy of coastal concentration. In 1910, accordingly, the Administration withdrew to the coast evacuating the interior – little of which was in any case under stable civil rule – and arming the Isaq clans – the 'friendlies' as they were called – thus leaving them to protect themselves against the Dervishes. Such misgivings as were felt by the Administration were soothed by the convenient assumption that, if left undisturbed, the situation would throw up a leader capable of rallying support against the Dervishes. That the Dulbahante were left utterly unprotected was considered justified in view of the fact that they had no treaty with the British. This, however, had not prevented Britain in the past from regarding the Dulbahante as part of the Somaliland Protectorate when it was convenient to do so.

This vain hope was based on a quite mistaken appreciation of the situation, for it assumed that Sayyid Muhammad was merely a regular, if rather outstanding, clan or tribal leader whose political rôle lay in the field of internal Somali clan politics. The truth of course was, on the contrary, that the Sayyid occupied a unique position as a national figure appealing to the patriotic sentiments of Somali as Muslims irrespective of their clan or lineage allegiance. It is true that internal clan rivalries weakened the Dervish movement, and that its compulsive appeal was also restricted by the divisions between opposing religious orders. But even the deeply alienated adherents of the Qadiriya Order could hardly be expected to rally in strength against the Sayyid, for this would have required them openly to assume the rôle of the Christian colonizers, and would greatly have detracted from their religious status. It was one thing to fight at British instigation against co-religionists; but to band together specifically for the purpose of destroying the Dervishes was another matter. Moreover, such unity against the Sayyid and his followers as had existed under the British leadership had caused internal clan jealousies and antagonisms to be temporarily bottled up; and now that the British had gone, and free supplies of arms were available, the urge to abandon this strained peace was overwhelming.

Consequently, far from throwing up a leader to lead the friendlies against the Dervishes, the clans now launched into a frenzied pursuit of old scores and feuds, and the interior of the country lapsed into a state of unparalleled confusion and chaos. Soon indeed the situation was so desperate that a large proportion of the population was reduced to a state bordering on starvation, and food was so scarce that people had to eat rats and other unclean animals.

The coastal Administration, deprived of effective military resources and greatly reduced in prestige, was totally incapable of restoring order: and the Dervishes were again on the move, and receiving a great access of new adherents, in circumstances which were peculiarly favourable to them. The new policy clearly was a complete failure.

By the end of 1912, when it was officially reckoned that perhaps a third of the Protectorate's population had perished in the 'Time of eating filth', as it is known to Somali, British policy again changed and the Administration was authorized to raise a local mounted camel constabulary. This force which was to police the immediate hinterland was organized under the command of Richard Corfield and soon proved highly successful, its mobility and tactics being well adapted to the needs and conditions of the country. The people, besides, had for the time being had sufficient of unlimited violence and welcomed the restoration of order. Hence, in quite a short time the new Camel Constabulary was able to bring conditions back to something like normality in the west and centre of the Protectorate – the Dervishes meanwhile remaining in the east. Corfield received careful and detailed instructions that his duties were to police the immediate hinterland, and that he was on no account to attack the Sayyid's forces. This, however, was not an easy task, since the Dervishes periodically raided the clans under his protection.

It is scarcely surprising, therefore, that eventually a situation arose where, after a fierce Dervish raid, Corfield and his constabulary were in a position to give chase. Thus in August 1913, disregarding his instructions, Corfield courageously if impetuously moved out from Burao in pursuit of a large Dervish force which he engaged at Dulmadobe in the east of the Protectorate. This rash action cost Corfield his life and both sides suffered very serious casualties. The result, which was announced on newspaper hoardings in London as 'Horrible disaster to our troops in Somaliland', has been immortalized in Sayyid Muhammad 'Abdille Hassan's savagely brilliant poem 'The Death of Richard Corfield'.[11] Despite this set-back, however, the effectiveness of the Camel Constabulary, which was now considerably enlarged, continued to increase and served, with from time to time additional military support, to keep the Dervishes at bay until their final defeat in 1920.

In the meantime, several new factors of significance entered the situation during the Great War. The ill-fated pro-Muslim prince Lij Yasu became Emperor of Ethiopia in December 1913, and moved his court from Dire Dawa to Harar amongst his Muslim subjects with whom his sympathies lay. With the not-disinterested support of the Turkish and German Consuls in Ethiopia, the new Emperor conceived the aim of creating a vast Muslim Empire in N.E. Africa. To this end he entered into relations with Sayyid Muhammad, probably supplying him with financial aid and arms, and arranged for a German mechanic called Emil Kirsch to join the Dervishes and work for them as an armourer at their new headquarters at Taleh where a formidable ring of fortresses had been built by Yemeni masons. Before his pathetically unsuccessful bid for freedom from his exacting masters, Kirsch served the Dervishes well. And it is a measure of the amazing resourcefulness and effectiveness of the Dervish tactics that, with the services of only one professional armourer for a restricted period, they could so successfully resist the long series of costly British operations. Apart from Kirsch's services, the extent of Turko-German support received by the Dervishes has not yet been fully elucidated although it seems to have been rather nominal. However, in 1917, the Italian Administration of Somalia intercepted a document from the Turkish government which assured the Sayyid of support and named him Emir of the Somali nation. But the Turks were in no position to give effect to this belated attempt to revive their old claims to the Somali coast.

Nevertheless, the Sayyid himself, on the basis that one's enemies' enemies are one's friends, certainly greeted the news of Turko–German successes with satisfaction, although he firmly repudiated any suggestion that their help was essential to his campaign. The following extract from a letter received by the British Commissioner at Berbera in March, 1917, expressed his views in no uncertain fashion:

'And you know, and I know, what the Turks have done to you and what the Germans have done to you, you of the British Government. The suggestion is that I was weak and had to look outside for friends; and if, indeed, this were true and I had to look for assistance, it is only because of the British, and the trouble you have given me. It is you who have joined with all the peoples of the world, with harlots, with wastrels, and with slaves, because you are so weak. But if you were strong you would have stood by yourself as we do, independent and free. It is a sign of your weakness, this alliance of yours with Somali, menials, and Arabs, and Sudanese, and Kaffirs, and Perverts, and Yemenis, and Nubians, and Indians, and Baluchis, and French, and Russians, and Americans, and Italians and Serbians, and Portuguese, and Japanese, and Greeks and cannibals and Sikhs and Banyans, and Moors, and Afghans, and Egyptians. They are strong, and it is because of your weakness that you have to solicit as does a prostitute.'[12]

Throughout the period 1914–18, on account of their military commitments elsewhere, the British could do little more than continue their defensive operations on a modest scale. However, in February 1915, the capture of the Dervish fort at Shimberberis left a considerable gap in the Sayyid's network of advanced posts and there were other minor successes. At the same time, the British blockade of the coast had become thoroughly effective, greatly reducing the Dervish supply of arms and ammunition, so that, by the end of the Great War, the local administration judged that the moment was ripe to mount another expedition. This London finally agreed to, and at the beginning of 1920 a carefully planned combined air, sea, and land attack was launched which at last routed the Dervishes. The formidable stronghold at Taleh was bombed and Sayyid Muhammad forced to flee into the Ogaden where, with characteristic fortitude, he proceeded to reorganize his scattered followers and seek new recruits. As on several occasions previously, the Governor at Berbera now sent a message to Sayyid Muhammad calling upon him to surrender and offering him a free pardon. The reply which was made in March was ambiguous, neither accepting nor rejecting the British terms.

It was then decided to dispatch a peace delegation of leading Isaq elders and religious dignitaries, including Sheikh Maddar's son, Sheikh 'Abdillahi, representing the Qadiriya Order. Also of the party was Sheikh Isma'il Sheikh Isaq of the Dulbahante clan, official representative of Sayyid Muhammad Salih in northern Somaliland. Like many another, this religious leader had played, apparently, a somewhat equivocal rôle in the intricate politics of the period. He is said to have clandestinely supported the Sayyid, but appears also to have been a party to the Salihiya letter from

Mecca denouncing the Dervishes. With this distinguished composition the party set off in some trepidation to treat with the Sayyid. They were authorized to persuade Sayyid Muhammad to surrender on the understanding that he would be allowed to establish a religious settlement in the west of the Protectorate and there, under the watchful eye of the Administration, live in peace.

After a series of alarming audiences in which they were treated with contempt and submitted to many degradations, they returned to report to the Administration that Sayyid Muhammad had rejected the offer of surrender with haughty disdain. Almost immediately afterwards, a Dervish force attacked Isaq clansmen grazing their livestock near the Ethiopian border. Despite their very heavy losses, the Dervishes were evidently not yet reduced to defeat. However, this attack aroused fierce Isaq resentment, and the outraged clans sought and gained the sanction of the Administration for a massive tribal onslaught on the new Dervish headquarters in the Ogaden. The Dervishes suffered a very heavy defeat, but as on so many previous occasions, the Sayyid himself and a few companions eluded capture and made good their escape to Imi on the upper reaches of the Shebelle River in Ethiopia. Arriving here in October 1920, the Sayyid and his followers built thirteen new forts and unsuccessfully sought official Ethiopian protection. This was their last gesture, however, for a few weeks later Sayyid Muhammad succumbed to an attack of influenza (or malaria) and died on 21 December, 1920, at the age of fifty-six. Thus, in the words of one Somali chronicle of Sayyid Muhammad's campaign, 'ended the life of the man who had fought great odds'. Of his many children from his numerous marriages only nine boys and one daughter survived him.

Sayyid Muhammad's movement and his achievements

Whatever his detractors have claimed, and notwithstanding the undoubtedly tyrannical character of his rule ultimately, there is no question that Muhammad 'Abdille Hassan's burning passion was to quicken his countrymen's devotion to Islam and to secure universal and absolute adherence to all the ordinances of their faith. To him the Salihiya brotherhood was the 'way' through which this was to be achieved. He had thus a deeply felt mission to fulfil amongst his people whose ancient belief in Islam he saw as perilously threatened by Christian colonization. It was this realization which fired his patriotism and convinced him that the first ideal would never be realized until his people were free. Thus the national movement which he felt himself called upon to inspire was primarily a means to an end. To argue, as has been customary in the past, that Sayyid Muhammad 'Abdille Hassan used religion merely as a cloak to advance his own personal aggrandizement is to make a cheap and shallow assessment which the facts do not warrant.

Yet, although he never lost sight of his primary purpose as his many religious poems and unpublished theological works testify, the pressure of circumstances made it inevitable that he should become increasingly preoccupied with the organization and military needs of the Dervishes. The theocratic rule which he established, founded on a rigid interpretation of the Shafi'i school of Islamic law, despite the fact that he allocated many civil and military responsibilities to the ablest of his adherents, remained always personal in quality and never developed into a strongly hierarchical organization. He did not establish, nor does he appear to have desired to establish a theocratic state which would survive him. He had no successor, many Salihiya followers did not support him, and he did not claim to be Sayyid Muhammad Salih's sole representative in Somaliland. Thus, although his organization perished with his death, the Salihiya brotherhood which had existed outside his movement as well as within it, continued on afterwards and greatly expanded in scope. Nor, probably despite his great gifts of leadership, could he have founded a stable theocratic state. It was difficult enough to create a highly fluid and loosely organized national movement. And what is remarkable is not that this collapsed with his death, but that he ever succeeded in establishing it at all.

For despite such favourable factors as the irritant of Christian mission activity and the hostile and zenophobic reaction of Somali to multiple colonization, the obstacles inherent in the very fabric of Somali society which he had to seek to surmount were formidable. Since Ahmad Gran's wars against Abyssinia in the sixteenth century there had been no tradition of political unity on anything approaching a national basis such as the Sayyid sought to inspire.

Particularistic clan rivalries and jealousies rooted in the exigencies of the eternal struggle for access to pasture and water were too strongly entrenched to admit of the possibility of widespread co-operation. Indeed, even in Swayne's well-informed and usually shrewd judgement, in the last decade of the nineteenth century these mutually contradictory forces seemed so overwhelming that the possibility of an organized rising against the British could be discounted.[13] Events proved otherwise, for Swayne had not calculated on the appearance of so uniquely charismatic a figure as Sayyid Muhammad.

And there is no doubt whatsoever, that notwithstanding the existence of favourable factors, these in themselves would have proved insufficient without the leadership of such a person as the Sayyid. It was more than anything else his magnetic personality, his ruthlessness and his complete and utter defiance of his enemies, that appealed to the Somali mind and deeply stirred the imagination of a people who with all their traditional democracy, admire, above all else, unswerving strength of purpose and un-wavering determination. Tyrannical he might be, but to many Somali, though not to all, his tyranny was directed towards a noble end. These qualities the leader of the *jihad* possessed abund-antly; and the magnificent rhetoric and poetry with which he denounced his foes so scathingly found a ready response amongst his countrymen. The excitements of battle and raiding, and the attractions of the spoils of war, also naturally exerted a strong appeal. But to suppose that the Sayyid's followers were motivated merely by the prospect of loot and livestock is to misjudge the Somali character and to ignore the real nature of the fascination exerted by Sayyid Muhammad's personality.

Yet although his task was to create a national movement transcending clan divisions, to accomplish his object he had of necessity to adapt his tactics to the realities of Somali life. Hence with consummate skill, he employed all the traditional devices of Somali politics; utilizing, when it seemed profitable, his ties with his paternal clansmen, while on another occasion appealing to his maternal relatives, and also taking full advantage of those direct links which he forged by his many political marriages. Although representatives of all the northern Somali clans were amongst his adherents, and his leading lieutenants belonged to no single clan, it was not surprisingly from his paternal clansmen of the Darod family that his most enduring support came. This was partly fortuitous, however, since the Isaq who proved generally less ready to follow the Sayyid lay much more firmly within the British sphere of effective control. Nevertheless, for this betrayal of his cause, as he regarded it, the Sayyid never forgave the Isaq and regularly berated them in his poetic polemics, saying of them in one famous poem: 'The fate of the Isaq is to remain forever as stupid as donkeys.'

While recourse to these tactics was necessary in building up his following, within the Dervish ranks the Sayyid sought to apply Islamic law, enforcing the law of talion and ignoring the traditional Somali practice of treating delicts according to their clan context. Thus amongst his followers he strove to replace traditional clan loyalties by allegiance to his cause, and the Dervish forces were organized into units largely on a non-clan basis. Another striking innovation was that women were sometimes trained as warriors, and a few were even mounted on horseback. All the daily prayers and calendrical ceremonies of Islam were strictly observed, defaulters being liable to correction and in extreme cases to the punishment of death and mutilation. Women also were obliged to adhere strictly to their religious obligations, to wear the veil, and relations between the sexes were stringently regulated according to the letter of the law.

In his dealings with his foreign adversaries as with those of his compatriots who denied him immediate support, he employed a mixture of violent denunciation and vituperation, alternating with soft words of conciliation and encouragement, a conjunction of extremes which often bewildered and sometimes bemused those to whom these varied exhortations were addressed. That he was able to engage in interminable wordy exchanges, by letter, and by word of mouth, and to compose innumerable poetic polemics which have immeasurably enriched the Somali poetic heritage, as well as controlling the political and military conduct of Dervish affairs is a further testimony to the Sayyid's truly extraordinary energy and resourcefulness. His letters, and such of his poetry as has been collected reveal a shrewd appreciation of the colonial situation. Thus, he was well aware of the Italian position in relation to the British, saying of the former in a poem addressed to the British Commissioner at Berbera: 'The Italians are your followers, the foundlings whom you drive before you . . . it is you who lead to pasture these weaker infidels. Can I distinguish between you (i.e. the British) and your cattle?'

It is interesting too, that the French with whom the Dervishes had no direct contact are apparently seldom referred to in Sayyid Muhammad's poems. Their attitude throughout the Dervish period seems to have been somewhat equivocal; and since they do not appear to have energetically prevented arms imported through their coastline from reaching the Dervishes, it is not beyond the bounds of possibility that they watched with interest the outcome of a struggle which might prove permanently prejudicial to British interests.

Finally, before passing on to examine the effects of Sayyid Muhammad's *jihad* in Somalia where the Italians were struggling to extend and consolidate their control, it is important to emphasize that, whatever Sayyid Muhammad Salih himself may have thought of his turbulent disciple, Muhammad 'Abdille Hassan remained, after his fashion, true to his Order. Thus it was with the words of a hymn in praise of the Salihiya founder upon their lips that the Dervishes attacked in battle. And although the true character of Sayyid Muhammad 'Abdille's relations with the headquarters of his Order at Mecca has not yet been, and may never be fully elucidated, Sayyid Muhammad Salih could surely have more decisively repudiated his pupil in Somaliland had he chosen to do so. Certainly Muhammad 'Abdille Hassan himself conceived his mission to be that of restoring to the straight path of devotion the Muslim faith of the Somali. Yet, as must now be clear, to many of his followers, to his adversaries, and sometimes even to himself, this basic aim became overshadowed by his call to national unity against his 'infidel' opponents. And with all the bloody campaigns in which the Dervishes fought, often against other Somali Muslims, it is in this light, as a national hero and forerunner of modern Somali nationalism, that he is remembered by the mass of his countrymen rather than as a sheikh or saint of great blessing.

In this guise his patriotic achievements are lauded today even by the descendants of those who suffered most in the Dervish period, and even by the followers of the Qadiriya. At the time, of course, the Qadiriya were amongst his most bitter opponents, and not without cause, reviled the Dervishes as heretics of whom it was claimed to be more meritorious to kill a single man than a hundred of the infidels. This rivalry, which naturally weakened Sayyid Muhammad's call to arms and limited its scope, was not restricted to the north of the Somali Peninsula where the main course of the twenty-years war unfolded. It reached also into the south of Somalia and the Benadir coast, despite the fact that, in their resistance to Italian colonization, many of the tribes and clans there looked to Sayyid Muhammad for deliverance and support.

The extension of Italian rule in the south

When Britain, not without reluctance, assumed Egypt's place on the northern Somali coast, there was no intention of extending her dominion into the interior and hinterland. Britain's interest was strictly limited to seeing that no hostile power held the shore opposite Aden and to ensuring that the Aden garrison's meat supplies from the Somali coast were unhampered. The long-drawn out, costly, and unrewarding operations against the Dervishes, which were not by-products of any attempt to carry the British flag inland, caused the British government to assume greater responsibilities in Somaliland than had ever been foreseen and which were out of all proportion to Britain's very secondary interest in this area.

The position in respect of Italian interests and hopes in Somalia was very different. From the beginning, Somalia was of primary concern to Italy, and in taking over direct responsibility for the Benadir coast in 1905 the Italian government did so with every intention of developing a true colony which could serve the mother-country both as a source of primary goods and as a convenient receptacle for some of Italy's surplus population. From the beginning, therefore, the Italian policy was to extend their effective authority within the widest possible territorial limits, the increasing penetration and opening up of the hinterland being a direct object, not as in British Somaliland an unlooked for consequence of the Dervish rising. However, in the early years after the disappointments in Eritrea, since public opinion in Italy was strongly opposed to grandiose and costly colonial adventures, by Italian standards the gradual occupation of the country and extension of Italian rule proceeded fairly cautiously. Nevertheless, the impact of the new colonizers was sufficient to arouse fierce resistance amongst many of the clans and tribes of Somalia to whom Sayyid Muhammad often appeared as a symbol of Somali resistance to colonization. Not, however, to all the Benadir peoples. The opposition to Sayyid Muhammad's movement on the part of the southern branch of the Qadiriya Order was as strong as it was in the north. Their leader, Sheikh Uways Muhammad of Brava vigorously denounced the Dervishes, branding them as murderous heretics destined to eternal damnation in many of his noble religious poems. His defiance of the Sayyid's cause cost him his life, for in 1909 he was assassinated by a party of Dervishes near Bioley, where his tomb has become one of the most important centres of pilgrimage in southern Somalia. Likewise, Sheikh 'Ali Maye Durogba of the Ahmadiya Order (d. 1917), today also venerated as a saint, if he did not so openly challenge the Dervishes, certainly offered them little support and was favourably regarded by the Italians.

As in the north, there were thus in the Benadir those who acquiesced more or less readily in their new situation, and those, especially but not exclusively with Salihiya connexions or sympathies, who resisted the colonizers with all the means at their disposal, some receiving arms and other assistance from the Dervishes. Resistance to Italian colonization was at the same time stiffened by the objection of some of the southern clans to the suppression of slavery. For as well as being employed in domestic duties in the Benadir ports, many slaves or serfs were also required to cultivate the fields of noble Somali land-holders who despised manual labour. Besides this, there was still some traffic in slaves to other countries, so that there were many with a vested interest in the continuation of these conditions which the Italians were obliged to seek to remedy.[14] Thus partly on account of this grievance, in 1904 the bellicose Bimal clan blockaded the hinterland of Merca, but after a series of engagements peace was more or less restored by 1905 when, having acquired outright control of the Benadir coast, the new government of the colony issued its first governmental decree. By this time, in addition to Mogadishu, the efforts of the two company regimes had resulted in the opening of administrative posts at seven other centres, mainly along the coast and at Bardera and Lugh on the Juba River.

In 1907 further trouble broke out with the Bimal who had now secured some support from the Dervishes. And in February 1908 a force of Dervishes armed with rifles swept down the Shebelle River causing considerable havoc. They were defeated, however, and the Italians took advantage of the occasion to occupy the Bimal centre of Danane, thus finally pacifying that clan. The same year saw the occupation of Afgoi, formerly one of the main slave markets, and this action won for the Italians the co-operation of the important Geledi Sultan. The Administration consolidated this significant access of support by creating an auxiliary force of tribal police called the 'Geledi Band' to aid their regular forces (made up chiefly of Arabs and Eritreans under Italian officers).[15] By 1909 the coastal area bounded by the Juba and Shebelle rivers and the sea had been effectively pacified and respect for Italian authority had grown. Slavery was also now virtually under satisfactory control. Prior to this date, Tommaso Carletti, Governor of Somalia from 1907-10, reports that hostility towards the new colonizers was such that a European could not venture outside any of the coastal towns without an escort of armed soldiers with fixed bayonets.[16]

In 1909 the first administrative post was opened at Obbia in the Obbia protectorate, and six years later the first Residency was established at Alula in the northern part of the Majerteyn protectorate. Meanwhile, a year previously, a party of Dervishes had established a fort at Beletweyn on the upper part of the Shebelle River and from this advanced post in 1916 they attacked Bulo Burti, being only finally dislodged from their stronghold in 1920. Thus, throughout this period of the extension of Italian rule, the threat of Dervish intervention was a constant though never fully realized menace. And it was only with the final defeat of the Dervishes in 1920, by which time Italian authority was thoroughly established, that this hazard was removed.

The frontier with Ethiopia

It was not only from the Dervishes and sections of the Benadir population that the Italians encountered opposition. In 1905, an

Ethiopian force descended down the valley of the Shebelle, raiding and pillaging as far south as Balad near the coast which was then not yet occupied by the Italians. Two years later, after an Ethiopian military party had been forced by the Dervishes to retreat in the Ogaden, a second and stronger expedition was sent out, which, failing to engage its elusive foes, turned south to descend on Lugh, raiding livestock and annihilating the Italian garrison. Seriously alarmed at the situation, the Italian government requested reparations, which were duly made, and then took advantage of the position to press the Ethiopians for a definition of the frontier. After the Italian débâcle at Adowa, it will be recalled that, in the Italo-Ethiopian peace negotiations of 1897, the Italian sphere had been defined as an area 180 miles in depth running from the Juba River north of Bardera to the confines of the British Protectorate. This agreement had left outside the Italian sphere the post at Lugh established by Ugo Ferrandi[17] in 1895 where, however, Menelik had agreed to an Italian commercial concession. In the interval, the Italian government had been pressing hard through its representative at Addis Ababa for the recognition of Lugh as lying within Italian territory. The Italian position had meanwhile been greatly strengthened by a tri-partite Anglo-Italo-French Agreement of 13 December, 1906. This treaty pledged the three powers to 'co-operate in maintaining the political and territorial *status quo* in Ethiopia' as determined by present conditions, and no less than nine separate agreements, treaties, and conventions – many of them mutually exclusive and contradictory, and including the Anglo-Italian protocols of 1891 and 1894, which had recognized the Ogaden region as a sphere of Italian interest.[18]

The purpose of this document was to provide the three powers with instruments which would safeguard their various positions and ambitions in the event of a collapse of the Ethiopian government – something that was considered as a distinct possibility since the Emperor Menelik was ailing. In the official Italian interpretation, the agreement – which naturally alarmed Ethiopia – accorded to Italy a sphere of influence in southern Ethiopia, and the right of armed intervention in the event of a politico-territorial change affecting the integrity of a bordering state (e.g. Somalia or Eritrea).[19] This significant enhancement of the Italian position was further consolidated by the effects of the Anglo-Ethiopian agreement of 6 December, 1907, which fixed the frontier between Ethiopia and north-east Kenya (then still the British East African Protectorate) at Dolo on the Juba River, a point well north of Lugh-Ferrandi.

With this substantial encouragement and a payment to Menelik of 3 million lire, Italy obtained by the Italo-Ethiopian treaty of May 1908 a frontier running from Dolo on the Juba northwards to the Shebelle where it joined the line agreed to previously. A perfunctory and rather nominal attempt was made to allocate different clans along the boundary to either Ethiopian or Italian control, with little regard for the grazing and watering needs of the people concerned who, of course, were never consulted. The Rahanweyn, for instance, were allocated to the Italian sphere, while the Digodia, Ogaden and others 'north of the frontier line' were to be dependent upon Ethiopia. With such scant definition of the new frontier, it is scarcely surprising that when in 1910 a joint Italo-Ethiopian boundary commission sought to delimit the boundary, agreement was reached only on a small sector running from Dolo on the Juba to Yet, some 130 kilometres to the north. Thereafter negotiations were abandoned, although the Italian survey party continued its work up to the Shebelle.

Nevertheless, Italy had safely secured Lugh within her colony of Somalia and a good stretch of territory besides, between the Juba and Shebelle, and in this area she now proceeded to assert her influence as well as along the 'frontier' as understood in the Italian interpretation of the 1897 and 1908 agreements. Ethiopia, by contrast, was in no position to establish administrative posts within the sphere which she claimed, except on the western side towards Harar and Jigjiga. Thus, it was the Italians who derived most profit from the fluid position which resulted, and which tended to reinforce the Benadir's traditional rôle as the natural outlet for much of the trade of western Ethiopia and the southern Ogaden. This rôle the Italians deliberately stimulated, adopting a policy of economic penetration which they advanced by building roads from the coast to the border and granting customs exemption on goods in transit between western Ethiopia and the Benadir. At the same time, the clans straddling the border on the Italian side were encouraged to move into the Ethiopian sphere freely, as their grazing and watering needs prompted, and were provided with armed protection by parties of the colony's frontier guards. By 1921, this policy of systematic infiltration had already reached a point where it was felt by the Italians that the division of Somali clans and territory effected by the 1908 treaty was no longer consonant with the prestige and majesty, as they put it, of Italian sovereignty.[20] But it was not until the celebrated Walwal incident of 1935 that matters came finally to a head.

The general position in 1920

By 1920, thus, the Benadir coast and hinterland had been brought under Italian sovereignty, partly by treaty, partly by the distribution of largesse, and partly by force, although, by the standards of the period, this last device was used with relative moderation. In the north, the two Italian protectorates had both local administrative stations, answerable now not to Aden but to Mogadishu, and the ground was prepared for their final incorporation in the colony with the abandonment of the old policy of indirect rule a few years later. Sayyid Muhammad 'Abdille Hassan's war, while it had sometimes delayed and impeded the gradual extension of Italian rule, had not caused the Italians to alter their colonial plans or deflected them from the purpose of creating an economically profitable possession whose agricultural potential might be exploited by settlers from the mother country. Not that economic considerations were the only factors; Italian prestige was already at stake and became an increasingly significant motive as time passed. Nor had the activities of the Dervishes prevented the Italians from appreciating the benefits of a policy of winning Somali goodwill as a means, not only of safeguarding their position in Somalia, but also of expanding their influence into the Ethiopian sphere.

By contrast, as has been seen, the extension of British rule to cover a large area of the hinterland of the Somaliland Protectorate was the result rather than the cause of the Dervish war. The Sayyid's campaigns had also engendered a tradition of Anglo-Ethiopian collaboration against Somali and had drawn the slender arm of Ethiopian rule farther into the Ogaden, thus considerably strengthening Ethiopia's position in relation to Somali. No doubt this would have happened eventually without British support and prompting, but its occurrence at this time, and in these circumstances, was one of the paradoxical consequences of the Dervish fight for freedom. Hence, although Sayyid Muhammad's image was at the time of his death, and still remains, that of a national hero and patriot, his holy war – despite all the courage and tenacity of his supporters – not only failed in its purpose of driving the 'infidels' into the sea, but actually led to a further extension and entrenchment of alien rule.

In French Somaliland, by contrast, neither these secondary effects nor the direct actions of the Dervishes made any sensible impact. And throughout this elsewhere turbulent period the French devoted their energies to the imaginative project of securing Ethiopia's transit trade for their colony by the construction of a line of rail from Jibuti to the Ethiopian hinterland. Despite the interruption of the Great War in which a French Somali battalion distinguished itself, the Franco-Ethiopian railway reached the Ethiopian capital by 1917. The successful conclusion of this great enterprise, the only line of rail in the whole area, guaranteed the future prosperity of the *Côte* and its capital and port, Jibuti. Equally, it ensured the gradual eclipse of Zeila as the traditional outlet for much of the hinterland's external trade. Thus, from the European point of view, France which had maintained consistently excellent relations with Ethiopia, though possessing the smallest of the Somali territories had so far gained most advantage from her colony. Britain, at the other extreme, had profited least. From the Somali point of view, the events of the period had merely further consolidated the partition of Somaliland, but, despite this, Sayyid Muhammad's vain struggle had left in the Somali national consciousness an ideal of patriotism which could never be effaced and which was to inspire later generations of his countrymen.

CHAPTER V

SOMALI UNIFICATION: THE ITALIAN EAST AFRICAN EMPIRE

Economic and social developments in Somalia

THE LONG-DRAWN out campaigns against the Dervishes in British Somaliland, and the gradual extension of Italian rule in Somalia, left little time or resources available for economic or social improvement. In Somalia, however, from the beginning of the period of direct control, the aim was to attract settlers from the mother country and to develop colonial plantations along the Shebelle and Juba Rivers. The scheme originally proposed by Carletti (Governor, from 1906–10) envisaged the settlement of groups of Italian farmers in co-operative colonies on the fertile land. With this in view, in 1908 Carletti instructed his Resident Commissioner at Giumbo to reserve some 10,000 hectares of arable land in the Gosha region of the Shebelle. This land had formerly been cultivated for the Tuni clan by their bondsmen and serfs.

With these resources at the Government's disposal, steps were taken to attract Italian settlers to open concessions and build farms. But those who hopefully responded to the lure of a bright future in Somalia soon found their efforts seriously impeded by the difficulties of recruiting local labour, which, contrary to all expectations, proved far from easy to attract. This led the Italian Resident in the Gosha District to force people – mainly former slaves and serfs – to work on the plantations which were being opened. Despite salaries which were not low, voluntary recruits were hard to come by, and those who were induced to work for the Italian farmers had to be supervised by guards otherwise they simply stopped work or fled.[1] This tradition of largely compulsory labour recruitment, mainly from the sedentary Bantu tribes of the riverine regions, continued throughout much of the Italian colonial period, although the conditions of service of plantation workers gradually improved, in theory at any rate, if not always in practice.

It was not, however, only labour problems which confronted the first concessionaries. Since there were no scientific studies of local conditions to guide them, the first Italian farmers had simply to follow a procedure of trial and error, which, with their lack of adequate capital or equipment, and in the absence of any serious Government support until the end of the Great War, in most cases proved disastrous. An agronomic research station was in fact opened at Genale, on the Shebelle, near Merca, as early as 1912 by Dr Onor where experiments were made with various tropical crops including bananas and rice, and systematic investigations undertaken of climatic and soil conditions. But the importance of this pioneering work was neglected at the time by the Italian government and did not bear fruit until the initiation of a more active colonial phase after the war. In the meantime, most of the early attempts at plantation farming had failed, and the prospect of settling large numbers of Italian farmers in Somalia had dimmed.

However, the arrival in Somalia in 1919 of that pioneer of tropical agriculture, the Duke of the Abruzzi, and the commencement of the fascist governership of De Vecchi[2] heralded new developments which in time came to change completely the colony's economy. After intensive technical research supported by adequate financial resources, the Societa Agricola Italo-Somala, founded by the Duke in 1920 with local headquarters at the station named after him on the Shebelle (Villagio Duca degli Abruzzi), rapidly developed into a highly efficient agricultural consortium producing cotton, sugar, bananas, oil and soap.[3] In large measure the success of this enterprise was due not only to the organizing genius of its founder, and to the rational scientific preparation which preceded each phase of the work, but also to the strenuous efforts which were made to overcome the traditional difficulties of labour recruitment. Unlike earlier attempts at plantation farming in Somalia where the settlers had obtained their land from the Administration of the colony, S.A.I.S.

acquired both its land and much of its labour by a direct contract with the local tribesmen (the Bantu Shidle) amongst whom the consortium was established. By the end of 1920, the company had at its disposal an area of 30,000 hectares of rich land granted directly from the collective tribal lands of sections of the Shidle. The tribesmen concerned retained possession of the gardens which were actually under cultivation, only conceding to the Society land which they held in reserve.

The Company thus broke new ground in the manner by which it acquired title to its lands from the traditional tribal owners, who contracted to supply much of the labour necessary for the work of irrigation and bonification which was to follow, and who also undertook to continue afterwards as paid employees of the Society. Each family was to cultivate for the Company an area not less than that worked for its own private use, and the produce was to be sold at rates fixed annually by joint agreement. However, while between 1920 and 1922, when the rains were poor, and poverty and lack of work at home drove many people to seek employment with the Company, after the floods which followed in 1923, the labour force melted away and a local out-break of bubonic plague provided little inducement to return. This marked reduction in the supply of labour during the critical work of bonification created a serious situation for the Company which was then driven to apply the old methods of coercing people into joining its labour force. By arrangement with the Administration, Shidle and other tribesmen from Afgoi, Awdegle, and Bulo Mererta were compelled to provide contingents of labour. At the same time, other voluntarily recruited workers were taken on at slightly higher salaries.

Nevertheless, the Society still experienced the utmost difficulty in securing a stable labour force. By 1924, however, the system of co-operative 'collaboration' by which labourers were established in cultivating settlements within the Society's lands was extended to all employees and began to prove successful. Each worker was allocated one hectare of land, of which half was for his own use, while the remainder was to be worked by him for the Company at rates which varied according to the yield produced. On this basis, a comprehensive labour code was elaborated under which recruits from different tribes and areas were grouped together in cultivating villages on the consortium according to their ethnic and tribal origin. Elementary health and social services were provided which, however modest and rudimentary, exceeded those generally available at the time elsewhere.

The eventual success of the S.A.I.S. scheme encouraged De Vecchi's government to create at Genale – the long neglected site of Onor's pioneering research station – a vast irrigation project for plantation cultivation. In regulating the conditions under which concessions were granted to Italian settlers and companies, the Administration produced a labour code modelled on that pioneered by the Duke of the Abruzzi. The aim was to attract whole families, as well as individuals, from the southern cultivating tribes (particularly the Bantu riverines), and to bind them to the land of the consortium in which they found employment by establishing them in labour colonies. As at Villagio, each man or woman was allotted land for his own use and entitled to keep a few poultry and cattle. The employer was obliged to provide seed for the worker's own use, and additional wages were paid during harvest and at planting time. During pregnancy, women were to be given light work, and to be granted one month's leave after bearing a child. Health and sanitary services were provided in the colonial villages in which the workers were forced to live—for having gained labourers it was clearly in the employer's interest to provide for their welfare.

The contract under which this bond was created between employee and employer had to be fully explained to the former, and signed by both parties.[4] Yet, however generous these conditions may have appeared to the Italian settlers and companies, there was marked reluctance on the part of many cultivating tribesmen to leave their lands and homes, neglecting their own subsistence farming, to work, virtually as prisoners, for foreign masters. Consequently in good seasons, especially, when there was plenty of work at home, the Italian concessionaries at Genale continued to be confronted with the problem of a reluctant and generally inadequate labour force which they overcame, with the connivance of the Administration, by forced recruitment. The consequent forages which were undertaken, to collect workers from the Baidoa and Bur Hacaba regions for this purpose, are still bitterly remembered today. Paradoxically, it was (and still is) precisely those clansmen of the nomadic areas who were least disposed to work on the land, because of their traditional contempt for cultivation, who were most anxious to obtain salaried employment. By contrast, the southern cultivating peoples, could, at this time certainly, satisfy most of their modest wants from the produce of their own fields and livestock without engaging in salaried employment except in time of scarcity and famine.[5]

Despite these difficulties, however, the definitive establishment of the S.A.I.S. estates and their emulation by other companies at Genale and other centres on the Shebelle, and later on the Juba, provided Somalia with a new pattern of trade. The export of bananas, attempted first experimentally by the Duke of the Abruzzi, soon came to be the main object of production at Genale and provided the colony with a new export product which rapidly came to rival in importance the traditional mainstay, hides and skins. The only other significant commercial venture launched in this period was the salt extraction plant at Ras Hafun, on the Majerteyn coast in the extreme north. Work on this enterprise began in 1920, financed by a group of Lombardy industrialists, and although interrupted by the military campaigns in Majerteynia in 1925–27, the plant was by 1933 producing 260,000 tons of high grade salt annually. The bulk of this was exported to East Africa, India, and the Far East.

There were also corresponding developments in other fields, particularly in communications, the Italians setting great store by the imperial Roman dictum that roads are the basis of successful war and expansion and of peaceful prosperity. Thus during the De Vecchi régime, the extent of motor roads trebled to cover some 6,400 kilometres. In 1928 a small diesel railway system was established linking the plantations at Afgoi and Villagio Duca degli Abruzzi with the capital and port of Mogadishu. In 1929, the first government geological survey was initiated to provide a basis for a badly needed well-drilling scheme to aid the nomadic sector of the economy to which little attention had previously been paid. And between 1932 and 1933, one hundred and fifty wells were constructed. About the same time, consideration was also given to the hitherto neglected problem of improving the traditional subsistence cultivation economy, and some bonification and irrigation works were undertaken in indigenous areas on the Shebelle.

In the meantime a certain extension of social services had taken place. A loose network of dispensaries, and, in the main centres, of hospitals, had been established, the Administration devoting perhaps more attention to this aspect of the welfare of the local population than to any other. A school for training Somali hospital orderlies was created in 1933.

Other educational services, although state-aided, were provided chiefly by the Catholic missions to whom, in the less refractory social climate of the south, there was less public hostility than in the north. Indeed, with their much more pervasive hold over the population, the Italian government of Somalia was even able to erect an imposing cathedral in Mogadishu without arousing any serious opposition. In such conditions, by 1929, the missions were running elementary schools – at Merca, Brava, Gelib, Afgoi, Villagio, Baidoa, Kismayu, and even Ras Hafun. There was also a government school for teaching Italian to Somalis at Mogadishu which had been opened in 1907; and in the same centre there was now a trade school. For the Italian Administration regarded education for Somalis as, in the main, preparation for such limited technical tasks as should conveniently be assigned to them. However, in the mission elementary schools, Somali and Italian children were initially taught together in the same classes. But in 1929 De Vecchi's successor Guido Corni, considering this practice incompatible with the proper relations between masters and 'subjects' – the status assigned to Somali – laid down that the two races must be taught in separate classes.

Nevertheless, the educational facilities open to Somalis continued to expand and the numbers of Somali and Arab pupils at elementary schools rose from 1,390 in 1930 to 1,776 in 1939; which, in the circumstances, was a not inconsiderable achievement comparing favourably with the position at the time in British Somaliland and the French Côte. This certainly would not have been possible without a more favourable public attitude towards Western education than that prevailing at the time in the British Protectorate. And in this connexion, in addition to the factors already mentioned, it is important to realize that, while the Italian Administration allowed considerable freedom to Catholic missionaries, at the same time it also openly supported Islam. Frequently funds were made available to aid in the construction of mosques and shrines.

The administrative system was, of course, after the fashion of Italian fascism, bureaucratic and highly centralized, and directed by the Governor and his immediate subordinates and secretaries at Mogadishu. In the Districts and Provinces, the Residents (equivalent to the English District Commissioners) were assisted by government stipended 'chiefs' and elders. And although the latter operated *vis-à-vis* the Administration in an advisory capacity only, or more often merely as the vehicle for directives and instructions, to those of these 'Capos' who proved loyal and co-operative Italian colonial decorations and financial rewards were distributed freely. Thus, for example, the Bimal clan which had earlier proved such a thorn in the flesh of the Administration, in official publications of the 1930s are praised for their loyal devotion to the Italian flag, and their notable leader Sultan 'Abd ar-Rahman 'Ali 'Ise, who was created a Cavaliere Ufficiale, is hailed as a staunch supporter of Italian interests.[6] Likewise, Sultan Ahmad Abu Bakr of the Geledi, renowned as a soothsayer and reputed to have been consulted by Italians in 1940 as to the outcome of the war in East Africa, was made a Commander of the Order of the Colonial Star for the part which, as nominal paramount of the Digil clans, he had played in the organization of labour recruitment for the Genale consortiums.

These and other Italian appointed 'Capos' were supported in their rôle as agents of the Italian Residents by an armed rural constabulary force known as the *Gogle*, first recruited under De Martino's governorship in 1914 and possessing by 1930 a strength of some five hundred men. This force was the Somalia equivalent of the British Illalos in the north. The Administration was also supported by a strong police force which, in the same period, had a strength of 1,475 natives led by 85 Italian officers and subalterns. Later, as the colony's military contingents increased in number, the police force was considerably reduced and became an official branch of the Colonial Carabinieri.[7]

In keeping with the expansionist spirit of the period, in 1925 the colony was considerably increased in size with the cession by Britain of Jubaland and the port of Kismayu. This was part of Italy's modest share of the spoils of the Great War, and though

Jubaland had been the scene of much turbulence in the past and had experienced several heavy-handed British punitive expeditions,[8] the transfer and the demarcation of the new frontier between Somalia and Kenya passed virtually without incident. The clansmen concerned, of course, were not consulted, and little or no account was taken of clan distribution or grazing needs.

If the transfer of Jubaland went smoothly enough, the case was very different with the extension of direct colonial rule to the two northern Italian protectorates. De Vecchi had urged this annexation from the time of his appointment; but authority was not given by Rome until July 1925, after a border incident in the previous year when a party of police from the British Protectorate had crossed over the frontier in pursuit of raiders from the Majerteyn Sultanate. The operations which were required to effect this change, though euphemistically described as a 'colonial police action', entailed strenuous efforts and the employment of more than 12,000 troops, including three battalions from Eritrea, and a division of Marines with naval support and reconnaissance planes. The first objective, the submission of the Obbia Sultanate, where the Sultan, Yusuf 'Ali Kenadid, was not a hereditary ruler but a breakaway scion of the Majerteyn clan, was accomplished easily enough; and by the end of October 1925, the sultanate had been declared a province with Residences at Galkayu, El Bur, and Illig. Yusuf 'Ali himself was deposed and pensioned off to Mogadishu.

In the subjection of the northern protectorate, the Majerteyn sultanate proper, even with the large military resources at their disposal, the Italians encountered serious resistance. *Boqor* 'Isman, though now an old man, was widely respected and his armed contingents had seen service during the Dervish period in which, like many of his countrymen, he had played a somewhat equivocal rôle. Faced with the demand to accept the new status assigned to himself and his people, he sought at first to temporize while mobilizing his followers. Hence, despite the overwhelming military superiority of his opponents, he was able to hold out against them for almost two years until the end of 1927, when all effective resistance was crushed and he gave himself up to receive the same treatment as that accorded to his kinsmen at Obbia. His son fled to Ethiopia, but returned after several years to Mogadishu where he died of smallpox.

Meanwhile, in the newly subjected Sultanate of Obbia a daring rising had occurred at El Bur, led by a Majerteyn clansman called 'Omar Samatar. After gaining control of the police armoury and murdering the Italian Resident, the leading insurgents crossed the border into Ethiopia, where, according to Italian reports, they proceeded to campaign against Italian infiltration in the Ogaden and to prepare attacks on Italian border posts. But apart from this, in the circumstances of the power of reprisal wielded by the Italian authorities, the rising left little tangible trace in the colony itself.

The incorporation of Jubaland and the two northern protectorates led to a corresponding extension of direct administration, and the colony was now divided into seven provinces or 'Regions' comprising thirty-three Districts presided over by Residents. The Civil Service as a whole now included no less than 350 expatriate Italians as well as 1,700 locally recruited Somali, Arabs, and others employed in a wide variety of subordinate posts such as those of medical orderly, technical assistant, and forestry guard, etc. The most important appointment, certainly in Somali eyes, remained of course that of interpreter, a key position in any system of direct rule where expatriate officials cannot speak the local language. With this formidable administrative machine, now strongly established, the ranks of salaried chiefs and notables were pruned to retain only those of proved loyalty and efficiency. Their position was also held in check by the appointment of official Muslim judges (Kadis) with authority to administer Somali customary law as well as Islamic law, wider powers of jurisdiction than those accorded to Kadis in the British Protectorate.

This consolidation of rule and construction of the basis necessary for economic exploitation proved exceedingly costly. From a figure of a mere 900,000 lire in 1905, the budget rose continuously, reaching 2,500,000 lire in 1908, and an average of 74 million lire in the early 1930s. Local revenue, derived mainly from customs and excise duties on imports and exports and licences – there was no significant direct taxation – also rose steadily but came nowhere near meeting expenditure. Indeed, in the same period, local revenue produced only 27 million lire, considerably less than half the colony's budget. However, by this time, the export trade – principally of hides and skins, and cotton and bananas, the latter taking precedence over the former after 1932 – had begun to show some return, reducing the adverse balance of trade from a peak of almost 131 million lire in 1927 to just under 29 million lire in 1934. Nevertheless, after thirty years of direct rule, despite a great expenditure of finance and effort, the colony was still running at a marked deficit, and was very far from being the economic asset to their country which the early Italian pioneers had forecast. And the concomitant expectation that Somalia would also provide a prosperous livelihood for large numbers of Italy's surplus population was now so patently untenable that it had been quietly discarded. This unsatisfactory economic position, which it was becoming fashionable to disregard in view of the reputed gain to national prestige which the colony afforded, was soon to be further aggravated by the far-reaching consequences of the unhappy incident which occurred at Walwal in the course of the Anglo-Ethiopian demarcation of the British Protectorate's boundaries in 1934.

Progress in the British Protectorate

The twenty-years Dervish war had been a period of stagnation when all the efforts of the Administration were directed towards overcoming Sayyid Muhammad's movement and there was virtually no time or money for anything more productive. Moreover, unlike the Sudan, where the British campaigns against the Mahdists had indirectly promoted the development of the country through the establishment of rail, road, and telegraphic communications, and had also drawn attention in England to the Sudan's needs and led to such imaginative achievements as Gordon College, in the Somaliland Protectorate the results of the *jihad* there were very different. Indeed, as Douglas Jardine, Chief Secretary during part of this period, has eloquently recorded, Somaliland's twenty-years war left nothing more tangible than a few ramshackle Ford cars and no decent roads or other means of communication. 'A still greater misfortune' was 'that the British public had forgotten the Somali war many years before it was brought to a successful conclusion.'[9] And having spent so much on military operations so completely out of proportion to their interests in Somaliland, the British government was not now disposed to make further funds available for development. To add to this sorry tale, the conclusion of the operations against the Dervishes, far from ushering in a new era of co-operation between the people and the Administration, left instead an atmosphere of sullen distrust and covert hostility.

Notwithstanding this gloomy picture, however, an extremely significant development had in fact occurred, almost unnoticed, and without any assistance or aid from the Protectorate authorities. This was the gradual adoption of sorghum cultivation in the western part of the territory (in Borama and Hargeisa Districts), far from the scene of the Dervish operations in the centre and east. From shortly before the turn of the century, the Gadabursi clan and sections of the Habar Awal (especially the Jibril Abokor) living in the higher and better-watered land in the west had begun to follow the example of their kinsmen in the Jigjiga region of clearing areas of bush and planting sorghum, the ground being tilled by ox-drawn wooden ploughs. This comparatively advanced system of cultivation, strikingly different from the hand hoe technique employed in southern Somalia, seems to have been pioneered locally by a few religious settlements from which it soon spread to the surrounding clansmen. Far from hindering this economic revolution, the effect of the Dervish war appears on the contrary to have stimulated it by creating a highly lucrative market for local grain. For those nomads who turned to cultivation still retained an interest in livestock and were not thus completely dependent for subsistence on their crops. To some extent at least, they produced a cash crop which was traded locally with the pastoral nomads in the centre and east of the Protectorate.[10]

The importance of this development was recognized by the Protectorate Administration in 1924, when an agriculture and veterinary office was opened, followed shortly afterwards by the establishment of a small experimental station. In 1928, however, a serious set-back occurred in the form of a locust plague which destroyed almost the entire harvest and led to widespread famine. Nevertheless, by the early 1930s, stable cultivation combined with pastoralism was firmly established in a wide area of the west of the Protectorate, and the Administration had completed the demarcation and mapping of the agricultural lands in Hargeisa District and in Borama District (definitively opened, after several false starts, in 1921). Elsewhere the all pervasive nomadic economy, providing the export trade in sheep and goats and skins, continued to prevail.

While in agriculture the initiative came from Somali, the position with education was very different. The effect of the activities of the Mission school at Berbera, and later at Daimole, in providing one of the irritants which promoted the growth of the Dervish cause has already been noted. This school was in fact closed in 1910, when all Mission proselytization was forbidden – the ban being strictly enforced, and never revoked in later years. During this early period, however, the Government entered the field on its own account and by 1905 had established small elementary schools at its three stations of Berbera, Bulhar, and Zeila, despite continued resistance and hostility. Unfortunately with the rise of Jibuti, the populations of Zeila and Bulhar dwindled, and the schools there were closed for lack of support.

A more systematic approach had to wait until the end of the Dervish war when, in 1920, plans were prepared for the institution of six elementary schools and an intermediate school. Since the home government refused to provide funds, it was proposed to raise the necessary capital by levying a direct tax on livestock. This striking, and, to the Somali public at the time, most abhorrent project, roused fierce resentment and led to a riot at Burao in which the District Commissioner lost his life. Since the Protectorate authorities were repeatedly instructed that any project which might spark off another 'Dervish war' was to be avoided at all costs, these plans were consequently dropped for the time being. Nevertheless, from 1919 onwards, funds were made available to enable a trickle of boys, whose parents desired their education, to be sent to the Sudan and by 1933 there were five boys at Gordon College. In the interval, in 1929, a government grant was made to selected private Islamic schools run by Somali sheikhs on condition that they taught Arabic reading and writing and arithmetic. In 1935, new proposals were adopted for introducing a rational system of education and work started on the construction of a new government school at Berbera. In the following year, the Protectorate's first Director of Education was appointed; but again religious feeling strongly opposed the scheme; and, after a riot at Burao in which three Somalis were killed and the new Director of Education was greeted with a shower of stones, the proposals lapsed and had to await the reoccupation of British Somaliland in 1941 after the Italian defeat in East Africa.

In other spheres, though perhaps less tempestuous, the record was on the whole similarly bleak. Following 1926, however, there was some road development, increasingly necessary with the opening of new Administrative stations, and also an extension of medical services. Apart from the activities of the veterinary office, the only other measure of direct benefit to the pastoral economy was the initiation of a small-scale well-drilling scheme in the 1930s. These restricted and altogether minimal developments in a territory where, in contrast to Somalia, there were fewer natural resources and neither the spur of imperial pride nor the needs of a European settler community to consider, cost very little. The budget remained pitifully small, amounting as late as 1937 to only £213,139. With the failure of the attempt to introduce direct taxation, which, had it been persevered with, would have been of tremendous value for the future, revenue was derived as in Somalia mainly from import and export duties and licences. The principal exports were still, of course, hides and skins and livestock on the hoof, valued in the late 1930s at £279,940, when imports cost £535,210.

That it was possible to govern so cheaply this Cinderella of the Empire, as it was well epitomized, despite its considerable territorial extent of 68,000 square miles and its estimated population of 350,000, is explicable not only in terms of the exiguous nature of government and of public services and development, but also in relation to the special characteristics of the Somali social system. Despite the presence of only a tiny complement of expatriate officials aided by Indian and Arab clerks, and despite the lack of any effective organization of chiefly authority which could have served as a basis for a system of indirect rule in the orthodox sense, the Somali clan genealogical system provided a pervasive framework through which every individual could be unerringly identified. This, with the fact that in contrast to Somalia the Protectorate's population was more compact and homogeneous, and divided in fact amongst three clearly defined groups of clans – the Dir, Isaq and Darod, made it possible for administration to be conducted with a comparatively light hand.

Yet, it must again be emphasized that the Administration's aims were extremely modest, and restricted in fact to little more than the maintenance of effective law and order. In the light of the intractable character of the local population who, despite the few thousand cultivators in the west, were as a whole overwhelmingly dedicated to the nomadic way of life, the effective implementation of any radical changes would have required a much more strongly established administrative machine. For the homogeneous and clearly delineated character of the population in the Protectorate which facilitated the maintenance of law and order on a limited basis, also meant that, notwithstanding the traditional rivalry of the Isaq and Darod clans, such radical innovations as western education could be resisted more effectively and on a wider front than in the much more heterogeneous and divided conditions of Somalia.·

At the same time, although there was no pervasive system of indigenous chiefs and consequently no basis for a true system of indirect rule, titular clan leaders and the elders of lineages were in many cases officially recognized by the Administration and granted small stipends. As in Somalia, these leaders, usually known by the Arabic title 'Akil', provided the link between the District Commissioner and the people of his district. And to aid the mass of court work to which District Commissioners found themselves unrewardingly committed by the Somali love of litigation and the frequent clan and lineage quarrels, these government Akils and 'chiefs' (as they were sometimes misleadingly called) were granted limited judicial powers and thus furnished a rudimentary system of subordinate courts. Their authority, however, was very small, and religious issues and matters of personal status involving Islamic law were left to the care of Muslim magistrates (Kadis).

Thus, despite some superficial concessions to the principle of indirect rule, in practice the Protectorate was governed as directly as Somalia, though with a much lighter hand and a more restricted purview. All effective power remained with the District Commissioners who also acted as magistrates, the territory being divided into six separate Districts, ruled from the secretariat and seat of government at Berbera. With the poor quality of communications and the remoteness of many out-stations from the capital, District Commissioners naturally wielded very great authority and their position was enhanced in this respect by the Illalo tribal police detachments assigned to their control. A separate police force was only created in 1926. But, while this aided the control of clan and lineage disputes, it did not seriously alter the District Commissioner's far-reaching powers; and in practice there tended often to be a certain rivalry between police and administrative officers and the Illalos and regular police which, with their genius for political intrigue, the clansmen were only too ready to exploit. This, with internal clan politics, and the playing off of one administrative official against another, a sphere of activity in which government interpreters played a crucial rôle, provided much of the excitement of local tribal life.[11]

From the end of the Dervish period until after the East Africa campaign during the Second World War, this remained the general character of life in the Protectorate. Yet, although the rudiments of law and order were now effectively established, there was during this period considerable turbulence in the west, particularly amongst the Gadabursi and 'Ise clans. This created serious administrative difficulties which were aggravated by the effects of the arbitrary colonial partition which divided these clans between Britain and Ethiopia and, in the case of the 'Ise, France also. Rival claimants for the leadership of the Gadabursi clan and their adherents sought to play off to their own advantage the Ethiopian authorities at Jigjiga and the British at Borama. In 1930, this dangerous game led to an unfortunate incident when, guided by the pro-Ethiopian Gadabursi claimant, an Ethiopian force crossed into the Protectorate and seized livestock. An encounter with the Borama authorities quickly followed in which shots were exchanged and four Ethiopians were killed. There were similar, though less serious, difficulties also on the eastern border with Somalia: but in the centre of the country these complications did not arise, for in the absence of any Ethiopian administration in the central Haud, the Protectorate authorities could dispatch police parties into the area with impunity as need arose.

Nevertheless, the time had clearly come to mark out on the ground the Protectorate's frontiers which had been defined so many years previously. In response to Italian pressure, attention was given first to the border with Somalia. This was demarcated without incident by an Anglo-Italian Commission led by Col Stafford and the Italian scholar and colonial Civil Servant Dr

Enrico Cerulli. The work was completed by September 1930, and the results were ratified by an Anglo-Italian Agreement signed in London in June of the following year. In the spirit of the original Anglo-Italian Agreement of 1894,[12] this ratification seemed to imply that the frontier of Somalia was recognized as extending along the south-eastern part of the Protectorate as far west as Do'mo in the (Ethiopian) Ogaden, i.e. to the 47th meridian east.

Having successfully settled the frontier with Italy, Britain now proceeded on the demarcation of her Protectorate's boundaries with Ethiopia, following the terms of the dubious agreement of 1897. This was the first clear indication which British-protected Somalis were vouchsafed of the partial withdrawal of British protection, and of the abandonment of their territory over which Ethiopia was now anxious to exercise jurisdiction. Consequently, it is scarcely to be wondered at that the joint-Commission encountered opposition from the clansmen in the area, or, that in the course of its work, one of the commissioners lost his life. This, however, was but a minor incident compared with the reception which was in store for the Commission, led by Col Clifford and Dedjazmatch Tessema Bante, when it arrived at Walwal in the eastern Ogaden in November 1934.

The Commission's appearance here calls for some explanation. What had happened was that, after completing its unpopular work of demarcation, the Commission had crossed into the Ogaden to survey the wells and grazing areas there to which British-protected Somali were entitled access. This brought the Commissioners to Walwal on 23 November where, to their alarm, they found their Ethiopian escort which had preceded them confronted by a well-armed Italian post.[13] Before following the local consequences of the well-known and tragic dénouement which led to the Italian invasion and conquest of Ethiopia, we must return briefly to survey the course of Italian and Ethiopian frontier activity in the years immediately preceding 1935.

The Walwal incident

It will be recalled that, following the unsatisfactory 1908 treaty which perfunctorily and arbitrarily assigned certain clans to the Italian sphere and others to the Ethiopian, the Italians had consistently pursued a forward policy of economic and political infiltration in the Ethiopian Ogaden. Thus Guido Corni,[14] Governor of Somalia in succession to the redoubtable De Vecchi, boasts how successful this policy proved during his term of office (1928–31). Several prominent religious leaders across the border had now been won to the Italian cause by generous gifts. Irregular Somali groups, who could be disclaimed conveniently as bandits, were also recruited and provided with arms to stir up trouble in the area.[15] Thus in the Mustahil region, Ololdin, the forceful Ajuran sultan, was paid and armed by the Italians to attack the Ethiopian tribute-gathering expeditions whose arbitrary activities constituted virtually all that there was at this time in the way of Ethiopian administration.

These auxiliaries represented the spearhead of the official Italian border patrols which, from 1931, organized into a 'Banda' command, and with a strength of one thousand armed soldiers under Italian officers operated from posts at Gardo, Goddere, and Galadi, on the Ogaden side of the disputed frontier. In the early 1930s other small posts were opened as far into the Ogaden as Walwal, which could scarcely be regarded as lying within the sphere assigned to Italy. Yet the Italian presence there went unchallenged until the tragic incident in 1934.

By contrast, as has already been noted, at this time the Ethiopians had still not established any administrative posts in the eastern part of the Ogaden into which these audacious Italian feelers were now being thrust.[16] The main centre of administration was in fact still far west at Jigjiga; although, as they had previously done in the Somali territory lying round this centre and the city of Harar, strongly armed tribute-gathering parties were pressing ever farther towards the east to pave the way for the eventual imposition of Ethiopian rule. At the same time, while the Italians played upon the ancient Somali antagonism towards the Amhara, the Ethiopians sought to depict the Italians in the light of ruthless alien usurpers and to turn internal Somali clan jealousies to their account. Thus, not only by arbitrary military raids but also by giving arms and other support to those Somali groups hostile to the Italians, the Ethiopians sought to accomplish the dual aim of countering Italian aggression and winning Somali territory. Typical of those on the Ethiopian side was 'Omar Samatar, who, after his daring attack on the Italian post at El Bur in 1926, had crossed the frontier and was now engaged in rebuffing Italian infiltration in the Ogaden.

Thus the Somali clansmen of the Ogaden found themselves caught between the rival attractions of the two opposing camps, both of whom were competing for their allegiance. And because of the exigencies of the nomadic life and the circumstances of the Somali clan system in which any widespread political collaboration cannot long survive, they proved an easy prey to the two powers seeking their allegiance and territory. On the whole, the Italians were the more successful because they were more free with gifts and blandishments and because it was easy for them to pose as the champions of Islam when the Ethiopians made no attempt to conceal their anti-Muslim sentiments.

The Ethiopians, meanwhile, were not content merely to seek to counteract Italian intrusion by actions which were limited to their sphere. Thus, for example, in September 1931, after evicting the Italian post at Mustahil, an Ethiopian force several thousand strong swept down the Shebelle to menace the Italian district headquarters at Beletweyn, administering to the Italians an unpleasant dose of their own medicine. Italian reinforcements were hastily marshalled, but after hurried diplomatic exchanges an open clash was avoided and the Ethiopians withdrew. Other incidents followed from both sides, culminating in the clash at Walwal in 1934, by which time preparations for the invasion of Ethiopia from Eritrea and Somalia were well advanced, and Italy was becoming increasingly confident of her position *vis-à-vis* Ethiopia. And not without cause.

It will be remembered how, many years previously, Italy's general position in the Horn of Africa had been strengthened by the tripartite treaty of 1906.[17] The effects of this had been further consolidated by an Anglo-Italian agreement of 1925, by which Britain recognized and agreed to champion Italy's claims to economic interests in western Ethiopia. Italy, in return, agreed to support Britain's aim of securing a concession to build a barrage on Lake Tana. Thus, as before, Britain was in fact preparing all possible safeguards for her interests in the event of a collapse of the Ethiopian monarchy. Three years later, to still Ethiopian fears and to advance Italian interests more directly, a treaty of perpetual peace and alliance was signed between the two states. Under the terms of this, both countries bound themselves to submit disputes between them to a procedure of conciliation and arbitration; a truly remarkable preparation for a war of colonial conquest. At the same time, in the councils of Europe, Italy had been lobbying quite successfully for Anglo-French acquiescence in the forth-coming act of aggression.

Without going into all the sordid details, the encounter at Walwal, between the Italian garrison and the Ethiopian escort party, led on 5 December to a battle in which by the employment of superior forces and weapons the Italians forced their opponents to withdraw. The futile negotiations[18] which followed through the League of Nations, Britain's tardy decision to abandon her sup-port of Italy's colonial adventures, the equivocation of the other powers, especially of France, and the final crushing Italian con-quest little impeded by the League's eventual decision to apply sanctions, have all been too often described and judged to be again retailed here. Up the imperial roads in Somalia and Eritrea which had been built first to attract trade and then to serve as a basis for expansion, with overwhelming numbers, arms, and aerial support, the Italian armies ruthlessly advanced until by 7 May, 1936, the war was over, the conquest complete. The ignominious Italian defeat at Adowa, which had always rankled, had at last been vindicated and Mussolini could boast that Italy had won her empire at last.

Somalia and the Ogaden within the Italian East African Empire

With the conquest of Ethiopia, Somalia was enlarged by the addi-tion of the Ogaden and the regions occupied by Somali on the upper parts of the Shebelle and Juba rivers. This added three new administrative Provinces to the territory and brought together Somali clansmen who had hitherto been arbitrarily separated by the Somalia–Ethiopia 'boundary'. The preparations for the cam-paign and the war itself brought a brief period of unprecedented prosperity to the colony. This, however, was quickly followed by the economic decline caused by Italy's participation in the Second World War, a period during which in Somalia no new develop-ments of importance were undertaken by the government.

Trade and commerce were now in any case strictly controlled by a rigid system of governmental monopolies and para-statal organizations which left little room for endeavour or enterprise and which, by fascist legislation, explicitly excluded the participation of Somalis or other colonial 'subjects' in any sector of the economy where they might be in competition with Italians. In the government of the colony itself, it is scarcely an exaggeration to say that fascist bureaucracy had run riot, leading to a proliferation of civil and military functionaries which markedly reduced the efficiency of administration. All the apparatus of fascist social life, their clubs and organizations – to at least one of which every Italian citizen, child as well as adult, belonged – had been imported from the mother country: and these permeated the life of the Italian community to an extent which, particularly in the local context of Somalia, seems today ludicrous in the extreme.

The non-Italian population was subjected to a complex body of discriminatory laws designed to uphold the racial status of the colonists; and, although mixed liaisons were common, officially they were frowned upon, and inter-racial marriage was totally forbidden. Fortunately, however, the Italian legal machine, though capable of issuing severe and arbitrary punishments for trivial offences, was at the best of times extremely cumbersome, and moreover tended often to be mitigated in its effects by the inducements in kind or in money to which Somali found many Italian officials open. And after the conquest of Ethiopia in which more than 40,000 Somali recruits had participated,[19] the Somali population at large was rewarded by the rather empty privilege of being officially designated as 'Somalis' or 'Natives' in place of the derogatory terms 'subject' and '*indigeno*' which had previously been the official usage. With this very limited gesture Somali interests had to be content, for no other significant developments were pursued to extend the range of those which had taken place prior to the Italo-Ethiopian war.

Yet despite the harsh character of fascist legislation and the mass of regulations and propaganda designed to promote and preserve the dignity and 'majesty' of the 'Aryan' conquerors, it would be quite wrong to imagine that the Somali population as a whole was at this time actively hostile to its rulers. Moreover, there were naturally many Italian officials who, while paying lip-service to the bombast of fascism, carried out their administrative duties conscientiously and well. And between not a few Somalis and Italians there were frequently bonds of friendship and respect, at least as deep as those between Somalis and expatriate officials in the other Somali territories. Equally, despite the paucity of schooling, knowledge of Italian, often of course very rudimentary, was fairly widespread and certainly more extensive than acquaintance with English in the Somaliland Protectorate. Partly, this is to be explained by the ease with which it is possible to pick up a tolerable speaking knowledge of Italian, as compared with the difficulties of English, and partly also by the fact that it was the policy in Somalia to regard Somali as a barbaric tongue which must give place to the civilized language of the rulers – an aspect of the Italian image of themselves as colonists with a civilizing mission worthy of the Roman tradition.[20]

Politically, of course, there was no avenue open for Somali activity except within the framework of the traditional clan system, or in dealings with administrative officials. Nor was there any direct participation by Somali in the government and administration of the colony save at the lowest levels, and then always in a subservient capacity. Thus though Tommaso Carletti, the first regular governor of the colony appointed in 1907, had compared Somali intelligence favourably with that of his own countrymen, and sensibly proposed the creation of Somali municipal councils, and eventually of an elected system of government,[21] these liberal ideas were far in advance of the spirit of his generation, and had to await the new ideals of the Italian trusteeship period of the 1950s.

Yet to do the Italians justice, whatever their motives, and notwithstanding the impress of fascism, decidedly more of benefit to Somalis had been created in Somalia than in the British Protectorate, French Somaliland, or, above all, in the Northern Province of Kenya which for long was destined to remain a stagnant backwater. In public buildings and roads, and in the plantation industry, the foundations of a modern colony had been created, the benefit of which, despite the many injustices committed against them, Somalis were to reap in the future. At the same time, in the less intractable conditions of their colony, a wider respect for law and order and a more modern attitude towards centralized government had been inculcated which was to prove of great importance in the future.

The first stirrings of modern Somali nationalism

In the same period, another phenomenon of significance had begun to become evident in Somalia. This was the rapid growth in urbanization which received a new impetus when, after the Ethiopian campaigns, large numbers of Somali soldiers were discharged and settled in the Benadir towns, especially in Mogadishu. This ancient port, with its long cosmopolitan tradition, had, in the decade between 1930 and 1940, more than doubled its population, and now boasted some 60,000 inhabitants. Equally, although no trade union activity was permitted, the employment of considerable numbers of workers by S.A.I.S. and other concerns helped to promote the formation of new social and political attitudes, and these, further stimulated by western schooling, now began to be apparent in the towns and principal centres of the colony.

In these centres, where the impact of western influence was experienced most keenly, and where the traditional system of collective indemnification for wrongs was now less necessary than in the nomadic world of the interior, amongst merchants and traders especially there arose a new feeling of dissatisfaction with the particularism of the past. This, with the traditional Somali national consciousness, which the experience of Italian patriotic fervour presented in a new light, and the long suppressed reaction to alien rule, all combined to provide conditions favourable to the emergence of new aspirations. Thus, in the last few years of the short-lived Italian East African Empire, the first definite steps towards the creation of a modern nationalist movement began to be taken in Somalia. These took the form of small clandestine meetings, organized mainly, it appears, by some of the new generation of Somalis who had been to school and were employed by the Italian government. This activity did not pass unnoticed, however, and the Administration took prompt steps to suppress what was regarded as a potential threat to Italian rule. The employees concerned were separated and posted to remote areas where they were thought to be out of harm's way.[22]

Meanwhile, in the British Protectorate, similar developments were occurring. Here, although there was no urban growth of consequence, there were very direct contacts with the outside world, through Aden and the small overseas communities of Somali seamen which were forming in the world's main ports. Of greater consequence still was the ever-present memory and example of Sayyid Muhammad's struggle for freedom. Again, the first impetus seems to have come from the few Somalis who, after education in Aden or the Sudan, had returned to find employment in the clerical grades of the civil service. One of the earliest of these to espouse the new aspirations and to seek to promote the general social and political betterment of his countrymen was Haji Farah 'Omar, a former employee of the Administration, who became active in the 1920s. After difficulties with the Protectorate authorities, he was exiled to Aden where, amongst the growing Somali community there, he participated in the foundation of the Somali Islamic Association. Through articles in Aden newspapers and letters and petitions addressed to the British government in London, Haji Farah and his associates contrived to bring Somali interests to the notice of people in Britain and thus helped to prepare the ground for further developments.

In the Protectorate itself, under much the same kind of inspiration as in Somalia, small groups of local merchants and traders began to organize political associations and clubs in the main centres of Berbera, Burao, and Hargeisa about 1935. From these tentative beginnings the Somaliland National Society emerged shortly afterwards. Its principal aims were to encourage modern education and progress in general and to seek to overcome the traditional particularistic rivalries which divided Somali society. Later, these general aims were elaborated into a more detailed programme which also included the aim of the unification of the Somali people and territories. While these aspirations, and particularly those approving western education, represented a distinct break with the past, the Society was in no sense anti-religious and indeed sought both inspiration and justification for many of its aims in Islam. In 1937 another movement, more limited in its political significance but still of considerable importance, came into being. This was the Somali Officials Union, formed principally to promote Somali interests in the Civil Service, and inspired by discontent at the Administration's policy of employing Indian and Arab clerks instead of training local Somali for these posts. These new currents of opinion, now for the first time assuming organized form, were, after the East African campaign and re-occupation of the Protectorate, soon to find issues capable of arousing a much wider public interest and concern.[23]

Finally, mention must also be made of a separate but related development in Somalia which, though cultural rather than political, was later to acquire a highly emotive nationalistic appeal. This was the invention, about 1920, by 'Isman Yusuf Kenadid, of a highly sophisticated and accurate alphabet and script for the Somali language. Although the Arabic script had long been in use in restricted circles as a medium for writing Somali, the differences between the two languages made this a makeshift expedient. And despite improvements introduced by Sheikh Uways and other early pioneers of writing Somali, Arabic still remained an imperfect vehicle for Somali. 'Osmaniya, as the new script was soon named after its founder, overcame these disadvantages by completely abandoning the attempt to rely on the Arabic alphabet, adopting instead an entirely new set of letters. This creation of a truly indigenous vehicle for the national language naturally appealed to the Somali national consciousness, although, from the start, it found opponents amongst conservative religious leaders who favoured Arabic. However, with its inventor's position as a member of the princely family of the Majerteyn clan, it soon gained a restricted currency in parts of the Majerteyn region and amongst other members of the clan living elsewhere. Later events were to create circumstances in which this ingenious writing was to be championed by the leaders of modern Somali nationalism as a symbol of Somali achievement, associated with perhaps the most prized of all things in the Somali national heritage – the Somali language.[24]

CHAPTER VI

THE RESTORATION OF COLONIAL FRONTIERS: 1940–50

Somali unification, 1940–50

ONE OF THE MANY side-effects of the Second World War was to stimulate a new conception of Somali nationalism, to foster the nationalist aim of unifying the several Somali territories, and to provide conditions under which this aim could largely have been realized. In the course of the fighting in Africa, in August 1940, the Italians captured British Somaliland and added that territory to the Somali portion of their East African empire. This, however, was a short-lived success for seven months later the Protectorate was recovered, and Somalia and the Ogaden were occupied by the Allies during the East Africa campaign and liberation of Ethiopia.[1] With the sole exception of French Somaliland which in 1942 declared for De Gaulle, all the Somali territories were now destined to remain for almost a decade under the British flag.

The occupied enemy territories administration, which had been temporarily established in Ethiopia after the Italian defeat, was terminated by an Anglo-Ethiopian agreement and military convention of January 1942. To aid the movement of Allied troops and to counter any danger from Jibuti, then still under Vichy rule, however, this agreement provided for the continuance of British Military Administration in the Ogaden and in the Haud as part of a series of 'Reserved Areas' and cantonments which also included the vital Franco-Ethiopian line of rail from Dire Dawa to the French Somaliland border. The Haud was ruled from the Ethiopian administrative centre of Jigjiga by a British Senior Civil Affairs Officer, and the parallel existence of the two authorities was a source of constant embarrassment to each. Continuing the

position under the Italians, the Ogaden remained attached to
Somalia and was administered with that territory from the headquarters at Mogadishu. British Somaliland, though part of the
same over-all administration, had its own separate military governor.

A further Anglo-Ethiopian agreement, signed in 1945,[2] returned the Franco-Ethiopian railway to its pre-war status along
with the British military cantonments in Ethiopia, but enabled
British military administration to continue in the Ogaden and
Haud without prejudice to Ethiopia's ultimate sovereignty over
these areas. With these arrangements completed, the Horn of
Africa was now to become the scene of a new scramble for Somali
territory; a conflict of interests in which for the first time the views
of the Somali themselves and their aspirations for the future
received some belated consideration.

The British military administration in Somalia and the Ogaden

In Somalia the Italians capitulated more easily and quickly than
had been anticipated, giving up a much larger area of territory
than the British authorities were ready to administer. Consequently, it was with the scantiest of resources and preparation that
a ridiculously small band of Civil Affairs Officers, many of whom
had no previous colonial experience, arrived in Somalia to deal
with the chaos left behind by the fighting.

Once the elements of civil order had been restored, the most
pressing problem facing the new administration was the serious
economic situation created by the collapse of the various Italian
para-statal monopolies. The plantations on the Shebelle and Juba
were in a sad plight, many of the Italian farmers having fled to the
towns; the Somali labour force had virtually disappeared, and
looting had caused widespread damage. Of the major concerns,
the least affected was the S.A.I.S. enterprise at Villagio which was
still in production and still enjoyed a considerable complement of
manpower, a tribute to the better conditions and labour relations
prevailing there. At Genale, by contrast, the British Administration found that only six out of 136 holdings were still under effective production, and after several weeks of strenuous effort only
500 of a required labour force of 8,000 had reported for work.

Later this situation was improved by an extensive grant of un-occupied land to the local Bimal clan. Along the Juba the position was even more desperate.

However, gradually, after the employment conditions of the former régime had been liberalized, an adequate labour force was forthcoming and the plantations were encouraged to concentrate on the production of sugar and grain to meet the territory's local needs. Capital loans and tractor fuel were made available to Italian farmers. Encouragement was also given to local Somali cultivators; and by 1943 Somalia was self-supporting in primary foodstuffs, although further serious food shortages occurred from time to time. Somalis and Arabs were also encouraged to partici-pate in trade and commerce more fully than had previously been possible under the discriminatory legislation of the past. Despite these economic achievements, however, a considerable amount of public assistance was required, particularly to meet the needs of the Italian community which in 1941 numbered 8,000 and consisted mainly of civilians and former civil servants and their dependants. This problem was eased gradually by the repatriation of women and children to Italy, to the extent that by 1943 there were only some 4,500 Italians left in Somalia of whom a tenth were still in receipt of assistance.[3]

Equally pressing was the question of security and the firm establishment of the new administration's authority throughout the territory. Here there were two main aspects to consider: the maintenance of law and order amongst the population as a whole; and the special problem of the enemy Italian community. These two issues could not be completely separated since, with its very inadequate resources in personnel, the new administration had, of necessity, to rely upon the services of many Italian officials, particularly those with specialist technical skills. In the event, while many junior technical officials continued to work under the British Military Administration, in more important key posts only those were retained who showed no fascist leanings and whose conduct indicated that no security risk was involved. Others were interned in prisoner-of-war camps.

At the same time, radical and sweeping changes were necessary. The Italian police force was disbanded because of its 'bad discipline and unreliability'[4] and completely replaced by a hastily recruited

Somalia Gendarmerie under British officers. By 1943 this new force had swollen to an establishment of 3,070 Somalis and African ranks (including some recruits from Tanganyika) with 120 British officers. With these resources the general disarmament of the population was satisfactorily achieved, and the activities of a number of pro-Italian irregular guerilla groups effectively controlled. To increase the force's efficiency and to provide for the future, a police school had been opened and was working extremely well, training Somali N.C.O.s and Officers, a few of whom by 1949 had reached the rank of Chief Inspector. At the same time, the appalling prison conditions of the fascist régime were drastically altered.

While the central police force was thus completely remodelled, the *gogle* tribal rural constabulary was taken over virtually in its entirety and without serious modification. On the other hand, the Italian provincial administration which had collapsed during the fighting, was completely replaced, all Provinces and Districts being placed in the charge of British Civil Affairs Officers. Other innovations were gradually introduced. The old clan chiefs and leaders continued to receive government subsidies as in the past, but vacancies in their ranks were generally not filled. Instead, in order to promote local government, and as a preparatory step towards autonomy and self-rule, tribal assemblies were encouraged to act as a liaison with the Administration; elections for assembly leaders were held; and District and Provincial Advisory Councils were created in 1946. These new Councils were encouraged to discuss such outstanding problems as water supplies, pastoral betterment generally, agricultural improvement, unemployment and food scarcities.

Modest advances were also achieved in education. When the British Military Administration assumed control of Somalia, it found in operation thirteen state-aided Italian mission schools providing some elementary education for Somalis and Italians. By 1947 nineteen government elementary schools had been opened, notwithstanding the difficulties of recruiting qualified teaching staff in this period. There were also three private schools, and a teachers' training centre for Arabs and Somalis with an average enrolment of fifty students. Thus, though education was still pitifully inadequate both in standards and extent, the number of children (still almost entirely boys) attending school had doubled since before the war.

While with its concern for imperial ambitions and the needs of its settler population the Italian government had done little to advance Somali interests, a large part of the energies and activities of the new administration was directed towards this end. To understand the atmosphere in Somalia at this time, and the nature of the relations between British officials and Somali, it has to be remembered that the new rulers saw themselves as liberators from fascist oppression and to a considerable extent were so received. Indeed, the generally friendly reception accorded to them reinforced the Administration's tendency to regard the Somali as allies against the Italians. And many British officials made no secret of their admiration for Somalis and contempt for the defeated Italians. Hence there was from the beginning a considerable bond of sympathy between the new rulers and the Somali public which, in the liberal currents of opinion of the times, found expression in a strong and quite explicit pro-Somali policy. Despite its small numbers, moreover, the new administration was not lacking in energy or initiative. And in some respects, the lack of previous experience on the part of many of its officials seems to have been more of an advantage than a handicap; for it brought fresh and unprejudiced minds to bear on the country's problems and further emphasized the break with the past, giving to the new government even more of the character of a new broom.

There was consequently a generally favourable response, with of course some exceptions, to the benevolent, and on the whole enlightened paternalism of the new rulers. And, if the British officials were sometimes more rigid in their official and private capacities than their Italian predecessors, there was little question of their progressive intentions. Moreover, British law, though strictly enforced with often unpopular but effective collective punishments to control clan and tribal warfare, soon earned Somali respect and indeed has left a legacy which is still valued for its impartiality. Above all, the defeat of their former masters who had seemed invincible not only gave the new British Administration great prestige in Somali eyes, but also prompted an increasing Somali sophistication in the evaluation of foreign nations.

In practical terms, the liberalizing effect of the British Military

Administration, while it did not lead to the promotion of Somali civil servants to the extent followed in Eritrea, led to the training of a cadre of junior Somali officials and a smaller number of more senior police officers. This, as later events were to show, provided a sound if modest basis for more extensive Somali advancement in the civil service in the trusteeship period preceding independence. Of even greater significance, however, was the Administration's attitude towards local politics. Once it had found its feet, the new government abolished the restrictions of the Italian régime on local political associations and clubs. Immediately, a proliferation of Italian societies arose, expressing all shades of metropolitan opinion from that of the extreme right to the extreme left. After the fall of the fascists, local branches of the Christian Democrats gained the largest affiliation amongst the Italian community. All these Italian groups were naturally interested in the question of the future status of Somalia, an issue on which all shades of Italian party opinion showed virtual unanimity, the strength of patriotism being apparently greater than that of party doctrine.

This issue and the upsurge of activity among the Italian clubs and associations attracted considerable Somali interest. In these conditions, the currents of progressive Somali opinion which had begun to seek expression in the closing days of the fascist period, took concrete form with the establishment of a number of Somali societies and clubs. The first and most important of these movements to achieve a formal existence was the Somali Youth Club opened at Mogadishu on 13 May, 1943, after several weeks of discussion with the local Political Officer on the form of the society's constitution. The Club had thirteen founder members representing all the main Somali clan groups. Much of the inspiration came from 'Abdulqadir Sekhawe Din, a prominent religious figure of Mogadishu, and from Yasin Haji 'Isman Shirmarke of the Majerteyn clan of northern Somalia. Another prominent religious leader who played an important part in the Club's early days was Haji Muhammad Husseyn, also of Mogadishu.

Thus, from its inception the new society contained representatives of the majority of the traditional clan divisions within the nation, and of men of religion as well as laymen, united in the desire to abolish the wasteful clan rivalries of the past and to establish a new conception of nationhood. These aims had always been present in Somali Islam, and forty years earlier, at the time of Sayyid Muhammad 'Abdille Hassan, this was the only means by which national patriotism could be expressed coherently. Now, however, these religious aims were married to a modern conscious-ness of nationhood, and strengthened by a desire for progress in general expressed through the new vehicle of the Somali Youth Club.

With these modernist and progressive aspirations to which the British Military Administration was sympathetic, the Somali Youth Club rapidly gathered adherents, its members' conduct be-ing officially described as 'exemplary'. Initially, it found most ready support amongst the younger educated officials, and soon also in the Somalia Gendarmerie. The Club's popularity in the Gendar-merie was no doubt partly due to the fact that at the time some of the most highly educated Somalis served in this force. Another significant factor was that by its very nature this organization composed of Somalis from every clan division, mixed by deliber-ate policy in even the smallest units, also sought to inculcate a code of loyalty transcending tribal and clan schisms. In these circumstances, reinforced by the gradual tendency of both organi-zations to acquire a majority of Darod clansmen in their ranks, there is little doubt that the Gendarmerie must be regarded as having played a significant part in the growth of modern Somali nationalism at this stage. And despite the British predeliction for that principle of government which discourages political activity in the civil service, the Somali Youth Club affiliation of many Gendarmerie and other officials was condoned because the new movement was progressive, co-operated with the government, and was anti-Italian. In other circumstances, the attitude of the British administering authority might well have been very different; as in fact, as will presently be seen, was the case in Kenya.

By 1946 the British Military Administration officially estimated the Club to number no less than 25,000 affiliates,[5] and by the end of 1947 it had changed its name to the Somali Youth League and was strongly organized as a political machine with branches throughout Somalia, in the Ogaden, Haud, British Protectorate, and even in Kenya where its activities, in a different administra-tive milieu, were viewed with distinctly less favour. The League had now a four point programme:

'To unite all Somalis generally, and the youth especially with the consequent repudiation of all harmful old prejudices (such, for example, as tribal and clan distinctions); To educate the youth in modern civilization by means of schools and by cultural propaganda circles; To take an interest in and assist in eliminating by constitutional and legal means any existing or future situations which might be prejudicial to the interests of the Somali people; And finally, to develop the Somali language and to assist in putting into use among Somalis the 'Osmaniya Somali script.'

These were aims with which, as will be evident, no reasonable, progressive administration could possibly find fault. Of particular interest in this programme is its realistic attitude towards modern education, so different from the traditional religious opposition to western schooling. Nor was the League's view on this matter merely verbal propaganda. Already, on its own initiative, and with the approval of the Administration, the S.Y.L. had opened a number of schools and classes in English. Now too, the ingenious Somali 'Osmaniya script, was no longer merely a cultural curiosity, but had acquired definite nationalist significance. The difficulties attending its wholesale adoption, partly practical and partly as a result of competition with Arabic, have proved more intractable than some of the other objectives in this initial S.Y.L. statement of policy.

Although the largest and best organized movement, the League was not the only organization to emerge in this initial period. Apart from a number of ephemeral smaller groups, mainly with limited local and particularistic interests, the most important rival was originally formed under the name of the Patriotic Benefit Union, or 'Jumiya', representing chiefly southern Rahanweyn and Digil tribesmen, the partly Bantu riverine peoples, and some of the local Arab community. This organization, with the welcome addition of Italian financial support, favoured a more conservative policy and sought particularly to protect the interests of the southern agricultural tribesmen from domination by the northern nomads who overwhelmingly supported the League. Out of this body, which was markedly less anti-Italian than its rival, developed the Hizbia Digil-Mirifle Somali, formed on 25 March, 1947, under the presidency of Sheikh 'Abdallah Sheikh Muhammad.

Meanwhile, the tempo of political activity and interest had

soared after the war with increasing speculation on the future status of the Somalilands, an issue which could only be resolved in the context of the whole tangled problem of the disposal of all the former Italian colonies. Already Ethiopia was pressing for the return of the Ogaden and Reserved Areas, her sovereignty over which had been recognized in the 1942 and 1944 Anglo-Ethiopian Agreements. Ethiopian pretensions extended also even to Somalia, which of course Italy was now claiming strongly. To the four Powers initially charged with the disposal of the Italian colonies, however, the British Foreign Secretary, Ernest Bevin, sensibly proposed in the spring of 1946 that the interests of the Somali people would be best served if the existing union of Somali territories were continued. A trusteeship, preferably under Britain, although this was not an essential condition, was suggested. Unfortunately for Somali aspirations but scarcely surprisingly, this solution was strenuously opposed by Ethiopia. Nor was Ethiopia to be distracted from her determination to regain the Ogaden by the promise of British support for her claims to Eritrea, or more directly, by the offer of the port of Zeila and parts of the north-west of the Protectorate in exchange for those areas of the Haud and Ogaden regularly frequented by British protected clansmen in their grazing movements.

This tardy British attempt to adjust the situation showed some concern for Somali nomadic interests, and a recognition of the real problems created by the partition of a nomadic people. Even under the unitary control of the British Military Administration these had proved singularly troublesome and had been a constant source of friction. This argument, however, had no appeal for Ethiopia. Nor did it carry much weight with the other three powers concerned with the problem of the disposal of the Italian territories. For they tended to be generally sceptical of British intentions, and their wider interests, in so far as they impinged at all on the Somali question, tended to run counter to the Bevin proposals. Thus from the start it was clear that if the British scheme for Somali unification was to have any prospect of success it would need strong advocacy. As matters turned out, it soon became obvious that the forces arrayed against the plan were such that to have sought to overcome them would have required a degree of effort and political sacrifice which was not warranted by Britain's very limited strategic interests in the area. By the end of 1946 the Four Powers had still not reached agreement on the whole turgid question of Italy's former possessions and it was decided to send out a commission to the countries concerned (Somalia, Eritrea, Libya, and Cyrenaica) to consult their own aspirations for the future.

The Commission arrived at Mogadishu on 6 January, 1948. By this time the local political scene had become complicated by the strenuous efforts of the Italians to secure a favourable pro-Italian front, and by the premature announcement of the Bevin proposals. Though still uncompromisingly opposed to any return of their territory to Italy, and still the party with by far the largest following, the S.Y.L. had experienced a split in its ranks in its former stronghold of Majerteynia, where the infiltration of Italian interests had secured the promotion of a rival splinter group called the 'Progressive Majerteyn League'. The Hizbia Digil Mirifle was more seriously divided internally: and all the other Somali societies had joined together in a catholic alliance called simply 'The Conference' – in which pro-Italian sentiments were fostered by Italian money. Nevertheless, despite the presence of this intrusive Italian influence, this configuration of interests had a basis in Somali political realities at the time. Notwithstanding the attempt to detach the important Majerteyn element, the S.Y.L. had now a strong Darod following and anti-Darod traditional interests were often suspicious of and hostile to the League. This was the case with many, though not all Somalis of the Hawiye clans, of whom an important group centring on Mogadishu tended to regard the Italians as potential allies against further Darod intrusion and pressure in their affairs. Similarly, many of the Rahanweyn and Digil tribesmen continued to accept Italian support in an effort to enhance and safeguard their interests against those of the predominantly nomadic clansmen of the north.

In addition to attempting to divide the ranks of their strongest opponents in the League and to sponsoring and encouraging the growth of rival organizations, the Italians were also engaged in a direct and forthright propaganda campaign for the return of Somalia to Italy. Towards the end of 1947 these manœuvres assumed formidable proportions, and local manifestations of Italian concern, backed by the metropolitan radio and press, had become increasingly vociferous and arrogant in tone. It was, more-over, difficult for the British Military Administration to deal fairly and also firmly with this upsurge of Italian national pride. For the future of the territory was still in question and already Somali hopes had been unjustifiably encouraged by discussion of the Bevin plan which, as was now becoming increasingly evident, could not be implemented. The local Italian community was, however, warned officially of the dangers which were likely to ensue if this exuberant campaign continued. But, apparently, the Italians relied upon the British Administration to uphold their interests, even if this meant unjustly suppressing Somali nationalist fervour. Certainly there was little if any modification in the con-duct of the Italian agitation for a return of Somalia to Italy, and events came to a tragic head with the arrival of the Four Power Commission of inquiry.

As soon as the Commission had assembled at Mogadishu it was greeted by a flurry of Italian flags and slogans. The British Chief Administrator warned the Commissioners of the danger to public order, and particularly to Italian lives and property, likely to follow if similar demonstrations were allowed to continue. The Com-mission, however, replied that it wished to observe such public manifestations of support, and asked that permission be granted for a large public rally to be held by the S.Y.L. on 11 January. This was granted, and on the appointed day the Youth League assembled a large number of its supporters at Mogadishu. On the morning of the same day, without prior notification or author-ization, members of the Italian community and their supporters and henchmen, many of whom had been hired for the occasion, thronged in lorry loads into the town. Many of the Italian party were armed with bows and arrows as well as other weapons and proceeded to apply these in a determined effort to break up the S.Y.L. demonstration. Tension rapidly mounted, and both sides were soon engaged in a full-scale battle in the course of which Italians shot at S.Y.L. supporters and threw hand-grenades into the crowd.

This rash action cost the Italian community dear; fifty-one Italians were killed and a similar number wounded. Somali casualties were less severe. Widespread looting also occurred, and further violence was only prevented by the action of the Somalia

Gendarmerie supported by contingents of the King's African Rifles.[6] After this unfortunate incident, hysterical allegations were levelled at the Administration which was accused of complicity on the Somali side and of failing adequately to protect Italian lives and property.

It was in this atmosphere of smouldering animosity that the Four Power Commission proceeded to examine, surprisingly nonchalantly in the circumstances, the cases of the various parties and groups, the Italians hoping to profit from the sympathy which their losses had attracted. The main spokesman for the S.Y.L. was 'Abdillahi 'Ise (later to become the first Premier of Somalia).[7] The League's President, Haji Mahammad Husseyn, also played a prominent part in the hearings; and the very detailed and impressive S.Y.L. programme for the future development of the country was drafted with the advice of Mr Salole, an Aden Somali lawyer employed in the legal department of the Administration, and of Michael Mariano, a former administrative employee from the north.[8] As on previous occasions, the party stressed its aim of bringing the Somali territories together under a single government, of working steadily towards full independence, and advocated a ten years' period of trusteeship for Somalia under Four Power administration. On no account would the League countenance a return of Italian rule.

The majority of the other Somali groups, organized with Italian financial support into a consortium under the name of the 'Somalia Conference', presented a less coherent programme in which they proposed a trusteeship period of thirty years for Somalia, under Italian rule, but subject to the radical reform of the country and its development in all spheres. The H.D.M.S., while previously supporting this view, had now broken with the Conference and favoured Four Power trusteeship for the same lengthy period. The opinions of all the local Italian societies and interest-groups were conscientiously heard, and treated indeed with greater respect and attention than their numbers might have seemed to warrant. These, needless to say, unanimously favoured the return of Somalia to Italy.

Having studied the views of a considerable cross-section of the population, the Commission[9] in due course submitted its findings on Somalia to the Council of Foreign Ministers, reporting, correctly, despite frequent jibes at S.Y.L. delegates during the hearings, that the League's programme commanded the largest public support in the territory. Nevertheless, notwithstanding the manifest opposition to a return of Italian authority, Britain, like France and America, had now definitely come round to supporting trusteeship under Italy, while Russia, although previously also advocating this, had now decided in favour of Four Power control. With this failure to reach agreement which involved also the other ex-Italian colonies, the whole turgid issue was passed for settlement to the General Assembly of the United Nations. And having now abandoned its earlier proposals for Somali unification, the British government proceeded to defend its new position·by seeking to discredit the S.Y.L. claim to speak for the majority of Somali. Statements in the House of Commons to this effect, drew a sharp reply from 'Abd ar-Rashid 'Ali Shirmarke[10] who had now become Secretary of the League and was later to lead an independent Somali government. 'Abdillahi 'Ise was dispatched to lobby the United Nations delegates: and the pro-Italian Conference now enjoying little public support, and largely controlled by the Italian Liaison staff at Mogadishu, sent representatives to promote the Italian case.

While the U.N. Assembly discussed the disposal of the Italian colonies at its meeting at Lake Success in 1949, having before it the Bevin–Sforza compromise plan proposing Italian trusteeship for Somalia[11] for an unspecified period, popular demonstrations against the Italians continued at Mogadishu and elsewhere in the territory. Somalia's fate was now clearly in the balance, and Somali hopes seemed likely to founder, as so often in the past, for quite extraneous reasons. This duly occurred, but, despite the strength of anti-Italian feeling, the Assembly's decision on 21 November, 1949, to entrust Somalia for ten years to Italian administration under U.N. tutelage was received calmly and without incident. As will be apparent presently, this unexpectedly peaceful acceptance of the decision was not merely a matter of resignation in the face of the inevitable. Due account has to be taken of the very firm provisions which the Assembly laid down ensuring that Italy would discharge her new responsibilities honourably, and, even more significant, of the limitation of the period of trusteeship to ten years.

In any case, Somali nationalism mainly expressed through the S.Y.L., which immediately gathered a fresh access of support, was now so firmly entrenched that, whatever happened, there could be no return to the stagnation and oppression of the fascist period.

The disposal of the Haud and Ogaden

Meanwhile, while in Somalia itself the majority of the population had been fighting to achieve independence and freedom from Italian rule, in the Ogaden a similar campaign was in progress against the surrender of that territory to Ethiopia. And despite its isolation and backwardness, the new aspirations spread by the League quickly found support. As early as 1942 there had been disturbances in the Harar–Jigjiga region connected with Ethiopian attempts to impose direct taxation. Two years later, leaders of the Ogaden clans petitioned the British Military Administration, urging Britain not to relinquish their territory to Ethiopian rule.

These attempts to preserve Somali independence were countered by Ethiopian moves designed to win Somali favour. To the embarrassment of the British authorities, the Ethiopian Governor at Jigjiga sought to solicit Somali goodwill by offering higher salaries to Somali elders and clan leaders than those paid by the Administration. The response to these overtures varied considerably. The official head of the faction-ridden Gadabursi clan, in receipt of a stipend from both sides, was gradually won over to the Ethiopian cause, leading many Gadabursi to defect from the S.Y.L. Others, however, and they were in the majority, flocked to the League which became so successful that the Ethiopians sought to ban it, but were prevented by the British Administration. Having failed in this direct line of attack, a counter-movement financed by the Ethiopian government was launched called the Somali Mutual Relief Association. This, however, did not attract much support. Full advantage was also taken of the occasion of the Duke of Harar's wedding in 1946 to which leading Ogaden clansmen were invited as official guests.

These various blandishments were of questionable value, but with uncertainty as to whether the Bevin plan would be implemented mounting, towards the end of 1946 a number of Ogaden leaders took the precaution of making contact with the Ethiopian governor at Jigjiga. This situation, indeed, was one with which the Ogaden clansmen were already only too familiar from their previous experience of Italo-Ethiopian competition. And in the present circumstances of continued doubt as to their future position, it was natural that the clansmen concerned should seek to provide for every possibility. Nevertheless, the general character of opposition to Ethiopian control was indisputable.[12] In 1947, this was amply demonstrated when, with the exception only of the 'Ise, all the clans of the Ogaden and Reserved Areas presented the British authorities with a petition against the surrender of their country to Ethiopia, requesting that their protests should be conveyed to the General Assembly of the United Nations.

Britain, as has been seen, had earlier sought to retain the Ogaden as part of the Bevin scheme for Somali unification. But as this plan had come to nothing, the British government decided that the time had now come to abandon the Ogaden to Ethiopia in fulfilment of the 1942 and 1944 Anglo-Ethiopian Agreements. This course of action was adopted despite the known strength of Somali feeling on the matter, and the natural repugnance of the British officials on the spot to participate in what many regarded as a betrayal of Somali interests. And when the decision was announced at Jigjiga, a riot occurred in which twenty-five Somalis lost their lives. Nevertheless, apart from this gesture of defiance, the population of the Ogaden as a whole bowed to the inevitable; and the transfer from British to Ethiopian control took place smoothly and without further incident on 23 September, 1948. This unexpectedly peaceful exchange, whether or not this was the intended effect, was no doubt facilitated by the disbursement amongst the Ogaden clansmen of some £91,000 by the departing British in settlement of all outstanding blood-dues and claims incurred during the period of British rule.[13] In any event, Ethiopia had at last gained the Ogaden which she had so long coveted, and, in contrast to the position at the time of the Italo-Ethiopian conflict in 1935, was now in a position to establish her rule throughout this vast area. The tribute-gathering sorties which Ras Makonnen had sent out from Harar and Jigjiga at the turn of the century, which had created a basis for Ethiopia's pretensions to sovereignty over the Ogaden, had at last borne fruit.

However, by agreement with Ethiopia, Britain retained a temporary civil affairs administration, directed from the British Protectorate, within that part of the Haud and Ogaden which the 1935 Anglo-Ethiopian boundary commission had established as being habitually frequented by British protected Somali clansmen in their further grazing movements. This, of course, did not in any way question Ethiopia's sovereignty in these 'Reserved Areas', although this rested ultimately upon the ambiguous 1897 Anglo-Ethiopian treaty, which despite the recent interpretation given to it had originally carefully refrained from acknowledging Ethiopian sovereignty over the areas in question.[14]

Thus Ethiopia had in fact done very well in these transactions, and had turned the Italian conquest of her territory to considerable profit. She had gained the Ogaden which she had never fully administered and to which her only international title was provided by the 1897 and 1908 Italo-Ethiopian agreements. And even if she was not at once to administer it fully, she had also now unambiguously acquired the Haud, to which her original legal, as well as moral, claim was tenuous and debatable. As the victim of fascist aggression, Ethiopia had naturally every right to the most considerate and generous treatment. But it was unfortunate that, in the process of satisfying her claims to reparation for the events of the past, protesting Somalis should be sacrificed and the collective Somali desire for national self-determination be cast aside almost as soon as it had achieved an articulate existence.

The rehabilitation of the British Protectorate

Having abandoned the Bevin plan for a Greater Somalia, and having relinquished the Ogaden to Ethiopia, the next step was obviously the return of the British Somaliland Protectorate to its pre-war status. This took place in November 1948 when Mr Gerald Reece (later Sir Gerald), formerly Provincial Commissioner in the Northern Province of Kenya, was appointed Governor of the Protectorate and also invested with the office of Military Administrator of the Haud and Reserved Areas.

Since the re-occupation of the Protectorate in 1941 much had occurred, the old care and maintenance policy of the past having been at last decisively abandoned in favour of more progressive policies. For this complete change of orientation much credit is due to the efforts of Sir Gerald Fisher, Military Governor from 1943 to 1948. Despite the more intractable character of economic and social conditions in the Protectorate as compared with Somalia, and the absence of the colonial basis which had been created there by the Italians, the upheavals of the war had not been without effect upon the local Somali population. These circumstances favoured an extension of the modernist trend which had begun to appear before the war; there was now appreciably less hostility to secular progress and social change.

On the return of the British in April 1941, the first problems were again those of re-establishing normal trade and commerce and of restoring law and order, which, as in Somalia, entailed the recovery of the large stores of weapons and ammunition discarded during the fighting. Since Berbera, as well as a number of other stations, had been seriously damaged in the operations, it was decided to build a new government headquarters at Hargeisa, the site of Sheikh Maddar's religious community, in the central hinterland of the Protectorate. This was a decision in full accord with the new forward policy of extending administrative and social services through the Protectorate: the old days of the coast administration based on Berbera had gone for ever. The reception accorded to the returning British was also propitious. On its own initiative the Camel Corps reported for duty armed with Italian weapons, and was at once dispatched to disarm the clansmen of the interior. By the end of the year, trade and commerce were back to normal and the primary disarmament of the whole population had been achieved without serious incident. By the end of the following year the police force had been completely reorganized and, with a strength of eight British officers and inspectors and some 800 Somali other ranks, was in a secure position to maintain civil order.

By 1945, with the aid of the new Colonial Development and Welfare scheme of grants, a co-ordinated programme for development was under way. A general survey of the resources and potentialities of the country, including a study of grazing and watering requirements, began in 1943 under the direction of Mr J. A. Hunt, an experienced geologist and administrative officer. Public health services were extended, and a training school for Somali nurses opened in 1945. The long-standing problem of secular education was also attacked. With three elementary schools opened at Hargeisa, Berbera and Burao in 1942, a concerted campaign by radio and mobile cinema was mounted two years later to win support for further educational developments. The response this received was favourable; and by 1945, seven elementary schools with an attendance of over four hundred boys were functioning. Assistance was also being given to nineteen private Koranic schools teaching Arabic and arithmetic. By 1950 there were two Intermediate schools and plans for starting secondary education. In the same period the scope of agricultural services expanded considerably; experiments with new crops and fertilizers were initiated, grazing control schemes were put into effect, and a number of small experimental date plantations were established.

It might be thought that the successful introduction of these new measures, and particularly of secular education, implied that all conservative resistance to change had been overcome. This, however, was far from being the case. There was still an under-tow of antagonism which the severe devastation caused by a plague of locusts in 1944–45 brought to a head. Anti-locust measures employing locust bait, which was regarded with suspicion, were interpreted by some elements in the population as a deliberate attempt by the government to kill Somali camels and stock; and in 1945 this issue provoked a serious riot at Burao and similar troubles at Erigavo. Order was restored without much difficulty, but the situation pointed to the need for a marked improvement in public relations and a tightening up in administrative control. In point of fact, at the time, the administrative establishment was quite inadequate, there being only five District Commissioners available to run six Districts, and only one of these officials could speak Somali. As will be evident, the Protectorate was still very lightly administered.

As in the past, the line of control ran through the District Commissioners to government stipended Akils, a few of whom were empowered to hold minor courts without any criminal jurisdiction. The Kadis Courts, regulating matters of personal status according to Islamic Law, continued to function under a Chief Kadi presiding over a court of appeal at Hargeisa. In 1945,

the Akils Courts, more appropriate to a more hierarchical traditional system than that characteristic of Somali society, and
which had never worked very well, were gradually abandoned
in favour of a new system of Subordinate Courts. These courts
consisted of a judge and assessors expert in customary law, but
also with sufficient education to record proceedings in English
or Arabic. This more flexible arrangement was more in keeping
with the spirit of Somali customary procedure. In the main
towns, new township committees were formed to provide for a
gradual devolution of authority, and a town planning board was
also set up.

The most notable experiment launched in this period, however,
was the creation of a Protectorate Advisory Council, which in
the presence of the Governor, held its first meeting in July 1946.
Delegates representing most sections of public interest, the new
as well as the old, attended from each District. The first meeting
lasted a week, and the Council's agenda included such topics as:
the development of agriculture, the problem of destitution and
juvenile delinquency in towns (very pressing at the time), the
extension of the Subordinate Court scheme, the opening of further
rural dispensaries, grazing control, and the more controversial
issue of grazing movements in the Haud and Reserved Areas.
This last item concerned the conflicting grazing movements of
the Isaq and Dulbahante clans from the Protectorate and those
of the Ogaden, a problem to become increasingly difficult of
solution after the surrender of the Ogaden and Haud to Ethiopian
administration.

These progressive moves were accompanied by a considerable
awakening of modern political interest which was further stimulated by growing concern over the future status of the Protectorate and the Somali territories generally. In this situation, the
Somaliland National Society which had emerged immediately
before the war, joined with another local association to form the
Somaliland National League. Although described in the official
records of the time as more conservative than the S.Y.L., this
body shared the League's aim for Somali unification as well as
championing the extension of education and the abolition of clan
particularism. Also in existence in this period was the more
narrowly based Isaqiya association, concerned almost entirely

with the needs and interests of the Isaq clans and particularly active in promoting these in Kenya. In the Protectorate, either through this organization, or independently of it, most of the Isaq supported the S.N.L.

The introduction of the Somali Youth League to the Protectorate, and its gradual growth in adherents in 1947, brought a new element into the situation, and one which was by no means welcomed by the local Administration.[15] For although the S.Y.L. was generally representative of all the Somali clans, to the dominantly Isaq population of the Protectorate it was tinged with a strongly Darod flavour, appealing therefore more immediately to the eastern Dulbahante and Warsangeli clans than to the central Isaq. However, the serious disturbances which marked the political scene in Hargeisa in 1947, though connected with a proposed merger of the S.N.L. and S.Y.L., were apparently not motivated by traditional Isaq–Darod antagonism. They were produced, in fact, it seems, by a split within the Isaq themselves, one party favouring the new alliance, while the other, being more conservative, supported the Isaqiya association. One of the two factions concerned consisted mainly of Habar Yunis clansmen who had recently lost their traditional position as the main source of employees in government service. The loss of this lucrative and influential monopoly, which dated from the earliest days of British rule, had been hastened by the new administrative policy of seeking to relate the employment of Somali personnel to the relative strengths of the various clans. This policy, while appealing to others, had little attraction for the Habar Yunis, and caused considerable bitterness.

This turbulent phase, however, quickly passed, and after the abandonment of the Ogaden to Ethiopia, the announcement of Somalia's future status, and the resumption of civil administration in the Protectorate itself, having no major and immediate issue to marshal public concern, interest in the new political associations temporarily flagged. Such interest as remained seemed for the present in the main content to co-operate with the Administration in the gradual development of the country. By 1950, indeed, it seemed that a new spirit of co-operation between the public and its government had been achieved, and the Protectorate appeared to be set fair on a course of gradual evolution and progress. And in keeping with this state of affairs the first decisive steps in the eventual Somalization of the civil service had been taken. Several police officers had reached the rank of Inspector, a Somali Inspector of Schools had been appointed, and two Somali officials had gone to England on Colonial scholarships. A modest beginning, but still a beginning.

The general situation at the end of 1949

Of all the Somali territories only French Somaliland,[16] with its rival Somali and 'Afar population, had experienced no major change of government and remained generally aloof from the momentous tide of events which characterize the decade in the area as a whole. This isolation and insulation coincides in a way with the particularism of the 'Ise Somali in the *Côte*, and their attachment, for the most part certainly at this time, to Ethiopia, a situation in conformity with Franco-Ethiopian co-operation. Although with its port of Jibuti extensively developed between 1926–39, and its salt factory in maximum production in 1936, the *Côte* had become the most profitable of all the Somali territories, very little in the way of social progress had been attempted. The pastoralists' needs had, it is true, been improved by a veterinary service started in 1939, health services existed on a rudimentary scale, and education by 1950 provided eight schools for some 720 pupils. But apart from the urbanized population of Jibuti, which had swelled rapidly to a town of 20,000 inhabitants, the traditional pastoral life of the interior remained virtually unaffected.

The system of administration, in which Commanders of Districts (*cercles*) were either military or civil officials, was otherwise similar to that in the British Protectorate and Somalia, although no attempt had yet been made to promote anything in the way of modern local government. Nor were there any Somalis in training for responsible positions in the civil service which continued to be staffed exclusively by expatriates. And although trade unions had come into existence amongst the working population of Jibuti, there were as yet no locally based political parties notwithstanding the fact that the S.Y.L. and S.N.L. had some support in the territory. Nationalist political activity indeed was not encouraged, in contrast to the position in British Somaliland and Somalia.

Nevertheless, a territorial Representative Council with statutory powers was established in 1945. This body contained an equal number of representatives of the local French community and of the mixed Somali, 'Afar, and Arab population, its members being appointed partly by election and partly by nomination by the *Côte*'s Governor. And in addition to its local functions, the Council appointed one representative to the Council of the French Republic, and another to the French Union Assembly. In the National Assembly itself, the *Côte* was directly represented by a Deputy elected from the combined native and French electoral colleges.

As in other French territories, this canalization of political activity towards the metropolitan country, profoundly affected the later development of political parties, serving to insulate political movements in French Somaliland from those in other parts of Somaliland. The general effect of French policy was thus the isolation of the *Côte* from the tenor of Somali advancement elsewhere. And the perpetuation of the old tradition of Franco-British rivalry in the Horn of Africa was very evident in the French mistrust of Britain's original plans for Somali unification, a deeply grounded suspicion of British motives which lost little of its savour after Mr Bevin's plan had been officially discarded. It was still a common view, in French official circles, given currency also by Ethiopian sources, that, to the detriment of Ethiopia, Britain still nurtured hopes of supporting the establishment of a Greater Somalia with a Somali government friendly to England.[17] Later events have not entirely supported this interpretation of British interest in N.E. Africa.

Thus, although by 1950 a measure of representative government had been granted to the *Côte*, and more in fact than was given at the time to British Somaliland or Somalia, both these territories had experienced a more profound and far-reaching political awakening. In addition, both these portions of Somaliland, and particularly Somalia, were now unambiguously launched on a course of development and progress leading to independence. Unfortunately for Somali national aspirations, however, the unique opportunity which had existed for welding these two territories together with the Ogaden and Haud, and preparing this national entity for self-government under a single system of rule, had been irretrievably lost. For the present, Somali nationalist activity was accordingly forced to concentrate most of its energies upon local issues in British Somaliland and Somalia, while elsewhere it was suppressed and condemned to a clandestine existence.

From the Somali point of view consequently, the advantages which had in fact materialized during Britain's period of military rule were slight compared with the expectations which had been aroused. And appreciation of the progress achieved during this time was mitigated by bitterness at the failure of the Bevin proposals. Those who did not know all the issues involved in the negotiations concerning the disposal of the ex-Italian colonies, and some of those who did, were left to muse upon this further instance of the fickleness of British policies. And far from gaining a rational national basis for preparation for self-rule, the divisive effects of the nineteenth-century partition of Somaliland, particularly in respect of Ethiopia's portion, had now become more firmly entrenched than before. This inevitably strengthened the barriers opposing Somali nationalist endeavour and consolidated the colonial legacy of fragmentation which could only lead to frustration and friction in the future.

But despite this, the centuries' old cultural nationalism of the Somali had at last found a powerful modern political expression. Somali nationalism in fact had gained an impetus and momentum which was to carry it increasingly forward, notwithstanding this continued partition and the continuing force of internal clan rivalries and factionalism. This new political development, moreover, opened a new field for the exercise of traditional Somali political expertise. And certainly few emergent nations could boast a more vigorous and exacting political tradition than that of the democratic pastoral social system where, perforce, every man is a politician and must exercise all his political talents to the uttermost if he is to survive and prosper in this demanding and hostile environment.

CHAPTER VII

FROM TRUSTEESHIP TO
INDEPENDENCE: 1950–60

The introduction of representative government in Somalia

ITALY'S NEW POSITION in her former colony of Somalia was
carefully and closely defined in the United Nations Trusteeship
agreement under which she assumed responsibility for the territory. The Italian Trust Administration (A.F.I.S.) was required
to 'foster the development of free political institutions and to
promote the development of the inhabitants of the territory
towards independence'. To achieve this end Somalis were to be
given increasing responsibility in the political and administrative
control of their country under the benevolent tutorship of the
Trust Administration. The Agreement, which was approved by
the U.N. Assembly on 2 December, 1950, also contained as an
annex a declaration of constitutional principles guaranteeing
Somali rights and the full implementation of the Trust Administration's obligations. To make assurance doubly sure from the
Somali point of view, a special U.N. Advisory Council was created
to sit in Mogadishu to provide direct liaison with the Italian
Administration and its wards. This body, which consisted of a
small committee of representatives of U.N. member governments
and a small secretariat staff, was available to make recommendations and reports on the progress of development in all spheres and
to provide tangible evidence of United Nations responsibility and
concern. The effect of this U.N. presence was also further strengthened by the provision of regular visiting missions which, like
the Advisory Council, reported to the Trusteeship Council of
the United Nations.[1]

These measures which left Italy little room for manœuvre or
evasion, coupled with the restriction of the trusteeship period to

ten years, helped to allay Somali apprehensions. Nevertheless, the first few years of the new régime were marked by animosity and suspicion on both sides. With memories of the 1948 disturbances very much alive, and conscious that they were unlikely to receive a very cordial welcome, the returning Italian authorities judged it prudent to ensure that they were adequately protected against any violent expression of Somali resentment. To Somalis, however, the strong military forces which were dispatched to support the establishment of the new administration, gave the handover much of the character of a military occupation. Nor was the position much eased by the heavy-handed manner in which the Italians tended, initially at least, to reassert their authority. Some prominent S.Y.L. members who had achieved responsible positions in the civil service under the British were reduced in rank, dismissed, and in a few cases imprisoned. Similar measures were also taken against leading S.Y.L. civilians, particularly those judged to be dangerously anti-Italian; and a determined attempt was made to discredit the strength and popularity of the League. Arbitrary acts of this sort led to S.Y.L. demonstrations and, on a number of occasions, to riots which were strongly repressed by the authorities.

This unfortunate vendetta, however, did not involve all the rank and file of the S.Y.L. and did not prevent some members from unostentatiously co-operating with the Italians in the implementation of new progressive developments. Hence, although the first two years of the trusteeship were marked by a series of incidents between the League and the Administration which reduced the immediate effectiveness of measures designed to promote Somali advancement, this equivocal period nevertheless saw the groundwork for progress firmly established. Nowhere was this more striking than in the field of education. An ambitious and imaginative scheme for general education crystallized in a five-year development programme launched in 1952 with UNESCO collaboration. New state schools providing free education replaced the mission schools upon which the Italians had relied in the past; and by 1957 some 31,000 children and adults of both sexes were enrolled in primary schools, 246 in junior secondary schools, 336 in technical institutes, and a few hundred more in higher educational institutions. This represented a not-

able advance on the situation in 1950 when little more than two thousand students were receiving education. It also testified to the new and widespread public appetite amongst the old and young alike, especially in the towns, for Western education.

Serious attempts to provide fundamental education for adults amongst the less accessible nomadic section of the population were also made, though with less success.[2] Priority was also given to higher and vocational education. Here the Italian Administration showed initiative and courage in opening a School of Politics and Administration at Mogadishu in 1950 as a training centre for Somali officials and political leaders. This bracketing together of the two skills most needed in an emergent country was also reflected in later legislation which, in marked contrast to the British tradition, encouraged members of the civil service to stand as candidates for election to the legislature, secure in the knowledge that if they failed they could resume their administrative careers without handicap. By 1957 the School of Politics had provided a cadre of officials with basic training in administration, and the emphasis then switched to the concomitant need for technically qualified staff in other fields. The School was transformed into a Technical and Commercial Institute. Meanwhile, in 1954, a Higher Institute of Law and Economics, later to become Somalia's University College, was opened to provide a two-year Rome University diploma course.

These local measures were reinforced by generous bursary provisions for study overseas, mainly in Italy, although Egypt also made considerable numbers of scholarships available as part of her aid programme.[3] These developments did much to dissipate what remained of Somali scepticism over Italian intentions and this effect was greatly enhanced by the progressive opening of senior posts in all branches of the civil service to Somali officials. Here advancement proceeded with rapidity, to such a extent indeed that by 1956 all Districts and Provinces were in the direct charge of Somali administrative officers. Although it would be unrealistic to imagine that in all administrative procedures the new Somali officials were as competent as those they replaced and there were certainly shortcomings in such matters as record keeping and paper-work – in their day-to-day administration, particularly in the Districts, they showed a high standard of ability

While in education, the Italian Trust Administration built essentially upon the efforts of their immediate British predecessors, in economics the groundwork went directly back to the fascist period. Unfortunately, however, advancement here on a scale and at a pace equal to that achieved in other spheres proved much more difficult. With an annual subsidy from Italy of over £3 million between 1950 and 1955, much of public expenditure was necessarily devoted to reconstruction and repair and applied to improve roads, communications, and other public works concerned with education, government, and health. In 1954, however, a comprehensive scheme for developing Somalia's economic resources was launched in the form of a Seven Year Development Plan based upon studies made by the Trust Administration, the United States I.C.A. mission, and U.N. agencies.[4] This scheme provided for a total expenditure of some £4 million, over half of which was allocated to agricultural and livestock development. In cultivation the emphasis was on the extension and intensification of irrigation farming along the middle and lower Shebelle River, the construction of flood basins along the middle Juba, and of catchment basins in the dry-land farming regions between the rivers. Provision was also made for the clearance of additional land, for the construction of public storage silos for grain, the opening of experimental farms, and for the introduction of modern farm implements. A more radical innovation was the formation of an agricultural bank, the *Credito Somalo*, designed to provide farmers with loans and credit facilities for agricultural development. For the nomads, the Plan proposed an extensive well-drilling scheme and the construction of water catchment basins. Whereas in the past Italian agricultural development had been limited to the plantation areas farmed by settlers, now the whole emphasis was on the realization of the potentialities of the indigenous economy. Considerable allocations of funds were also made, however, to improve road communications which would be of some benefit to the banana and fruit export trade.

Obviously the full effect of these improvements would not be felt for many years after the termination of the trusteeship period; but the initial results were nevertheless encouraging. This was particularly so with the production of cereals and cotton. Although

irregular in succeeding years, cotton exports reached a peak figure as early as 1952; and, with a more steady rate of progress, cereal production by 1957 was sufficient to permit an export surplus. Over the same period almost £3 million were invested by Italian concerns in plantation agriculture and industry, the main Italian company, S.A.I.S., producing by 1956 sufficient cane sugar to meet Somalia's own needs and to provide a margin for export. The principal export asset, however, remained the banana industry which, since it had been an Italian state monopoly, had languished during the period of British military administration. This was revived after the Italian return on a similar basis under the title of *Azienda Monopolio Banane*. By 1955, although still hedged about with tariff restrictions and judged by some economists[5] to be operating uneconomically, banana exports had risen to over 50,000 tons annually – almost five times the figure achieved in 1937. This monopolistic trade now occupied a crucial position not only in relation to its direct trade return, but also since it was indirectly a principal source of Italian grants-in-aid to Somalia. The industry's control by the Italian state not only ensured a steady and uncompetitive market in Italy – which on the long term might retard its potential growth – but also provided in its profits from the sale of bananas at high and uncompetitive prices to Italian wholesalers a source of revenue applied to make grants to Somalia. This was an arrangement which, though possibly ultimately detrimental to the development of Somalia's banana export industry, satisfied for the time being many different interests.

With these developments Somalia was thus greatly expanding her production for both local and foreign markets. As a whole, however, the country remained desperately poor and continued to run at a serious deficit. While local revenue, derived as in the past principally from import and export dues with little help from direct taxation, rose from just over £1 million in 1950 to double that figure in 1956, expenditure, although decreasing from £7 million in the first year to £5 million five years later, continued to remain far in excess of receipts. By 1956 there was still a considerable and persistent adverse balance of payments, and the general economic picture was such as to lead the World Bank mission which visited the territory in 1957 to conclude that exceptional financial assistance might be required for as many as twenty years after independence. Although later fiscal improvements suggest that this assessment might be unduly pessimistic, the outlook clearly left much to be desired.

If by 1957 it was still too early to be certain of what could be achieved with the resources available in economic progress, in the field of politics there was little doubt as to the outcome. Unlike the position in many other evolving African territories, in Somalia political advancement proceeded in step with the replacement of expatriate by Somali officials in the civil service and police. There was thus a smooth and regular devolution of authority in both the administrative and political spheres at the same pace of advancement. This sensible matching of the two lines of progress towards full autonomy was greatly facilitated by the success of the new educational measures which, if they did not produce an immediate cadre of university graduates, at least ensured a wide spread of general education. In politics, the first important step was the creation of a national Territorial Council in 1950 with consultative functions for which the ground had already been prepared under the British Military Administration. This was not merely a decorative or nominal body, but an active forum to which governmental decrees and draft ordinances were passed for scrutiny and discussion by the Trust Administration. Between 1950 and 1955 little short of a hundred ordinances, covering a wide range of subjects, were thus considered by the Council. Hence, although this body which contained some thirty-five members representative of both traditional and modern interests (including the political parties) was in composition similar to the British Protectorate's Advisory Council, it was more truly an embryonic legislature than the latter organization. A further step in this direction was taken when, on the advice of the U.N. Advisory Council, legislative committees and offices were created to prepare the way for a fuller devolution of political authority.

At the same time, at a local level, governmental responsibility was progressively devolved through two types of local government body: District Councils in the rural areas, and Municipal Councils in the towns and main centres. These organs were a direct development of what had already been established under

the British Military Administration. Although elected membership in the rural councils was introduced in 1955, the District
Councils tended to be less effective than their urban counterparts
and remained essentially consultative bodies providing a useful
adjunct to the system of direct administration through District
Officers. The municipal councils which were not so directly
affected by the exigencies of the nomadic life developed very
successfully, their members showing a marked desire and aptitude
for increased responsibility. Thus by 1956, 48 of these councils
had been established with a fair degree of financial as well as
political autonomy This rapid progress was assisted by the
Administration's policy of attaching as secretaries to the councils
officials with a training in municipal administration. Initially
council members were nominated by the Administration, but in
1954 the first municipal elections were held and no less than sixteen parties presented candidates. Seventy-five per cent of the
male electorate voted, suffrage being then confined to men, and
the S.Y.L. won over half the available 281 seats.

In 1956 when Somalis were replacing Italians in all senior
administrative positions, these developments were crowned by
the transformation of the Territorial Council into a legislative
assembly composed of 70 seats, ten of which were reserved for
ethnic minorities: the Italian and Arabian communities being
allocated four seats each, and the Indian and Pakistani groups one
seat each. The new assembly was given full statutory powers in
domestic affairs, although the head of the Italian Trust Administration retained the right of absolute veto. Initially Italian coun-
sellors were to be attached to the Somali Ministers in the cabinet
appointed after the elections, and draft legislation had to be
approved by the Italian authorities before passing to the assembly.
Candidates for election were required to be literate in Arabic or
Italian, a qualification which indicates the spread of education
which had already been achieved by this time. As was to be expected, the new assembly was much more representative in composition than the old Territorial Council, and included a wider
coverage of modernist opinion.

Voting which was still confined to men, was conducted by
different procedures in the urban and rural constituencies. In the
municipalities, voters had to be registered on the municipal lists

and votes were cast by secret ballot. In the interior where the conditions of nomadic life made this procedure difficult and uncertain, voting took place through traditional clan and clan section assemblies. These meetings passed block lists of votes to the recorders, a procedure which lent itself to manipulation. It was therefore no surprise to find that the total recorded vote was far in excess of what might have been predicted from the estimated strength of the population, although the latter figures themselves were by no means definitive.

Whatever shortcomings may have marred the conduct of the elections in the rural areas, the exuberance with which the general population seized this first opportunity to express its political will was remarkable. Of the 60 seats available to the Somali electorate, 43 were won by the S.Y.L., 13 by the H.D.M.S., three by a small group called the Somali Democratic Party, and one by a frankly clan organization called the Marehan Union.[6] From fifteen opponents at the previous municipal elections, the League's rivals had now dwindled to five, largely as a result of amalgamations amongst the smallest and most narrowly based groups. With this impressive consolidation of their position, the party was called upon to form a government under 'Abdillahi 'Ise as Somalia's first Prime Minister. By this time, little trace remained of the earlier antagonism between the Italian Administration and the League; a good working basis of agreement had now been reached between the two sides, which was strengthened with the appointment in 1955 of the highly respected liberal Dr Enrico Anzilotti as Administrator. Henceforth, in so far as it was in a position to do so, the Italian Administration confined its participation in Somali politics to seeking to encourage those elements within the S.Y.L. which it considered most 'moderate' and favourable to a continuation of the Italian connexion.

At the 1956 elections the League was estimated to have a mixed national membership distributed amongst the main clan groups as follows: Darod, 50 per cent; Hawiye, 30 per cent; Digil-Mirifle, 10 per cent; and others, 10 per cent. When the British withdrew from Somalia the principal cleavages within its leadership (which the Italians had sought to exploit) had been amongst its Darod adherents. Now although it still did not command an absolute monopoly of Darod support, the party's following from this major group of clans was exceedingly strong. The Hawiye, however, were divided in their attitude towards the party. Division within the leadership between Darod and Hawiye members, had led to the formation prior to the 1956 elections of an organization originally calling itself the Hawiye Youth League which sought to detach Hawiye support. These differences within the S.Y.L., however, were resolved in time to present a united front at the elections (in which the Hawiye Youth League won no seat). But the extent of the party's difficulties in patching up this cleavage was evident in the composition of 'Abdillahi 'Ise's government. In addition to the Premiership itself, two of the remaining five ministries were assigned to politicians of the Hawiye clans, while the Darod gained two ministries, and the Dir one. This allocation of portfolios, which seemed to meet the needs of the moment, later caused the pendulum to swing in the opposite direction, thus favouring the formation of Darod break-away groups.

Certainly no other party could boast the same national following. But, as later events were to show, the more effectively the League widened its base, and the greater its electoral success, the more profound became its internal divisons. In the circumstances of Somali political realities, any party with strong national support could not but be essentially a consortium of rival clan interests. The League's weakest following was still amongst the southern Digil and Rahanweyn who remained strongly attached to their own particularistic party, the H.D.M.S. This party did not campaign on a national basis; yet by winning 13 seats in its own electoral areas of Upper and Lower Juba Provinces, it found itself the main block on the opposition benches in the Assembly. Relations between the H.D.M.S. and the League continued to be coloured by the traditional hostility between the two factions of the nation which the rival parties tended to represent, and by their earlier differences in their attitudes towards Italy. Thus the H.D.M.S. accused the S.Y.L. government of discriminating against its supporters in the public service: and some conception of the depth of feeling between the two sides can be gathered from the assassination, in obscure circumstances, of the prominent H.D.M.S. deputy Ustad 'Isman Muhammad Husseyn in 1956. Later, H.D.M.S. members in the Assembly succeeded in having their 'martyred' colleague commemorated by the naming of a street after him near the principal mosque in Mogadishu. But although in 1956, the H.D.M.S. was still a force to be reckoned with, its lack of national appeal gave it little prospect of victory in a political atmosphere increasingly charged with the nationalistic fervour of a people moving rapidly towards independence.[7]

The British Protectorate and the Haud

While in Somalia the limitation of the period of trusteeship to ten years imparted a strong sense of urgency, in British Somaliland, where no date had been set for independence, and where indeed the matter had scarcely been raised, progress proceeded at a much more leisurely pace. This coincided with the general view prevalent in British circles that development was likely to be all the more effective if conducted at a slow and steady pace. This gradualist approach was, it may be argued, well adapted to the particularly intractable economic and social circumstances of the Protectorate. But as events turned out, the last days of colonial rule in British Somaliland ended in a hectic scramble which might have been partly avoided had the pace been quickened earlier. And certainly it was unfortunate that there was not more official contact and co-operation between the British and Italian authorities in the two neighbouring territories prior to their independence and unification. This, it should be added, is not merely to be wise after the event. Already by 1956 and 1957 the probable course of later developments had become fairly clear, and opportunities which might have been taken for profitable collaboration were irretrievably lost.

In the period immediately after the return of British Somaliland to its former civil status in 1948 perhaps the most striking evidence of progress was in the field of education, although the spread of schooling was concentrated within a much smaller section of the population than was the case in Somalia. Building upon the successful experiments of the war years, educational opportunities were gradually extended. A trades-school was opened in 1952 at Hargeisa, and a vocational training centre in the cultivating centre of Borama in the west. A year later, the opening of the first government school for girls at Burao constituted a notable innovation which, despite some continued resistance to secular education in general and to girls' education in particular, was generally welcomed. Indeed, favourable interest in the school took the very tangible form of many pressing requests to the girls' parents for the marriage of their daughters, and extremely high marriage payments were offered. The same year saw the establishment of the Protectorate's first secondary school for boys, which was a considerable advance for it enabled students to take the General Certificate of Education examination in their own country without having to go overseas. Increasing public interest in and support for these new ventures led to the establishment in 1954 of a standing committee on education; and, in that year also, the territory's first Somali Education Officer was appointed. By this time in Somalia, the Deputy-Director of Education was an Italian trained Somali, whose qualifications and experience, however, were by no means superior to those of the single Somali education officer in the British Protectorate.

In other spheres there was less to report. The territory's exports of hides and skins increased, but no new product was found to strengthen the economy. Agricultural and veterinary services were expanded; and in this direction the most striking achievement was perhaps the excavation of a series of much-needed water-storage basins along the southern boundary of the Protectorate.[8] In 1953 a hydrological survey of seasonally flooded waddies which might permit irrigation cropping commenced near Burao. Geological surveys were also intensified in the search for exploitable minerals.

In the political field up to 1955 progress was restricted in the main to local government. A Local Authorities ordinance enacted in 1950 empowered the Governor to appoint selected Akils – the salaried headmen who provided a link between District Commissioners and their people – as Local Authorities. This invested these lineage representatives with certain limited judicial powers, and in theory, strengthened their traditional authority beyond that customarily enjoyed by lineage elders. Consequently, there was at first widespread public resistance to the new scheme; but by the mid-1950s, when it was clear that the position could be accepted without applying its statutory powers, the new arrangements had come to be generally accepted. In practice there was hardly any appreciable change in the pattern of authority, except in the titles which clan headmen now bore. Yet the modest salary of not more than £15 monthly which went with the title attracted many rival applicants, and the position of Local Authority soon came to be regarded as synonymous with group independence.[9] In the same period, with less ostensible opposition, town and district councils were opened. By 1954 elected representatives were serving on the Protectorate's two town councils at Berbera and Hargeisa, and both these bodies had acquired a measure of financial responsibility. At a national level, the only vehicle for the expression of public opinion remained the Advisory Council. This usually met twice yearly to discuss a widening range of issues, including the vexed question of the abolition, or curtailment, of collective responsibility for blood-compensation. This problem which goes to the very roots of the Somali clan system was thrown into relief by the bitter clan fighting between the Dulbahante and Habar Tol Ja'lo in the years 1951–57, and was of increasing concern to all nationalistically minded Somali.

In the years immediately following the return of the Italians to Somalia, party political activity in the Protectorate declined temporarily. The S.N.L. and S.Y.L. continued their regular weekly meetings at branches in different parts of the territory but, with no burning cause to command attention, public interest flagged. At the end of 1954, however, an event occurred which changed the whole course of political life and led eventually to the Protectorate's advancement to full independence. This precipitant was the final liquidation of British administration in the Haud and Reserved Areas and the complete surrender of these vital grazing lands to Ethiopian control. In the period since the resumption of civil administration in the Protectorate, British control in the Haud had gradually been reduced until, by 1954, only two British Civil Affairs Officers remained there. Without prior notice or consultation with her Somali subjects, on 29 November Britain signed a new agreement with Ethiopia which provided for the complete withdrawal of British authority and replaced the remaining officials by a British Liaison staff with headquarters at Jigjiga. The duties of the British Liaison Officer (Mr J. G. S. Drysdale) and his assistants were to facilitate the exercise by

British-protected Somalis of their rights to graze and water their livestock in the Haud, rights which were enshrined in the original Anglo-Ethiopian treaty of 1897 and reiterated in the new Agreement.

The gradual withdrawal of British authority had attracted little attention or criticism. But when the terms of the new Agreement and its implications became public knowledge there was an immediate and widespread outcry. Massive demonstrations occurred throughout the Protectorate to express the deep sense of Somali outrage, and hastily organized protest delegations were dispatched to London and New York, where they were received with gratifying publicity and sympathy, but achieved little satisfaction. With the support of other prominent national leaders (notably Mr Adan Ahmad), Michael Mariano, who had earlier played an important rôle in the hearings before the Four-Power Commission in Somalia, succeeded in forming a national convention called the National United Front. This body which drew support from all sections of organized public opinion, including initially the S.Y.L. and S.N.L., launched a vigorous campaign with the twin objectives of recovering the Haud and obtaining independence for the Protectorate within the British Commonwealth.

These activities were regarded with every sympathy by the local British administrative officials many of whom deeply regretted the transfer of the Haud to Ethiopia and who soon found the terms of the new Agreement extremely difficult to apply. With the Ethiopian authorities seeking to claim sovereignty over those British-protected clansmen who exercised their rights to pasture their herds in the Haud, the work of the British Liaison Office at Jigjiga became impossibly complicated. The Ethiopians, for their part, found the continued British presence intolerable and only the utmost tact and patience prevented the situation degenerating into bitter open conflict. As it was, frequent incidents in the region and repeated representations by both sides, which found no satisfactory conclusion in a series of joint Anglo-Ethiopian conferences, reinforced the N.U.F.'s campaign for the return of the Haud to British Administration. The surrender of the territory was based, of course, upon the current British interpretation of the vexed treaty of 1897, an interpretation which, although at variance with Britain's original desire to avoid recognizing Ethiopian sovereignty in the Haud, had been reinforced by the 1942 and 1944 Agreements during the period of military occupation. Defending his government's decision (which reflected the Foreign Office's continued support for Ethiopia) in the House of Commons in 1955, the Colonial Secretary explained that he regretted the original 1897 treaty but that it was 'impossible to undo it'. However, as difficulties with the Ethiopian authorities multiplied and the strength of Somali feeling became fully apparent, the British government did make an abortive attempt to adjust the situation. In April 1956, the Joint-Parliamentary Under-Secretary for Foreign Affairs was sent on a fruitless mission to Addis Ababa to intercede personally with the Emperor and to offer to buy back the disputed territory. As in the past, the Ethiopian government stuck to its guns and no progress was made. Similarly, the N.U.F. failed in its attempts, extremely embarrassing to Britain, to have the issue debated at the U.N. Assembly and brought for judgement to the International Court at The Hague.

The new nationalist fervour which had been aroused, however, was not to be quenched and received further impetus from the Ethiopian Emperor's speech on 25 August at Qabradare in the Ogaden when he claimed that the Somali people were part of the 'Great Ethiopian family' and asserted that, inevitably, the future advancement of Somalis lay with Ethiopia.[10] There was consequently a renewed upsurge of political activity, and the former mood of quiescent acceptance of British Administration began to give place to increasingly urgent demands for fuller autonomy. In response to this pressure the British Government announced in 1956 that the pace of advancement would be accelerated and representative government gradually introduced. Britain, it was also indicated, would not oppose the eventual union of the Protectorate with Somalia if this was desired. Events now snowballed, gradually at first, but with increasing rapidity as the date of Somalia's independence drew near. New schools were opened; at rates of pay equal to those of their expatriate European equivalents, Somali officials were more rapidly promoted to senior positions in the police and administration, and in 1957, the Protectorate's first legislative council was established with six unofficial members nominated by the Governor from a list of twenty-four candidates proposed after a series of fiercely debated political meetings in Hargeisa. These candidates represented not the political parties, but the main clan groups in the country, as was to be expected in the light of the continuing vitality of clan ties and the failure of the parties at the time to represent the majority of clan interests.[11] Meanwhile, having failed in its primary aim of recovering the Haud, the N.U.F. had gradually lost support, the S.Y.L. and S.N.L. had drifted away, and what had originally been a national convention was rapidly becoming a political party in its own right.

Although the Haud campaign had not succeeded, the Protectorate had at last taken its first decisive step towards independence, and the political parties began actively to consider the possibilities of eventual union with Somalia. More immediately, requests for elected Somali representation were made as soon as the legislative council began its sessions in 1957; and following the report of a commission of inquiry (two of whose five members were Somali),[12] the legislature was reconstituted to provide for this early in 1959. The new Council contained twelve elected members, two nominated unofficials, and fifteen official members with the Governor, Sir Theodore Pike, as President. Elections were held in March, by secret ballot in a small number of urban constituencies and by acclamation in the rural constituencies: suffrage was restricted to men.

Since their request for an immediate unofficial majority had not been accepted, the S.N.L., at this time representing the most forward nationalist position in the Protectorate, officially boycotted the elections leaving the field clear for the S.Y.L. and N.U.F. In the event, however, no S.Y.L. candidate was returned; and of the twelve elected members of the legislative council seven supported the N.U.F., four had no definite party allegiance, and one was a member of the S.N.L. All the parties shared the same aims of independence and unification with Somalia, and differed only in their attitudes towards the speed with which these goals should be accomplished. With the exception of the Habar Tol Ja'lo clan who provided the main leadership and much of the rank and file support of the N.U.F., the majority of the other Isaq clans followed the S.N.L. which now enjoyed the strongest membership. The Darod clans in the east, and the Dir clans in the west, jointly numerically weaker than the Isaq, had still no binding party allegiance, although the S.Y.L. tended to find its greatest support, such as it was, amongst these groups. With their head-quarters at Mogadishu and their natural preoccupation with events in Somalia, the League had still not succeeded in creating a firm local basis of interest in the Protectorate. The Protectorate branches of the party remained the poor relations of the movement, and as such failed to make any wide impact.

In response to the S.Y.L. boycott and increasing public pressure for fuller Somali representation, a new constitution meeting these demands and providing ministerial responsibility was introduced at the beginning of 1960. In the elections for this new legislative council held in February, the S.N.L. gained twenty of the available thirty-three seats; the N.U.F. in alliance with the S.Y.L. one; and the United Somali Party, a new organization which associated itself with the S.N.L. and represented the Darod and Dir clans, twelve. This result marked the eclipse of the N.U.F. which had previously been regarded generally by the Administration as the future government party. Nevertheless, although the S.N.L. in alliance with the U.S.P. now held thirty-two seats as opposed to the single seat shared between the N.U.F. and S.Y.L., the number of votes which they obtained was only a little more than twice that of their opponents. But although those who supported the N.U.F. and S.Y.L. might justly claim that their voting strength was not matched by the allocation of seats, there was no doubt that the S.N.L. and U.S.P. jointly represented the majority of the Protectorate's population. Two members of each party were accordingly appointed as Ministers, Muhammad Haji Ibrahim Igal, leader of the S.N.L., assuming the title of Leader of Government Business in the legislature.

This sudden constitutional step forward was accompanied by a corresponding acceleration in the pace of Somali advancement generally. An examination of the whole question of the replacement of expatriate by Somali officials in the government service had been initiated in August 1958.[13] Some conception of the rapidity with which this process had now proceeded may be gathered from the fact that, while in 1959 there were only two Somali District Commissioners as well as a number of District Officers and Assistant Superintendents of Police, by 1960 all six

Districts were in the direct charge of Somali officials and the Assistant Commissioner of Police was a Somali. Over 100 Somali students were now studying overseas, some of them at British Universities, and the Protectorate's second secondary school had been established.

British Somaliland had come a long way towards realizing Somali nationalist aims, despite the tardy beginnings of the early 1950s, and with official British approval for eventual union with Somalia already indicated in 1957 and reiterated more strongly in 1959, the territory seemed now set fair on a course of a few years' final preparation for independence. Few observers, certainly, anticipated that the Protectorate was to be thrust into independence in a matter of months, thus in the event forestalling Somalia. This view which envisaged a calm and gradual final phase of British tutelage, however, seriously underestimated the great surge of nationalist interest generated by Somalia's forthcoming independence. Already in 1959, delegates from all the parties and political groups in the Protectorate had participated in the formation at Mogadishu of the National Pan-Somali Movement. In its charter this organization embraced the twin aims of campaigning by peaceful means for the independence and unification of all the Somali territories, and of creating firm ties with other African and Asian states. With these political manoeuvres towards unification gathering increasing momentum it was evident, in the wider context of Somali affairs, that the Protectorate's independence could not long be delayed.

The final phase in Somalia

The government formed in Somalia by 'Abdillahi 'Ise in 1956 was confronted by all the problems of a country moving rapidly towards autonomy. Interest naturally centred on those internal issues of vital concern to the future stability and prosperity of the state. External affairs being outside his government's purview, the only gesture towards the fulfilment of the abiding goal of Pan-Somali unity which the Prime Minister permitted himself was the announcement, given first place in his programme, that every effort would be made to settle the disputed frontier with Ethiopia – a subject on which more will be said presently. Of more immediate moment was the stabilization of the country's precarious economy, the attraction of foreign capital and aid, and the raising of increased revenue by wider taxation. The perennial and vexed question of deciding upon an official language – Somali being still in the main unwritten – also received attention, but, as will be seen later, remained unresolved. In social affairs the government pledgd itself to examine ways of extending voting rights to women, and to promote the further Somalization of all branches of government and administration, including the judicial system. In this latter field satisfactory progress was in the main achieved, and a number of other progressive measures were successfully launched.

The statutory authority of chiefs, in practice greater amongst the southern cultivators than the northern nomads, was reduced; and the procedure of applying collective punishments in the control of inter-clan feuds was modified in the direction of placing a stronger burden of responsibility upon the individual criminal. This move was designed to weaken the continuing vitality of collective clan solidarity. At the same time, in an effort to separate secular from religious authority, the considerable criminal powers wielded by Muslim magistrates (Kadis) under the Italian system were reduced in order to restrict their jurisdiction more unambiguously to matters of personal status. As far as the Somalization of the judiciary was concerned, pending the training of the necessary Somali staff, Somali District Commissioners were temporarily granted judicial powers to be exercised subject to the overriding authority of higher courts presided over by Italian judges.

On a different plane, in a climate of opinion increasingly hostile to the disruptive effects of clan particularism, legislation was passed making it illegal for political parties to bear tribal names. This measure, was, no doubt, partly directed against the opposition Digil-Mirifle party which adroitly changed its title to that of *Hizbia Dastur Mustaqil Somali* (Somali Independent Constitutional Party) thus taking advantage of the plurality of languages in Somalia to retain its original initials. Legislation was also enacted forbidding the use of the traditional derogatory names applied to the *sab* specialist occupational groups who, in any case, were now rapidly acquiring a considerable degree of emancipation from their former status as bondsmen. As well as such issues as these, the government was also soon preoccupied with the important question of preparing a constitution for the independent state. To this end a decree passed in September 1957 set up two committees to study the problem, one political, and the other which included Italian advisers, technical. The intention was to draw upon the experience of other African states which had already achieved independence.[14]

In the light of the prevailing Pan-Somali aim shared by all nationalists, the constitution had to provide for the possibility of the eventual union of Somalia with other Somali territories. and provisions fulfilling this requirement were incorporated in the final proposals. Here the S.Y.L. government and the H.D.M.S. opposition held very different views. The League favoured, indeed insisted upon, a unitary state with a high degree of centralized authority. In the light of its own particularistic interests, the H.D.M.S. on the contrary sought a federal relationship which would permit a high degree of regional autonomy. Already the opposition had advocated the creation in its own southern area of a separate Digil-Mirifle state, and in conflict with the government's firm repudiation of them had expressed sympathy towards the Ethiopian Emperor's overtures contained in his speech at Qabradare.[15] Here as in other matters such as the discrimination against Digil and Rahanweyn clansmen alleged to exist in the public service, the H.D.M.S. position proceeded directly from its own particularistic interests and general opposition to the S.Y.L. But with only thirteen members in the Assembly its voice was naturally weak.

The real threat to the League's authority came from within its own ranks, both through the independent-mindedness of its deputies in the Assembly, and through the wider cleavage between Darod and Hawiye supporters. The issue which best served as a vehicle for the expression of these internal differences was the imputed moderation of 'Abdillahi 'Ise's government's policies. Critics of the government accused it of being too ready to cooperate with Italy, of not showing sufficient Somali independence, and above all of doing nothing tangible to advance Pan-Somalism. This discontent, concerned essentially with rivalries within the League, came to a head on the appointment in July 1957 of Haji Muhammad Husseyn – then absent in Cairo – as President of the party. On his return to Somalia, Haji Muhammad assumed leadership of that faction within the League which took as its slogan a more militant advocacy of Pan-Somali unity. This group within the party now openly attacked the government, and the President of the Assembly, Adan 'Abdulle 'Isman, who was dubbed 'Shamun' after the pro-Western Lebanese leader. Strong demands were made for a more open pro-Arab and pro-Egyptian stand. This line of attack seemed favoured at the time by the public sympathy provoked by the recent assassination of the Egyptian member of the U.N. Advisory Council at Mogadishu. Earlier, some Somalis had volunteered for service with Egypt during the Suez crisis; but since then there had been Somali protests at alleged Egyptian interference in Somalia's internal affairs. Now, however, opinion seemed again generally favourable to a more definite pro-Egyptian alignment and this was strongly advocated by Haji Muhammad and his associates. In keeping with this position, they also urged the adoption of the Arabic script as the most appropriate national medium for written Somali, a question on which with its earlier enthusiasm for 'Osmaniya, and also on the part of some members for a Roman orthography, the League was still profoundly divided.[16]

The League's new President was a severe embarrassment to the government and its supporters, and his influence was such that an open split in the party seemed imminent. This, however, was narrowly averted, for in April 1958 those behind the Prime Minister and the President of the Assembly achieved the expulsion from the party of their troublesome adversary after a series of frantic meetings. Much of the credit for this successful manœuvre, which involved maintaining the support of both the Darod and Hawiye wings of the League, appears to lie with Adan 'Abdulle, later to become Somalia's first President. Faced with this defeat, Haji Muhammad Husseyn, who enjoyed a formidable reputation as an orator and who had in the past played an important part in the development of Somali nationalism, struck out on his own to form a new militant party called the Greater Somali League. To this new organization, known locally as 'Great', Haji Muhammad sought to attract support from the dissident flanks of the League and to exploit what remained of the Darod-Hawiye breach, after Adan 'Abdulle's intervention. The October 1958 municipal elections – in which for the first time women participated equally with men – provided an opportunity for assessing the extent of the new movement's appeal. Of 663 seats the S.Y.L. won 416; the H.D.M.S. 175; while Great came in third place winning only 36 seats but nevertheless beating the only other national party which contested the elections, the Liberal Party, which gained 27 seats.

Clearly the G.S.L. did not as yet constitute a serious threat to the League with its massive national following. But, taking into account its very recent formation, it could by no means be dismissed altogether, particularly in view of the forthcoming elections for the national assembly due the following spring. The S.Y.L. consequently intensified its efforts and sought particularly to gain a fresh access of support amongst the Digil and Rahanweyn who had so impressively demonstrated their attachment to their own party in the municipal elections. To appreciate the League's prospects in this direction it is necessary to recall that, although these tribes possess a strong sense of separate identity, in their ethnic composition they are a mixture of many different clan elements, and include large numbers of people of Darod and Hawiye origin. Whether this was the intention or not, the implications of this fact acquired new significance from legislation promulgated in 1959 to abolish the traditional status of client-tenant amongst the Rahanweyn and Digil tribes. For the effect of this was to encourage the more recent client elements – mainly of northern Darod and Hawiye origin – living amongst the Rahanweyn to assert their independence and thus weaken the solidarity of the Digil and Rahanweyn as a whole. At the same time, many Rahanweyn politicians who aspired to high office were becoming convinced that their best chance of success lay with the League rather than the *Hizbia*. Finally, since the H.D.M.S. had secured control of most of the municipalities in the Digil and Rahanweyn area, the need to present a united front against the S.Y.L. in the Assembly may have appeared less urgent. It was certainly an arguable proposition that local Rahanweyn interests might best be safeguarded from within the all-powerful League. Although it is impossible to determine the relative importance of these different factors, it seems beyond doubt that their general effect was to facilitate the new S.Y.L. drive for Digil and Rahanweyn votes.

The Greater Somalia League, in its turn, played into the hands of the government by indulging in acts of violence which led to its partial suppression and greatly reduced the success of its electoral campaign. Both the G.S.L. and the H.D.M.S. lodged strong protests against the conditions under which the electoral campaign took place and officially boycotted the elections.[17] Further confusion was caused by the action of the Darod Minister of the Interior who, allegedly in response to Egyptian representations, revoked a cabinet order closing the headquarters of the G.S.L. A cabinet crisis followed in which the Minister offered his resignation and this, apparently to his surprise, was accepted, his portfolio being assumed by the Prime Minister. The remaining Darod Minister, as a gesture of clan solidarity, then also tendered his resignation. This, however, was not accepted, and he – to the confusion of those who interpret Somali national politics purely in terms of clanship – remained with the government. These events followed immediately after the elections and indicate that 'Abdillahi 'Ise's government felt itself to be in an exceedingly strong position. And not without cause: of the 90 seats in the newly expanded Assembly only 29 were contested and of these the League won 22. Of the remaining seven seats, two went to the Liberal Party, and five to a break-away fragment of the H.D.M.S. which had ignored the official party boycott. Many former H.D.M.S. deputies had in fact changed sides and entered the new Assembly on the S.Y.L. ticket.

Despite this sweeping victory, or perhaps rather because of it, there were still wide cleavages within the ranks of the League. And 'Abdillahi 'Ise, chosen again as Prime Minister by the party conference in May, was faced with a formidable problem in rewarding all those very disparate elements which had contributed to his party's success. The new and enlarged government, formed in June after protracted negotiation, consisted of fifteen Ministers and Under-Secretaries evenly distributed amongst the Darod, Hawiye and Digil and Rahanweyn groups of clans. The two most prominent figures in the last category were Muhammad 'Abdi Nur, Minister of Industry, and 'Abdi Nur Muhammad Husseyn, Minister of General Affairs and former Vice-President of the H.D.M.S. The generous allocation of portfolios demonstrates better than anything else the success of the S.Y.L. campaign amongst the Digil and Rahanweyn.

In terms of the prevailing sectional interests within the country the new government could hardly be attacked for being unrepresentative. But it was precisely for so openly acknowledging the force of these political realities that it was soon under fire from the modernist wing of the important Majerteyn Darod faction in the party. Here the leading critics were Dr 'Abd ar-Rashid 'Ali Shirmarke who had recently completed a Rome University degree in political science and who had been Secretary of the League in its formative period in 1949, and 'Abd ar-Razaq Haji Husseyn who had been S.Y.L. President in 1956. The caucus led by these men suffered for a short time the fate which had earlier befallen Great's leader Haji Muhammad Husseyn. But the support which they were able to muster was such that they were soon re-admitted to the party, and the force of their views was partially acknowledged in a cabinet re-shuffle early in 1960. Further developments in what, put in its simplest terms, was partly a matter of conflicting policies, partly a struggle for power between individuals, and at the same time also a question of competing clan interests, had to await the sweeping government changes which took place after Somalia's independence and union with the British Protectorate.

Independence and unification

In February 1959, when announcing the new constitution to be introduced in the Protectorate in the following year, the British Colonial Secretary (Mr Alan Lennox-Boyd) had stated that his government was prepared to facilitate negotiations for the union of the Protectorate with Somalia after each territory had become independent. In July of the same year, 'Abdillahi 'Ise in explaining his government's programme to the Somalia Assembly had given first place to the unfication of the Somali territories. 'The Somali,' he told the Assembly 'form a single race, practise the same religion and speak a single language. They inhabit a vast territory which, in its turn, constitutes a well-defined geographic unit. All must know that the government of Somalia will strive its uttermost, with the legal and peaceful means which are its democratic prerogative to attain this end: the union of Somalis, until all Somalis form a single Greater Somalia.' In the same month, the informal discussions which had already been proceeding from time to time between political leaders in Somalia and the Protectorate received direction and stimulus with the formation of the National Pan-Somali Movement at Mogadishu when delegates of all the Somali territories attended and pledged to strive for the common goal. In December of the same year, the U.N. General Assembly adopted a resolution determining that Somalia's trusteeship should terminate on 1 July, 1960, several months before the end of the stipulated period. This announcement had immediate repercussions in British Somaliland.

Already, following the February elections in the Protectorate, which introduced ministerial government, the pressure for independence and union with Somalia had greatly increased. There, were however, differences of opinion within the S.N.L.– U.S.P. coalition government as to the timing of these events. One view, held amongst others by the Leader of Government Business, was that union should not be precipitate, but that time should be allowed for the Protectorate to narrow the gap in development and progress with Somalia. The very extensive differences in almost all aspects of government between the two territories would also clearly require many rearrangements and adjustments before union could be fully consummated. It fell to Michael Mariano as the sole opposition member in the legislative council to press the opposite view, which was also shared by some members of the government, and particularly by leaders of the U.S.P. This assessment considered that if union was to take place it was better that it should take place as soon as possible, differences in the administrative traditions of the two territories being left to sort themselves out afterwards.

Whatever the respective merits of these two schools of thought, and each clearly had much to commend it, the strength of public nationalist feeling was now such that the latter view must prevail. Consequently previous ideas about some form of Commonwealth connexion were dropped, and on 6 April, 1960, the legislative council, with the unanimous support of all its elected members, passed a resolution calling for immediate independence and union with Somalia. The motion requested that 'bold and definite action be taken, and that the date of independence and unification with Somalia must be 1 July, 1960, the date when Somalia will attain its full freedom'. Five days later, the British Prime Minister announced in the House of Commons that his government was sympathetic to the Somali request and that the Colonial Secretary (now Mr Iain Macleod) would hold a constitutional conference to discuss independence early in May. Faced with this decision, the Protectorate Administration, which had hoped to gain time for further development and preparation, and which had consequently encountered bitter hostility, was left to make the necessary precipitate arrangements.

With this behind them, delegates from the Protectorate conferred with government leaders in Mogadishu in the middle of April. By this time the preparation of Somalia's constitution for independence had been completed, and the Protectorate delegates agreed to its general terms that the Republic which they would join should be a unitary state, with an elected President as Head of State, and be governed by a Prime Minister and Council of Ministers responsible to a single legislative assembly. In short, there was to be one flag, one president, one parliament, and one government; and until they could be fully integrated the former administrative, judicial, and economic systems of the two territories would continue to function separately.

This decided, the Protectorate leaders assembled in London on 2 May for the conference which was to sever their colonial connexion. For once British and Somali interests seemed to coincide. The British government was now anxious to relinquish responsibility for what in relation to its size and significance had undoubtedly been one of Britain's least rewarding possessions. All Britain sought for herself, apart from measures to protect the pension and compensation rights of British personnel, was the continuation of the lease for the BBC Middle Eastern Service relay station at Berbera. This caused no difficulty, and the conference, which was conducted in a most cordial atmosphere, was told on 4 May by the Colonial Secretary that his government had decided to arrange for the Protectorate to become independent by 1 July, 1960.[18] Only one proviso, of a nominal rather than substantive nature, was attached. This was that while the British government did not consider it necessary to have a written agreement abrogating the 1884 and 1886 Anglo-Somali treaties, it desired that clan headmen and traditional leaders should publicly demonstrate their acceptance of the decision to grant independence.

This was readily agreed to by the Somali delegation, and provision was made for a meeting on 24 May of the Council of Elders.[19] What is of particular interest here is that the British government should have felt it appropriate and necessary to make this stipulation: earlier British governments had shown little scruple in acting unilaterally against the intention and content of these same treaties.

The constitutional conference was followed by a hectic scramble in the Protectorate to carry out its decisions, and in the event British Somaliland became fully independent on 26 June, 1960. Five days later, on 1 July, Somalia followed suit, and having previously concluded separate agreements with the British and Italian governments, the two territories united on the basis to which their leaders had agreed. The two legislatures met in joint session at Mogadishu and formally amalgamated to form the National Assembly of the Republic, electing Adan 'Abdulle 'Isman (former President of the Somalia Assembly) as provisional President of the Republic. The Republic's constitution was to be ratified by a national referendum to be held a year later: the former British Somaliland was to be known as the Northern Regions, and the former Somalia, the Southern Regions. Six days later, on 7 July, Jama' 'Abdillahi Qalib, a leading member of the northern S.N.L., was elected by the Assembly as its new President in place of Adan 'Abdulle.

This left the more difficult question of the composition and leadership of the new government to be resolved. After a series of delicate manœuvres lasting two weeks, this was successfully accomplished, and on 22 July Dr 'Abd ar-Rashid 'Ali Shirmarke, who had emerged as the leader with the most acceptable qualifications, announced the membership of his government. Of fourteen ministerial positions, four were allocated to the northern S.N.L. and U.S.P. Amongst these, 'Abdi Hassan Boni of the U.S.P. assumed the important position of Deputy Premier; Muhammad Haji Ibrahim Igal, the northern premier, accepted the portfolio for Defence, and 'Ali Gerad Jama' of the U.S.P., who had been one of those most strongly in favour of immediate unification, became Minister of Education. Of the southern S.Y.L., 'Abd ar-Razaq Haji Husseyn, the Prime Minister's close associate, was given the Ministry of the Interior, while 'Abdillahi 'Ise who had stepped aside in favour of Dr 'Abd ar-Rashid assumed responsibility for Foreign Affairs. Thus, three weeks after Somalia's proclamation of independence, the new Somali Republic was provided with a government which represented a reasonable balance of northern and southern interests, closely paralleling the ratio of northern (33) and southern (90) seats in the National Assembly. And after the enthusiastic celebrations which marked independence and unification had subsided, in an atmosphere still heavily charged with nationalist jubilation, the new government settled down to deal with the many problems posed by the new state's dual colonial heritage and its pressing need for financial assistance.

Although the United Nations 'experiment' in Somalia, as it has often been called, had certainly succeeded in providing the new state with an effective administrative and political framework, neither the southern nor the northern regions were yet economically viable. In recognition of their outstanding economic requirements both former colonial powers had agreed to continue to supply aid and assistance. Britain had promised £1½ million for the first year after independence, and thereafter an annually negotiable amount. This financial aid was accompanied by a six months' programme of technical assistance such that Britain would for six months continue to pay the salaries of those former colonial officials who elected, at the request of the Somali government, to stay on after independence. Italy promised a more substantial annual grant of about £3 million, paid partly in the form of salaries to a team of Italian 'experts' serving with the Somali government. The commercial link between the two countries, which brought the southern regions into the European Common Market, was to be continued through the banana monopoly and the heavy dependence of Somalia upon Italy for imported goods. With this backing, and a growing range of aid and loans from other countries, notably America, Egypt, and the Communist bloc, as well as generous help through the various U.N. agencies, the newly installed Somali Republic was in a position to face the future with better economic prospects than had ever been envisaged in the past.

CHAPTER VIII

THE PROBLEMS OF INDEPENDENCE

The balance of particularistic interests in the new state

HOWEVER PRECIPITATE and incomplete it may have appeared at the time, the union of the former British Somaliland and Somalia had at once a profound effect on Somali politics. Since the focus of all political interests was now ultimately a single national legislature, the marriage of the two territories entailed significant, and in some cases quite drastic changes in the political status of the various clans and lineages within the state. To appreciate the full import of this immediate consequence of union it is necessary to realize that, despite the patriotic fervour which acclaimed the formation of the Republic, the most all-pervasive element in politics remained the loyalty of the individual to his kin and clan. There was not, of course, a political party to represent the interests of each clan; the trend which had once existed in this direction had long since passed and the presence of such powerful national consortiums as the S.Y.L. made it impossible for narrowly based clan parties to achieve any effective position in national politics. Nor was clan particularism by any means the only political tie of significance. With the increasing spread of western education, the growth of modern towns, and the gradual but quite unmistakable formation of new social classes, clan loyalties now fell into place as one component in a complex of diverse political attachments. Yet within this cluster of allegiances, for the majority of the population those bonds based on clanship – now extended much more widely than in traditional Somali politics – remained the most pervasive, the most commanding, and above all the most insidious. No other single line of communication and common interest connected so directly and incontravertibly the pastoral nomad in the interior with his kinsmen in the civil service, in the

National Assembly, or in the cabinet itself. No other bond of mutual interest had so many far-reaching ramifications in all aspects of private and public life.[1]

Nationalists, party politicians, and traditional religious leaders alike, had for long inveighed against those aspects of kinship which perpetuated wasteful sectional rivalries, which weakened and sometimes vitiated necessary collaboration, and which led to the preferment of individuals and of policies irrespective of their intrinsic merits. While acknowledging the associated values of generosity and assistance, and the highly democratic traditional political process where policy-making is not the monopoly of a small privileged class but the natural right of every adult man, the other divisive aspects of their political heritage were fiercely condemned. This 'problem of tribalism' as it came to be known had already been the subject of much public controversy and debate. Prior to independence and union, both the Protectorate and Somalia legislatures had frequently discussed the question and, over-optimistically in the light of the realities of the situation, had sought to find a means of extirpating what nationalist leaders now regarded as the supreme impediment to effective national unity.[2]

Here of course Somali nationalists were at one with nationalist leaders in every other territory in Africa: and the divisive influence of Somali 'tribalism' was felt as more, rather than less frustrating by the fact of its persistence within an already achieved cultural unity. Nationalist leaders saw only too clearly how clan differences and jealousies had in the past facilitated the partition of their people by foreign powers. Now these same factors, with little diminished vitality, impeded not only the full realization of the Pan-Somali goal, but also seemed to imperil the stability of the Republic itself. Here Somali fears may seem exaggerated; for sectional interests and differences of one kind or another exist in all countries. Yet it has to be borne in mind that what is specific to the Somali case is the strength of these particularistic divisions, their universal appeal, their pervasiveness, and their organization along a single principle of grouping. And, despite the efforts of some nationalists to deny their existence, there could be no doubt of their continuing importance in the political life of the new state. The emotion which the whole issue of clanship engendered was itself evidence of the compelling force which clan ties still exerted.

However unwillingly, all politicians and parties had, perforce, to utilize these bonds of kinship in attaining their political aims.

Perhaps the best illustration of this necessary ambivalence in nationalist attitudes is provided by an ingenious sophistry which had grown up in Somalia prior to independence and which was now gaining wider currency. In the past, and still largely in rural areas, a person's general placement in society and clan allegiance was elicited by asking what clan he belonged to and what section within it, thus tracing his range of genealogical and political allegiance until a point was reached significant to the inquirer. Now, however, since it had become the accepted etiquette amongst the élite to refuse to reveal clan identity and to profess no more definite allegiance than that of 'Somali', people began increasingly to refer to their present loyalties as though they had only historical significance. It thus became acceptable to discuss clan allegiance, and even to inquire into the clan particulars of a stranger, in terms of his 'ex-tribe'. Indeed, the word 'ex' was adopted into Somali, and now provided a perfectly acceptable means of establishing those details of clan affiliation which are in a way similar to, but so much more important than what is conveyed by a Londoner's 'address'. In the predominantly nomadic social system of the Somali no other means existed, nor would it seem easy to find one, to so unequivocally identify the individual.

It is in this situation of continuing, if reluctantly acknowledged, particularistic divisions that the true political significance of the union of the Protectorate clans with those in Somalia is revealed. Prior to this, politics in the Northern Regions had been dominated by the numerically predominant Isaq supporting the S.N.L., with the local Dir and Darod clans combining in opposition as the U.S.P. Union with Somalia, however, not only greatly reduced the political status of the Isaq, but also made it possible for the U.S.P. Darod to acquire new influence through joining the all-powerful S.Y.L. For the Dir wing of the U.S.P., traditional associations suggested the possibilities of alliance with the Hawiye, either within or outside the League: or alternatively, of combination with the Isaq.

These were by no means the only potential regroupings which presented themselves as new and advantageous lines of political collaboration. On a basis of common interest other than clanship, as long as the S.Y.L. represented a moderate position on the question of Greater Somalia, those parties such as the S.N.L., U.S.P., and G.S.L. which shared a more militant policy and which also represented a strongly pro-Arab nationalist position might be expected to join together against the League. Again, the possibility of sharp regional cleavages between north and south could not be ruled out. For despite the underlying cultural unity of the Republic as a whole and the all-pervasive character of clan ties, the long experience of two distinct colonial traditions had left quite different imprints in north and south, to a greater extent indeed than was immediately apparent.

British exclusiveness and empiricism, the accent on quality rather than quantity in educational and social advancement, attachment to British conceptions of justice and ideals of administrative conduct, and the strict separation of politics from administration, all contrasted in northern eyes with the apparently less rigorous standards of political and public service morality in the south and with the involute Italian bureaucratic tradition. Nor was this all. The presence in the past of a sizeable settler European community in the south, coupled with a wider degree of economic development and education and a tradition of a more pervasive system of rule, reinforced by traditional cultural distinctions between the two regions, had produced subtle but none the less significant differences in their social climates. As a result, on the whole, the traditional attitudes of pastoral Somali society were more strongly entrenched in the north, while the south, by contrast, appeared in many respects more modernist in outlook. To northerners these distinctions provided a set of standards well adapted to express their traditional pride and aloofness.

These several bases for potential re-alignment and division did not, of course, appear as distinct and separate alternatives, nor did they all converge in a single line of cleavage. Rather they presented a cluster of overlapping bonds of affinity which could be utilized in various ways as seemed most advantageous to the leaders and rank and file of the different parties. This gave a degree of flexibility and room for manœuvre which the political parties of the new Republic were not slow to grasp. Since some of these lines of alignment were mutually contradictory they also contributed to the stability of the state. Thus, for example, clan solidarity amongst the Darod of the ex-Protectorate and Somalia was to some extent offset by differences between north and south stemming from the separate colonial traditions of the two regions, and vice versa. On the other hand, this regional cleavage was reinforced in the case of the Isaq by the circumstances of their distribution which was restricted to the former Protectorate and did not extend into Somalia.

The mechanics of integration

This in its most basic terms was the background against which the union of the two parts of the Republic remained to be consummated and something more binding than mere political integration achieved. Here it would be difficult to minimize the problems posed by their dual colonial heritage which confronted the leaders of the new Republic. In administration, although the functions of British and Italian trained officials were similar, whatever their relative standards, each staff operated under different conditions of service and on rates of pay which differed radically. This was true of all officials in every branch of government, including the national police force and the national army (formed by the amalgamation of the former Somaliland Scouts with the Somalia military forces). Less personal, but no less complicated problems arose in relation to the separate legal traditions of the two regions. The northern legal system was based primarily upon English Common and Statute Law and the Indian Penal Code. In the south the system depended mainly upon Italian Colonial law.[3] In addition, while before union Somalia had her own appellate system, appeals from the High Court of the British Protectorate were heard by the East African Court of Appeal. Hence, until a unified judiciary could be introduced, separate sections of the Supreme Court of the Republic had to be established to deal with litigation in the two regions. In fiscal and accounting procedures the position was equally complex for wide differences in procedure distinguished the British system in operation in the north from that founded by the Italians in the south. And to round out the picture, considerable variations in tariffs and customs dues and in patterns of trade divided the north from the south.

These and other divergencies contained in the Republic's dual colonial experience presented a wide range of intricate problems which would have to be solved before the new state could function with proper efficiency. These differences were further aggravated by linguistic barriers which, as well as entailing an Italian teaching tradition in southern schools and an English one in the north, affected all spheres of activity, private as well as public. Since agreement had still not been reached on a national script for Somali,[4] and since only a small section of the population was fully literate in Arabic, the two colonial languages continued to be used in the transaction of business. Many southern politicians and senior officials had acquired some knowledge of English during the period of British Military Administration, but few knew the language sufficiently well to use it regularly as a means of written communication for official purposes; and in the north virtually no one was proficient in Italian. Hence, while with other political considerations, this seemed to tip the balance in favour of English in the long term, it did not resolve the immediate problem of communication for the government and civil service, many of whose members could not write to each other directly without the aid of English-Italian interpreters. And competent translators and interpreters were hard to find. At the same time, even without this linguistic problem, physical communications between the two regions of the Republic left much to be desired. There was no direct telephone link between Hargeisa and Mogadishu; and although the two centres were connected by irregular police flights, and by a regular twice weekly air-service, the journey by road frequently took three days to accomplish.

Finally, the various Italian and British expatriate officials who remained in the country after independence as technical experts, were naturally strongly attached to their separate systems of administration and hence, no doubt unintentionally, tended sometimes to hinder rather than to facilitate integration. This conservative effect was most noticeable in the south where there was a much larger expatriate community. These Italian officials feared and resented developments which seemed to threaten not only the primacy of their mother-tongue, but also the whole metropolitan connexion with its important trade and cultural links.

With this very mixed legacy, and with the added inducement

of the strong clan cleavages which existed between north and south, it is hardly surprising that difficulties should have arisen, between the two halves of the Republic. Shortly after the flush of patriotic enthusiasm which marked independence and union had abated, a certain disenchantment became apparent in the north. That the north should take the initiative in questioning the value of union requires little explanation. The north had sacrificed more than the south. The south, with the capital and National Assembly at Mogadishu, was still the hub of affairs; but from its former position as the capital of a small state Hargeisa had declined to a mere provincial headquarters remote from the centre of things. Even though many northern officials now held key positions in the government, northern pride found it hard to stomach this reduction in prestige. This dissatisfaction was also directly stimulated by the marked increase in unemployment which accompanied the withdrawal of expatriate officials and their families after independence.

This growing mood of discontent and resentment was clearly expressed in the national referendum which was held on 20 June, 1961, to approve the provisional constitution under which the two territories had joined together a year previously. The referendum became in effect a test of confidence in the government; and despite the presence of some of their members in the government at Mogadishu, the S.N.L. in the north decided on a boycott. As a result, of a total recorded vote of just over 100,000 in the north, more than half opposed the constitution.[5] In the south by contrast, where the main opposition came from the G.S.L. and H.D.M.S., considerably more than a million and a half votes in favour of the constitution were recorded and little more than 100,000 against.

The significance of this obvious danger signal was not fully appreciated by the government at Mogadishu, which, despite generous disbursements of largesse in the Italian tradition, was having a difficult time in the Assembly, and not merely from northern members. Disagreements within the S.Y.L. were very apparent in the Assembly elections for the President of the Republic, held on 6 July. These Adan 'Abdulle 'Isman, the provisional President, won by a narrow majority from his opponent Sheikh 'Ali Jumaleh after three ballots. Three weeks later, Dr

'Abd ar-Rashid 'Ali Shirmarke, who had again been invited to form a government, announced his new and expanded administration of sixteen Ministers drawn from the S.Y.L. and S.N.L.–U.S.P. (these two parties had joined in formal coalition in September 1960). The National Assembly, however, felt that the government was too large: and on 14 August, with great independence of mind, passed a bill limiting the number of ministries to twelve before debating the new government's statement of policy. Dr 'Abd ar-Rashid resigned. Yet he was still the favourite leader, and having been prevailed upon to reconsider his decision, returned to confront the Assembly on 19 August with a cabinet pruned to twelve members. His programme of internal development and integration, and non-alignment in external affairs, backed by loans to the value of £25 million (mainly from Egypt, West Germany, the U.S.S.R., and Czechoslovakia) and direct aid (from Italy, Britain, and the United States) was overwhelmingly adopted by the Assembly.[6]

With this success to its credit, and with work proceeding on the preparation of a unified legal code and other measures designed to integrate more fully the two regions, the government apparently felt little need to give urgent consideration to the situation in the north. Attention was in any case soon sharply diverted by the disastrous floods which swept the south of the Republic in the autumn and which, following hard on the heels of two exceedingly poor rain seasons, threatened widespread hunger and disease.[7] Such sympathy as this unkind stroke of fortune aroused in the north was scarcely strengthened when the members of the National Assembly chose this moment to pass legislation doubling their salaries to a figure (£100 monthly) considerably in excess of that received by southern Provincial Commissioners and other senior officials. Despite the participation of their elected representatives, to northerners this was but one of a long series of irresponsible actions taken by the government in distant Mogadishu.

Matters came to a head with the short-lived and abortive military *coup* of December 1961. The full circumstances of this northern gesture of defiance are still far from clear. The revolt was led, however, by a group of Sandhurst-trained lieutenants who, after independence, found themselves serving under Italian-trained superior officers who had been posted to the north. Directly inspired, it seems, by a mixture of personal ambition and northern patriotism, these British-trained junior officers quietly arrested their southern superiors whom they regarded as unjustly promoted over their heads. They then gave out publicly that, following widespread rioting against the government in Mogadishu and elsewhere, General Da'ud, commandant of the national army, had assumed control of the state. This news seems to have been not unfavourably received. But on the following day suspicions began to be aroused by the conspicuous absence of superior officers, and word soon leaked out that the real object of the revolt, no doubt strongly sympathized with, if not directly aided and abetted, by elements within the S.N.L., was to break with the south and destroy the Republic. For many people this was too much; and led by private soldiers and non-commissioned officers the rebellious lieutenants were all arrested. By the time government reinforcements and police arrived in strength from Mogadishu the whole affair was over.

This incident, in which certain high-ranking officials and members of the government were suspected of complicity, and which, incidentally, pointed to the need to improve communications between Hargeisa and Mogadishu, at last spurred the government to action. The ring-leaders were arrested (and brought to trial a year later),[8] a number of officials were dismissed or reduced in rank, while those who had remained loyal were rewarded and new efforts were made to integrate the two regions more fully. Northern and southern personnel in all branches of government service, including the forces and police, were posted much more extensively on a national basis than had been the practice previously. Further measures took more time. The new Civil Service Law unifying salaries and conditions of service throughout the Republic was not ratified until March 1962. From the point of view of northern civil servants, although absolutely necessary, this was a mixed blessing; for, while it raised the salary scales for the lower grades of employee, the top salaries of senior officials were decreased to a point roughly midway between the two extremes of north and south.[9] (Prior to this, District Commissioners in the north on the old British rates received salaries considerably higher than those of Provincial Commissioners in the south and twice as much as southern D.C.s.) Later in 1962 new fiscal and accounting procedures on the (British) northern pattern were adopted throughout the Republic. At the same time, the former British practice of the purchase of government equipment through tender boards was also introduced, an innovation which seriously perturbed Italian companies in the south and encouraged competition by Somali firms.

Of more direct benefit to the north was the government's drive to see that the region received a greater share of development projects and new industries. Already the ambitious Tug Wajale mechanized wheat and sorghum farming scheme, which had been launched in September 1960, was proving highly successful, and with as much publicity as possible further efforts were made to expand production. With British aid, Hargeisa airport was to be modernized and improved; Russia and the U.A.R. were to provide funds for new local industries; and as a counter-part to the £2½ million U.S.-aided port development scheme at Kismayu in the south, Russian engineers were to examine the possibilities of improving harbour facilities at Berbera. New hospitals were also under construction.

These provisions, however, were not sufficient to silence the continuing discontent in the north. Most profoundly perhaps this stemmed from a conjunction of northern pride and political isolation: the basic difficulty being that the Isaq, who made up the majority of the region's population, no longer supported their elected members in the government. Moreover, although there was talk of having the National Assembly meet periodically at Hargeisa, nothing came of this, and the sense of northern remoteness continued much as before. In this situation it was natural that the G.S.L. should seek allies in the north, and indeed in the summer of 1962 a new party (the Somali Democratic Union), attempting to amalgamate the G.S.L., S.N.L., and some of the U.S.P. and H.D.M.S. (in the south), made its appearance under the leadership of Haji Muhammad Husseyn. However, the S.N.L., or at least its now rather nominal leaders in the Assembly, were hampered by their association with the coalition government; and the time was rapidly approaching when those S.N.L. members in the government who had maintained a dangerously ambiguous position would have to choose between retaining the support of their electors and their places in the government. A formal split between the S.N.L. and U.S.P also seemed indicated.

Both these things happened later in the summer. Dissatisfaction in the north had assumed such proportions that the government was moved to dispatch a special team of three northern Ministers (two S.N.L. and one U.S.P.) to sort out the situation which now threatened to lead to the breakdown of normal administration. The President himself was also thrown into the breach, and made a prolonged and much publicized tour, the general success of which must be partly attributed to his own high personal reputation. The investigating team of Ministers was less fortunate. Difficulties arose over the interpretation of their terms of reference; and the Minister of Agriculture (U.S.P.) did not agree with his colleagues as to the measures which should be taken (which included suspending a number of northern administrative officers[10]) to meet the situation. As a result, at the end of the summer the two S.N.L. members, one of whom was Muhammad Haji Ibrahim Igal, Minister of Education, resigned from the government. This action restored to these two prominent S.N.L. figures much of their former popularity in the north and encouraged other S.N.L. members in the Assembly to come out openly and concertedly against the government. A more organized and powerful parliamentary opposition was now emerging. Political leaders began to discuss the formation of a new party to include the rump of the S.N.L. under Muhammad Haji Ibrahim Igal, and those (predominantly Hawiye) members of the League who supported the defeated presidential candidate Sheikh 'Ali Jumaleh. It was also hoped to include other minority groups. These moves culminated in May 1963 in the creation of the Somali National Congress led by some twenty members of the Assembly from both north and south.

The immediate precipitant on this occasion, ironically enough from the point of view of the government, was the introduction throughout the Republic of a unitary system of tariffs and customs dues which, though intended to lower transport costs in the north, had quite the opposite effect.[11] Food prices in the northern regions immediately soared causing widespread public indignation which led to a riot at Hargeisa on 1 May. This assured that the new party received much public support in the north. In the south the position was less clearly defined, and it remained to be seen whether the S.N.C. or S.D.U. would emerge as the dominant opposition party, or whether both would join forces against the League. Would either or both these parties amalgamate with the H.D.M.S. and other minority organizations? These were questions which, in the extremely fluid and shifting political situation current at the end of 1963, only time and the approaching municipal and Assembly elections could settle. Certainly, if all the opposition groups were to merge, the S.Y.L. would be in a difficult position. But it was impossible to gauge whether, as in the past, the League would recapture its resilience and succeed in defeating its rivals. Here much would depend not only upon the balance of clan interests in the party, but also upon possible changes in its leadership.

Already the League, very much the backbone of the still nominal coalition government, had reacted to this mounting tide of opposition by seeking to close its ranks and by assuming a more militant and vigilant rôle in the management of the state. At its annual congress in July 1963, the new young Secretary-General, replacing the elderly traditional religious leader who had preceded him,[12] made a fiery speech urging that the party must act more effectively as the arm of the government. This was typical of a new tendency in S.Y.L. policy suggestive of the single-party state philosophy,[13] and came at a time when the League felt its position to be seriously threatened. Other pointers in this direction, at least in the eyes of the opposition parties, were provided by the controversial Public Order bill passed by the Assembly after stormy scenes in July.[14] If, however, it was still too early to assess this trend with any confidence, it was typical of the Somali political scene that it should develop at a time when the Republic was more amply provided with opposition parties than ever before. And in this uncertain situation there was one constant upon which all the parties could rely: that the present members of the Assembly would do all in their power to retain their highly paid positions. How the electorate would behave was another matter.

Thus by the end of 1963 northern particularism appeared more and more to be finding an outlet in the Somali National

Congress, and its objectives were less the division of the Republic than the downfall of the S.Y.L. government. It was this more limited, and of course entirely constitutional aim which explained the failure of the attempted *coup* in 1961 and the readiness with which the new northern political organizations sought to ally with those who opposed the S.Y.L. in the south. Hitherto, indeed, the integrity of the Republic had been much less seriously in danger than foreign observers had sometimes supposed. Moreover, by the end of the year, further progress had been achieved in the fuller integration of the two regions. In May, by 52 to 42 votes, the Assembly had passed legislation extending the existing southern pattern of universal suffrage to the north, where previously only men had enjoyed the right to vote.[15] In June, Article 29 of the Constitution was revised to prohibit proselytization except by Muslims, thus standardizing the previous British Protectorate practice throughout the Republic. In August, legislation was passed unifying the regulations governing municipal and rural district councils. And by the end of the year, the lengthy and intricate task of establishing a uniform legal code was almost complete.

Thus, by the end of 1963, in the three and a half years which had elapsed since the proclamation of the Republic, much of the work of integration had been accomplished. The most significant political forces in the state were also working towards a more satisfactory pattern of grouping. To what extent their conflicting interests would receive direct representation in the forthcoming Assembly elections, due in the spring of 1964, remained to be seen. It appeared likely, however, if current trends continued, and in particular if the Isaq could achieve a stable alliance with southern clan interests, that the division between north and south would lose much of its force.

The Pan-Somali issue

The creation of the Republic still left outside the fold those Somali nationals living in French Somaliland, in the contiguous eastern regions of Ethiopia, and in the Northern Frontier District of Kenya. The situation thus confronting the newly formed Republic in 1960 is best described in the Prime Minister's own words. 'Our misfortune', Dr 'Abd ar-Rashid wrote,[16] 'is that our neighbouring countries, with whom, like the rest of Africa, we seek to promote constructive and harmonious relations, are not our neighbours. Our neighbours are our Somali kinsmen whose citizenship has been falsified by indiscriminate boundary "arrangements". They have to move across artificial frontiers to their pasturelands. They occupy the same terrain and pursue the same pastoral economy as ourselves. We speak the same language. We share the same creed, the same culture, and the same traditions. How can we regard our brothers as foreigners? Of course we all have a strong and very natural desire to be united. The first step was taken in 1960 when the Somaliland Protectorate was united with Somalia. This act was not an act of "colonialism" or "expansionism" or "annexation". It was a positive contribution to peace and unity in Africa.'

The union of the Protectorate with Somalia, however, was one thing. The further extension of Somali unification to embrace French Somaliland, the Ethiopian Haud and Ogaden, and the Northern Frontier District of Kenya, although boldly enshrined in the Republic's constitution,[17] was an altogether different matter. Both the Northern Frontier District of Kenya, and the Haud and Ogaden, were part of neighbouring states which had shown no enthusiasm for the Somali cause and could hardly be expected to agree readily to territorial changes which would diminish their size and prestige. With French Somaliland the position might be thought to be more hopeful, since, theoretically at any rate, assuming that a majority of the territory's mixed population desired it, there would be no constitutional impediment to an independent ex-French possession joining the Republic in much the same way as the British Protectorate had joined Somalia. In 1960, however, French Somaliland was far from being independent. In the Gaullist referendum of 1958 the *Côte*'s population had voted against complete emancipation and had chosen to remain an oversea territory of France.

This requires some explanation. Since the formation of the *Côte*'s Territorial Council in 1945, the political life of the territory had received a new impetus with the establishment under the *loi cadre* in 1957 of an elected legislature with responsibility for internal affairs. This represented a notable constitutional advance but one which was not, however, matched by developments in other spheres comparable to those taking place at the time in Somalia or British Somaliland. The first elections for the new assembly were won by the Union Republicaine, an electoral coalition representing sections of both the Somali and 'Afar communities and the Arab population, and led by Mahamud Harbi. The principal rival organization, with a similarly mixed composition, was led by Hassan Guled, who, like Mahamud Harbi, belonged to the 'Ise Somali. After the elections, a Council of Ministers was formed under the presidency of the colonial Governor. In addition to its Vice-President, Mahamud Harbi, this body included three other Somalis; two 'Afar, one Arab; and one European. If it did not correspond exactly to the relative strengths of the Somali and 'Afar populations, this composition which reflected the greater political involvement of Somalis, suggested that, despite their traditional rivalry, the two main elements in the *Côte*'s population shared sufficient common interests to co-operate in the management of internal affairs.

As the tide of Somali nationalist feeling mounted in the British Protectorate and Somalia, however, the position began to change. The 1958 referendum in fact was interpreted as offering a choice between working for independence and union with Somalia, and remaining with France. Mahamud Harbi campaigned on a Somali nationalist platform, while Hassan Guled, with the powerful support of the French electorate, canvassed for a vote in favour of continuing the connexion with France. When, with Mahamud Harbi still in office, it was announced that this latter aim had prevailed, an extremely confused situation developed. This was resolved by the intervention of the French authorities who dissolved the assembly and arranged for new elections to he held on 23 November, 1958.[18] In the confusion, Mahamud Harbi's party largely disintegrated, while Hassan Guled's group changed its composition. Five electoral groupings eventually emerged; two of them frankly 'Afar organizations, and two others Somali-'Afar alliances led by the two principal contenders, Hassan Guled and Mahamud Harbi. Under a new system of allocating seats on a proportional basis,[19] Hassan Guled, commanding the majority of 'Afar support, defeated Mahamud Harbi's Union democratique Somalie. Mahamud Harbi subsequently fled to Cairo, and later

to Mogadishu where, in 1959, he participated in the formation
of the National Pan-Somali Movement. His short but eventful
political career ended in October of the following year when he
was killed in an air crash while on his way back to Mogadishu
from a visit to China and Eastern Europe.

In the *Côte* itself, Hassan Guled had succeeded Mahamud Harbi
as Vice-President in the Council, but vacated this office to Ahmad
Diini, an 'Afar member, in April 1959 when he was elected to
the French National Assembly. Later, in June 1960, Ahmad
Diini was replaced by another 'Afar tribesman, 'Ali 'Ariif Burhan.
Thus, although Somali members still made up the largest block
in the Territorial Assembly (14 out of 32 seats: 'Afar, 13) and
also in the Government Council, the leadership had now fallen
to the 'Afar and the most strongly nationalist Somali were in
opposition, or exile. Meanwhile, on a brief visit to the *Côte* in
July 1959, General de Gaulle had announced categorically, with
his usual command of rhetoric, that France attached extreme
importance to the port of Jibuti (which now rivalled the British
port of Aden) and had no intention of relinquishing control.[20]

Thus in 1960 when the government of the Republic began to
take stock of the prospects facing Pan-Somalism, the position
in French Somaliland was far from promising. Although there
was still no absolute division of opinion between the Somali and
'Afar communities on the question of eventual union with the
Republic, it was difficult to gauge the extent of Somali nationalist
interest, and even more difficult to assess its appeal to the 'Afar.
French policy, moreover, was evidently determined for the
present at least to make no further concessions of sovereignty,
and clear indications had been given that the French Government regarded the Pan-Somali movement as a threat to be resisted
as firmly as possible. In addition, new French measures in the
Côte, undertaken with the object of advancing the previously
neglected 'Afar community, had the effect – which in Somali eyes
they seemed designed to promote – of driving a wedge between
the two peoples. Finally, and perhaps most significantly of all,
in their hostility to the Pan-Somali aim, French policies were
closely allied with those of Ethiopia, and sustained by the mutual
interest of both countries in the prosperous port of Jibuti and
the line of rail connecting it to the Ethiopian hinterland.

In the Ethiopian Haud and Ogaden, the prospects of any further extension of Somali unification seemed even more remote. Here, following the Emperor's speech on Somali affairs at Qabradare in 1956, a few modest developments in schooling and medical services had been introduced, but nothing on the scale promised. And the appeal of such innovations was greatly weakened by the Ethiopian government's insistence that Somalis who wished to advance themselves should do so through the medium of Amharic. No party political activity was permitted and any overt expression of Somali nationalist sentiment was firmly dealt with. Thus, despite the fact that by 1960 there were six Somali deputies and one Senator in the Ethiopian parliament, and also a number of locally recruited administrative and police officials in the Ogaden, there was no avenue open for the expression of Somali nationalist aspirations. The extent of nationalist support consequently could only be estimated from the growing incidence of rebellious incidents and from the news brought to Mogadishu by political refugees and clandestine delegations. This uneasy situation was exacerbated by the failure of the two countries to reach agreement on their mutual frontier which, in practice, remained the provisional administrative line left by the British in Somalia in 1950.

During the Italian trusteeship period, at the instigation of the United Nations, repeated negotiations had taken place to define a frontier acceptable to both sides. The Italians claimed that the frontier lay to the west of the provisional line, while the Ethiopians maintained that it ran to the east, nearer the coast. After the Italian government had refused to accept an Ethiopian compromise on the provisional boundary, an arbitration tribunal of three jurists was appointed in 1958. Difficulties arose, however, over the tribunal's terms of reference, and the United Nations Assembly sought to overcome these by calling upon the King of Norway to nominate some outstanding international personality to act as an adviser to the tribunal. This delicate rôle was assigned to Mr Trygve Lie, the former U.N. Secretary-General, who was asked to propose terms acceptable to the two parties. A draft compromise was accepted by both Italy and Ethiopia in 1959 as a basis for discussion; but amendments subsequently made by both sides were mutually unacceptable and the matter remained in dispute.

The main issue was that, while Ethiopia insisted that the frontier should be determined on the basis of a strictly legalistic interpretation of the 1908 Italo-Ethiopian Convention, Italy maintained that other international agreements should also be taken into account as well as ethnic factors relating to the distribution of different Somali clans in the disputed area. The Italian position thus favoured a more liberal interpretation in the direction of Somali national aspirations. Prior to independence no further progress was made; although, in December 1959, both Ethiopia and Somalia agreed that the British provisional line should remain in force until a final settlement was reached.[21]

After independence, the union of Somalia with the British Protectorate added a new complication. In their negotiations with the British government the Protectorate leaders formally refused to endorse the provisions of the Anglo-Ethiopian treaty of 1897 which they were considered to fall heir to in succession to Britain. However questionable in international law, their attitude was that they could hardly be expected to assume responsibility for a treaty which, without Somali consent and in defiance of prior Anglo-Somali agreements, eventually led to Ethiopia's acquisition of the Haud.[22] With these two frontier disputes outstanding, both of which related directly to the wider Pan-Somali issue, it was clear that the Republic could expect no support from Ethiopia for her campaign of Somali unification. It was also evident that relations between the two neighbouring states would remain difficult in the extreme.

The Kenya dispute

This left the situation in the Northern Frontier District of Kenya to assess. This ethnically and administratively distinct region of Kenya contained a population (according to the 1962 Census) of just under 400,000, considerably more than half of whom were Somali. The 'District' in fact comprised six separate administrative Districts with headquarters at Mandera, Wajir, Garissa, Isiolo, Marsabit, and Moyale. Widely dispersed and thinly concentrated on the ground, the Somali pastoral nomads occupied almost the whole of the eastern part of the region (Garissa, Wajir, and Mandera Districts), being cordoned off from their neighbours and ethnic kinsmen the Orma and Boran Galla by the 'Somali line', which ran southwards from east of Moyale to the Tana River. The Pokomo cultivators, numbering some 6,500 and straddled along the banks of the Tana, provided another ethnic element in the composition of the District. And the fairly clear-cut division between Galla and Somali, although complicated by the fact that many Oromo had adopted Islam and were in process of assimilation to Somali, was offset by the presence in Marsabit District, in the extreme west, of the part-Somali Rendille tribe who formed a distinct wedge between pagan and Muslim Galla and numbered some 10,000 persons. Thus although the eastern part of the District clearly belonged to the Somali, the position in the western areas was less well-defined.

As a whole in 1960 the N.F.D. still remained the most isolated, and the most backward portion of Kenya, and indeed, with the exception only of the Ogaden, the least advanced of all the Somali territories. Since the proscription in 1948 of the S.Y.L. in this 'closed District', as it was defined in Kenya's legislation,[23] nationalist activity had to remain dormant until 1960 when some belated recognition was given to the political rights of its tax-payers. Immediately prior to that, although there had been no direct participation by the people of the District in the 1957 Kenya elections, in 1959 a Somali-nominated member had been appointed to 'look after' their interests on the legislative council. The lifting of the ban on political organizations in 1960, although not at once accompanied by a relaxation of the other special restrictions in the District, and the prompt mobilization of Somali nationalist support behind the Northern Province Peoples' Party, heralded a new era. Or so at least it seemed at the time. The Somali tribesmen of the District had already announced their intention of seeking self-determination independently of the rest of Kenya in order that they could unite with their kinsmen in the Republic. With the long administrative tradition of treating the area and its people differently from the rest of the colony, and with British approval for the union of Somalia and British Somaliland, Somali nationalists felt that they had good reason to hope that their aspirations might be realized. For, if in response to the wishes of the people of the Somaliland Protectorate Britain was prepared to facilitate their union with Somalia, how could she refuse to do less for her Somali subjects in Kenya? This may seem a simple view of the matter. But in the minds of the tribesmen concerned, Britain had committed herself to a line of action to which, in similar circumstances, it was only logical to expect she would adhere. The position of the British government, however, was far from clear. With vivid memories of Mr Bevin's attempts, however unsuccessful, to promote Somali unification, Britain's willingness to facilitate the union of her Protectorate with Somalia had, predictably, seriously disturbed Ethiopia. Since Britain's first guarded indication in 1956 of her intentions in respect of British Somaliland and Somalia, the Ethiopian government had launched a spirited campaign against Pan-Somalism. The strategy adopted was to accuse the British government of seeking to establish a pro-British Greater Somalia and to press for an elucidation of Britain's policy. The Emperor's visit to Moscow in 1959 and his acceptance of a $100 million Russian loan indicated the possible repercussions of disregarding Ethiopian interests. In these circumstances, and faced with the Protectorate's request for independence and union with Somalia by 1 July, 1960, Mr Macmillan judged it necessary to offer some clarification. Thus, in April 1960, having accepted the Protectorate's request for independence, the Prime Minister made the following statement to the House of Commons. 'Her Majesty's government' he said, 'did not and will not encourage or support any claim affecting the territorial integrity of French Somaliland, Kenya, or Ethiopia. This is a matter which could only be considered if that were the wish of the governments and peoples concerned.' Evidently this declaration was primarily intended to mollify the fears of Ethiopia and France and to reassure the Kenyan African leaders. At the same time, however, when this message was relayed by the Governor of Kenya to chiefs and elders in the N.F.D. two months later, it seemed to open the door to the attainment of Somali aspirations. For the statement acknowledged that their wishes would be considered, and they believed that apart from Somalis the only government which was 'concerned' was that of Britain. This was also the official view in the newly formed Somali Republic.

With the rapidly evolving political situation in Kenya, it was therefore this segment of the Somali nation in the N.F.D. which appeared to afford the best hope for an early extension of Somali unification. Thus, while in the two years following independence the government of the Republic kept a watchful eye on events in French Somaliland and the Ogaden and sought to publicize Somali efforts there to gain independence, its main preoccupation was with the Northern Frontier District of Kenya. Here there was certainly much to occupy Somali nationalists; for the situation developed very rapidly. In the 1961 Kenya elections the predominantly Somali Districts of Garissa, Wajir, Mandera, and Moyale, formed a single constituency (Northern Province East). But only 1,622 people registered as voters: Somalis had generally decided to boycott the elections on the grounds that to participate in them would imply that they accepted Kenyan citizenship. The sole candidate, Mr 'Ali Adan Lord (later killed in a motor accident and replaced by Mr A. R. Khalif), was returned unopposed.

After the 1961 elections the tempo of political activity rapidly mounted and the Somali campaign for self-determination independently of the rest of Kenya gathered momentum. Frequent delegations of Somali party leaders and tribal elders visited Mogadishu to seek support. In November, the National Assembly responded to these requests for help by passing a motion welcoming the union of the Northern Frontier District with the Republic and urging the government to press for this by all possible means. This encouraged the Mogadishu government to mount a publicity campaign in support of its kinsmen in Kenya; and although it could not be represented itself, to give strong moral backing to the N.F.D. delegation at the Kenya constitutional conference held at Lancaster House in February 1962. By this time, as well as a number of organizations which opposed the Somali aim, there were three principal nationalist parties in the District. These, although divided in their bases of affiliation along tribal lines, were united in seeking independence separately from Kenya in order to join the Somali Republic. The N.F.D. delegation was led by Mr A. R. Khalif. He asked that: 'before any further constitutional changes affecting Kenya were made, autonomy should be granted to the area which they represented as a territory wholly independent of Kenya, in order that it might join in an Act of Union with the Somali Republic when Kenya became fully independent'.[24]

This request was naturally firmly opposed by the K.A.N.U. and K.A.D.U. delegations, who, notwithstanding their lack of unanimity on other issues, were adamant in refusing to concede any right of separate self-determination to the Somali and associated peoples of the N.F.D. Such a concession, they claimed, would jeopardize the territorial integrity of Kenya and would encourage tribal separatist movements throughout the colony. In assuming this position, the K.A.N.U. leaders were fortified by the knowledge that they enjoyed the support of Ethiopia and that African governments in other territories had little sympathy for the Somali case. The N.F.D. delegation on the other hand asked why they should not be accorded the same rights as their kinsmen in the former British Somaliland Protectorate whose independence and union with Somalia had taken place under British auspices. If the principle of self-determination meant anything, they urged, it certainly could not mean the enforced suppression of their national and legitimate integrity.[25]

In reply, the K.A.N.U. delegation asked why those non-Somali tribesmen of the N.F.D. who might not wish to leave Kenya should be sacrificed to the Somali demand for secession. The solution to this problem, they claimed, was simple. Let those Somalis who desired it, leave Kenya and join the Somali Republic: no one would stop them. The fact that the Somalis found their livelihood in the District was not important, for they were nomads: and in any case in the K.A.N.U. view they possessed only a slender claim to the territory.

Faced with this conflict which involved different conceptions of nationhood and nationality, the Colonial Secretary (Mr R. Maudling) told the conference that he had decided that an independent commission 'with appropriate terms of reference' should be appointed to 'ascertain public opinion in the area regarding its future'. It might, he added, be necessary to hold a plebiscite or even a referendum in part of the N.F.D. On the understanding that the commission's findings would be implemented before Kenya became internally self-governing, this solution was accepted by the N.F.D. delegation. And with this, as it appeared substantial achievement, the delegation returned to Kenya to prepare for the investigation of opinion which, they had been led to believe, was to determine their future status. Knowing well the strength of Somali feeling in the N.F.D. on the matter, they were in little doubt as to the outcome.

Meanwhile, the Somali government in Mogadishu, having guardedly welcomed this news, anxiously watched the course of events through a specially appointed ministerial committee. Public opinion, particularly in the north where, with the common British connexion and similar circumstances prior to union, interest was most strongly marked, demanded that the government should pursue the matter energetically. Widespread public demonstrations in different parts of the Republic expressed moral solidarity with the N.F.D. delegates as they presented the Somali case at the Kenya Conference. In keeping with this mood, the Prime Minister made a fiercely anti-imperialist speech in March attacking Ethiopia and France, and warning Britain that she would be held responsible if the 'mistakes of the past' were repeated and the peoples of the Northern Frontier District denied the right to 'freely decide their own destiny'.[26] Words, however, no longer sufficed. The public clamour for action was loud and increasingly strident in tone. The prevailing feeling was reflected in a motion of no-confidence in the government tabled by thirty-one members of the Assembly (from both north and south) at the end of March. Their primary criticism was the government's 'lack of courage' in pursuing the Pan-Somali issue.

Nevertheless, despite these exhortations, Dr 'Abd ar-Rashid's cabinet decided to follow the principles laid down in the Republic's constitution and to limit action for the present at least to peaceful diplomacy. In the unexpectedly protracted period before the appointment of the N.F.D. commission towards the end of the year, the Mogadishu authorities sought accordingly to maintain what pressure they could upon the British Foreign Office. They made it clear that they intended to abide by the findings of the commission, or of any other impartial record of public opinion in the disputed territory. Once this had been established, however, it was up to Britain to take the necessary action, for the issue was primarily one between Britain and the Somali people. However, it was by no means easy to deal with Britain on this matter. For the British government found this direct approach from Mogadishu extremely embarrassing, and did all it could to avoid making any direct response beyond advising the Republic that it would have to wait for the results of the commission.

This evasive action concealed a most significant shift of emphasis in British policy. At the Lancaster House conference, the Colonial Secretary had shown that he had an open mind on the dispute and was prepared to see it settled by secession according to the evidence collected by the N.F.D. commission. Statements made then by the K.A.N.U. delegation too suggested that it would not have been impossible to have gained their acceptance, however reluctant, for this solution to the problem. Since the conference, however, the British government had apparently had second thoughts, partly at the instigation of the Foreign Office with its perennial concern for Anglo-Ethiopian relations, and partly in response to pressure from the Uganda and Tanganyika governments as well as from Kenya itself. Thus with the many other pressing problems confronting Kenya, to say nothing of other areas of British activity, the actual appointment of the N.F.D. commission was allowed to drag on while Kenya's African leaders acquired further authority and began to display increasingly militant attitudes towards the Somali secessionists.

These and other circumstances made it more and more attractive for the British government to pass over the Colonial Secretary's assurance and to incline towards the position of the Kenyan nationalists. Hence Britain's line was now to stress that part of her stated policy on Somali unification which held that in the case of the present dispute nothing could be decided without the consent of the government of Kenya. Accordingly, while officially maintaining the 'correct' attitude of refusing to treat directly with the Republic, unofficially members of the British embassy at Mogadishu put forward the convenient if somewhat disingenuous argument that ultimately the Somali government would have to settle the problem itself with Kenya. Only thus, it was urged, could a lasting solution be achieved.

Doubtful of the result, but willing to see what could be gained by this approach, the Somali government took advantage of the 1962 July Independence Day celebrations to invite leading members of the two Kenya African nationalist parties to Mogadishu for informal talks. Jomo Kenyatta and his party arrived first, their visit being followed shortly afterwards by that of Ronald Ngala and other leading K.A.D.U. figures. Socially the visits were a great success: the distinguished guests were fêted, the utmost cordiality prevailed, and most ironically in the circumstances, Mr Kenyatta and Mr Ngala were each awarded the Star of Somali Solidarity.

In a number of discussions and public speeches, Jomo Kenyatta stated emphatically that he regarded the N.F.D. as an inalienable part of Kenya and the whole issue as a domestic matter. Mr Ngala's position was similar, if less resolutely stated. Spokesmen for the Somali side challenged the argument that the disputed area was 'part and parcel of Kenya', and emphasized how throughout Kenya's administrative history the territory had been treated as a separate entity. Reiterating that the Somali government intended to respect the wishes of the N.F.D. tribesmen, they insisted upon the latter's right, as they saw it, to separate self-determination. And with both sides thus in disagreement, but vying with each other in their expressions of enthusiasm for the projected East African federation, which was ultimately to include both Ethiopia and the Republic, the President judged it necessary to intrude a note of caution. The basic obstacle impeding effective African unity, he sadly concluded in an assessment of Pan-Africanism as poignant as it was eloquent, was the 'unwillingness of African rulers to curb their powers and to lift their artificial colonial boundaries'.[27]

Thus these direct talks produced no progress, and preliminary discussions on the Republic's participation in the East African federation had already run into difficulties. Here the problem, no doubt theoretical in the light of the many other obstacles which would have to be overcome before even the nucleus of federation was achieved, was one of timing. Both sides agreed that if the Republic joined the projected federation, the Somali territories should form a single territorial unit within it. But the Kenyan leaders considered that this local Somali unification should take place *after* the Republic had entered the federation, while the Somali leaders, influenced by their difficulties with Ethiopia, insisted that the order of events should be reversed. This may seem a trivial dispute, but as the East African federation remained an unrealized aim, for the present both parties were adamant and showed no inclination to modify their positions.

In these circumstances the government at Mogadishu, confident that its kinsmen in the N.F.D. would opt for independence and union with the Republic, continued to press Britain to expedite the appointment of the commission and to give effect to its anticipated findings. In the interval, anxious that the N.F.D. should be shielded from any other changes which might prejudice the issue, the Republic judged it necessary on several occasions to remind the British government of its Lancaster House undertaking that, in the meantime, 'there would be no change in the status of the Northern Frontier District or in the arrangements for its administration'.

The long-awaited commission, consisting of a Nigerian judge and a Canadian General, at last arrived in Kenya in October; and having completed its work of hearing evidence with commendable alacrity, and – what was perhaps more surprising – without incident, published its report some six weeks later. The Commissioners found[28] that the Somali who they estimated made up 62 per cent of the N.F.D.'s population 'almost unanimously' favoured secession from Kenya with the object of 'ultimately' joining the Somali Republic. This desire was shared also by the majority of the other smaller Muslim communities in the District (principally Muslim Galla). The contrary wish to remain with Kenya and to participate in its constitutional development was recorded amongst some of the Oromo in Marsabit District, among non-Muslim Boran in Moyale District, and with the Pokomo cultivators along the banks of the Tana River in Garissa District. There were also several smaller areas of mixed opinion. The general division, however, coincided with the division between Muslims (Somali and associated peoples) and non-Muslims (principally Galla). A significant indication of the force of the Somali desire for union with the Republic was that although the main strength of the Oromo people lay in Ethiopia, there was 'no suggestion' in the verbally recorded evidence, that Ethiopia had 'any concern' with the issue of the territory's future status.

The Commission's findings were largely as had been anticipated, but the report contained one phrase which was particularly disquieting to Somali nationalists. This was that evidence had been collected 'on the premise that there can be no question of secession before Kenya gets independence'. This assumption derived, apparently, from the Commissioners' confidential instructions. It was not included in the previous Colonial Secretary's announcement of the decision to set up the Commission made at the Kenya conference, and it appeared to be in conflict with the undertaking given then that a decision would be taken before Kenya became independent. Whatever might be thought of the British government's conduct of the whole issue, this direction to the Commission seemed to imply a definite hardening of opinion against the Somali desire for secession. This was also suggested by the way in which the British Foreign Office was handling the matter through its embassy at Mogadishu. At the same time, although championed by a number of British newspapers, the Somali case had acquired no new appeal for the nationalist leaders in Kenya or as far as could be judged for those of other African states. The general atmosphere was scarcely promising.

Nevertheless, still hopeful that the British government would honour the undertakings given at the Kenya Conference, and encouraged by the N.F.D. Commission's findings, the Somali government intensified its efforts to press Britain for her promised decision. To this end, despite British reluctance, the Somali Prime Minister visited London at the end of the year for brief talks with Mr Macmillan and the Foreign Secretary. These did little to clarify the situation.

At last, in March 1963, it fell to Mr Duncan Sandys, the new British Colonial Secretary, to announce his government's decision. To the satisfaction of the Nairobi and Addis Ababa governments, but to the chagrin of Somalis, this was that the N.F.D. was to be brought into Kenya's regional constitution. A new, predominantly Somali, North-Eastern Region was to be created in which Somalis would enjoy the same degree of local autonomy as had already been accorded elsewhere in Kenya's other six Regions. This decision, which gave effect to the recommendations of the Kenya Regional Boundaries Commission[29] rather than to the findings of the special N.F.D. Commission, not only ignored the Somali secessionist demand but also cut off from the new Region several Muslim tribal groups which shared the Somali aim. Moreover, although no doubt with the intention of leaving some room for manœuvre it was not made clear whether this represented the British government's final decision on the issue, it was difficult to see how Britain could hope later to concede secession without seriously endangering her relations with Kenya and Ethiopia.

Whether, at the time, the British government considered the matter finally closed or not, the announcement of the new arrangements merely further antagonized Somali opinion and led to the resignation of all stipended chiefs and local authorities. The tribesmen concerned also made it clear that they would not participate in elections for a regional assembly under these conditions. With equal inevitability, relations between the Somali Republic and Britain which had been subject to serious strain over the previous months, now rapidly deteriorated. Public opinion was vociferous in its demands that the Republic should break off diplomatic relations with Britain, and in the face of mounting opposition Dr 'Abd ar-Rashid's government had little alternative if it was to remain in office. However, at the eleventh hour in a round of unusually active diplomatic exchanges, the British Ambassador told the Somali Prime Minister that he had been advised that new proposals were on the way. The British government, apparently, had decided to alter its position. What the new proposals were must remain a matter of academic interest only, for this hopeful message to the Prime Minister was later countermanded with the announcement by the Ambassador that, after all, his government had nothing more to say. With remarkable restraint and a pardonable ignorance of British diplomatic history, Dr 'Abd ar-Rashid permitted himself the observation that he doubted if any other British Ambassador had ever been similarly treated.[30] Relations between the Republic and Britain were formally severed on 12 March, 1963.

The rupture involved loss of privileges for both countries. The Republic relinquished her small but useful annual subsidy of £1½ million from Britain, while Britain lost over-flying rights and was forced to close down her powerful BBC Middle Eastern service relay transmitter at Berbera. Britain had evidently decided that, whatever interests she might have in maintaining friendship with the Republic, and whatever responsibilities she might be held to owe to her Somali subjects in Kenya, or to her former subjects in the Northern Regions of the Republic, these were not such as to justify endangering the long-standing *entente* with Ethiopia or alienating the new Commonwealth territory of Kenya. This decision no doubt assumed that the disputed Northern Frontier District of Kenya would probably not erupt into violence, or that if it did the resulting situation could be satisfactorily contained without danger to British interests. How accurate these assumptions would prove in the long term could not be predicted with certainty.

What could be said, however, with some degree of confidence was that the breach between Britain and the Republic need not have occurred. This, of course, is not to make the facile and uncomprehending judgement that the Somali Republic acted too precipitately: but rather to suggest that the British government acted too indecisively and too slowly. For several years prior to the 1962 Kenya conference, the Provincial Administration of the N.F.D. had consistently reported on the direction and strength of Somali feeling. Had these reports received serious attention it would clearly have been possible for the British government to have prepared the ground for the eventual secession of the N.F.D. without, at that stage, incurring serious opposition from African opinion in Kenya. This, however, was not done and the problem was left until it became insoluble except at the cost of alienating one side or the other.

At a much later stage in the development of the affair, it is also questionable whether the middle course of, in effect, passive resistance adopted by the N.F.D. Somalis with the concordance of Mogadishu was the best strategy to pursue in the circumstances. It is, of course, easy to be wise after the event. But it might well have been more profitable for the N.F.D. Somalis to have adopted more violently intransigent tactics, or alternatively, to have participated wholeheartedly in the new constitutional arrangements with the aim of using the new Region's Territorial Assembly as a mouthpiece from which to press their secessionist aims in a manner which the British government might have found it possible to accede to more readily. To have been acceptable, however, this latter course would have required a degree of mutual confidence and understanding which the British government's conduct of the dispute rendered difficult.

Lastly, it is not without interest to speculate how differently this dispute might have turned out had the Somali Republic entered the Commonwealth on the basis of the Somaliland Protectorate's long connexion with Britain. Such circumstances would no doubt have made the British government's position even more difficult; but they would perhaps also have provided a setting in which the aspirations of the Kenya Somalis would have received more sympathetic attention.

Pan-Africanism and wider issues

The Somali Republic's concentration of interest on the N.F.D. issue during the three years since independence had proved singularly unrewarding. Not only had the specific objective of union with her kinsmen in Kenya eluded her grasp, but also, in the process, the Republic had been manœuvred into a position of unenviable isolation in the Pan-African world.

This development was not without irony. In the particular setting of their nationalist movement in the past, Somalis had shown, on the whole, little interest in African nationalism elsewhere. But since the formation of the first Somali government in 1956, and particularly since the establishment of the Republic in 1960, the position had changed. These events had greatly widened the range of Somali interests and experience and had forced Somali nationalists to seek to come to terms with, and to play their part in, the rising tide of Pan-Africanism which was sweeping the continent. This new trend was already foreshadowed in the Republic's constitution which enshrined the twin aims of promoting Pan-African and Pan-Somali unity, as well as the obligation to maintain friendly relations with the world of Islam. Between Pan-Africanism and Pan-Somalism there seemed no incompatibility; for Somali nationalists regarded these goals as complementary and saw Somali unification as a legitimate regional application of the general and wider principle of Pan-African unity. On this basis, the union of the ex-Protectorate with Somalia was hailed by Somali as a Pan-African, as much as a Pan-Somali achievement, and indeed, despite the problems of integration, as one of the few successful examples of African unification. Outside the Republic this view at first received some favourable attention, but did not attract as much notice or interest as it might have seemed to merit.

The Somali view of the necessary preconditions for effective African unification owed much to the special circumstances of their cultural heritage. The assumption that viable political union required to be under-pinned by a commonality of cultural identity was fundamental to their thinking. Thus, as the President himself put it in a speech during Jomo Kenyatta's visit to Mogadishu in July 1962:

'We have learned of a cardinal principle underlying the effectiveness or otherwise of a political union between two Independent States. It is this: the ordinary person must be able to identify himself and his interests with the new order, on economic, ethnic, and cultural grounds.'

Moreover to Somalis there seemed a connexion between cultural homogeneity and democracy. Thus in the same speech, President Adan added:

'It is this lesson that is perhaps the hardest to learn but if we Africans are proud to take our place in the comity of Nations, we must do more than pay lip-service to the feelings of the ordinary man and woman in our society.'[31]

This view of African unity which expresses the long tradition of Somali cultural unity, and the desire to move from nationhood to statehood which is the crux of the Pan-Somali aim, runs counter to the process of national unification in other African states. For the general problem elsewhere in Africa is the construction of nations from the polyglot and polytribal territorially defined states, with their arbitrary frontiers, which are the legacy of colonialism. This difference between Somali nationalism and African nationalism elsewhere, however, while of academic interest, would in itself hardly have been important enough to isolate the Somali people at the bar of Pan-African opinion. The real difficulty lay in the conflict between the Somali aim to unite with their kinsmen across the frontiers of Kenya and Ethiopia, and the passionate attachment of the new African leaders to such colonially defined boundaries. To Kenya and Ethiopia, and by analogy elsewhere, the Pan-Somali movement threatened African territorial sovereignty. Kenyan leaders could hardly be expected to surrender readily something which, in their eyes, was part of what, as nationalists, they had struggled to win from the British colonizers. Ethiopia's position was rather different; although again, the Somali aim questioned the frontiers over which she had long struggled with Italy. And it was in this light, ignoring Ethiopia's rôle in the partition of Somaliland, that the leaders of other African states seemed disposed to view the problem. Moreover, the Somali case was put forward by men who had not played any striking part in the continental movement of African nationalism, but whose opponents, Jomo Kenyatta, Tom Mboya, and the Emperor of Ethiopia, had in their various ways most emphatically done so. Another significant factor weighing against the Somali was the hostility aroused by their traditional attitudes of ethnic superiority.

These were some of the wider considerations involved in the Pan-African assessment of the Somali dispute and those with which Somali representatives had to contend as they canvassed for support at successive meetings of African states. Over the period between the attainment of independence and the rupture of diplomatic relations with Britain the results were far from encouraging. Although prior to independence, the All-African People's Conference at its Tunis meeting in January 1960 had passed a favourable resolution on Pan-Somalism, it was this organization's next meeting at Cairo, in March of the following year, where the Somali delegates encountered stiff opposition, which set the tone for other all-African occasions. Thus at Monrovia two months later, all that was achieved was a motion urging the Republic and Ethiopia to settle their boundary disputes; and at Belgrade in September, the Somali case again attracted no tangible support. In the following month, however, President Adan 'Abdulle's state visit to Ghana produced a glimmer of hope from this influential quarter. A joint communiqué issued by the two Presidents advocated African federalism as the general solution to border problems but also stressed 'the imperative need to restore the ethnic, cultural, and economic links arbitrarily destroyed by colonization'. Here Dr Nkrumah was apparently influenced by his own interest in the Ewe problem on the Ghana-Togo frontier.[32] Such comfort as might be drawn from this statement, however, soon disappeared as it became evident that no African state was prepared to see Ethiopia's rôle in Somali partition as that of a colonizer. Even more emphatically, no one was prepared to view the Kenyan African nationalists' claim to the N.F.D. as in any sense colonialist.

Subsequent African meetings were equally disappointing, although more practical suggestions for settling the issue were soon forthcoming. The Lagos conference in January 1962 urged that the Somali dispute should be placed before the arbitrating body which was to be established to deal with conflicts between African states. The February meeting of the Pan-African Movement for East and Central Africa, endorsing Nkrumah's federalism, offered the more radical, if idealistic solution of uniting the Somali territories in an extension of the projected East African federation to include the Republic and Ethiopia. This proposal led to the later technical difficulty, mentioned previously, as to whether Somali unity should be restored before or after the Republic had joined the federation. While negotiations along these lines were proceeding with little success, the anomalous Afro-Asian solidarity conference held in Tanganyika in February 1963, despite bitter disagreement provoked by the presentation of the Somali case, surprisingly passed a motion in support of the N.F.D. secession movement. The conference's refusal to endorse Somali references to Ethiopian imperialism was much more in character with the general tenor of other African meetings.

Finally, such slender comfort as this ambiguous result seemed to offer was completely destroyed at the important Addis Ababa summit conference in May. With the long legacy of border incidents and recriminations between Ethiopia and the Republic and tension still continuing, the Somalis at first refused to attend the conference, but later decided to compromise. But there was no concealing the position of isolation into which they had been manoeuvred or the icy reception accorded to those passages in the Somali President's speech which, with more courage than tact, referred to Ethiopia's part in the division of Somaliland.[33] Ethiopia had scored a notable tactical victory; and with her recent discomfiture on the N.F.D. issue and the concerted rebuttal of her Pan-Somali aspirations, the Republic began to seek a rapprochement with her powerful neighbour despite growing resistance to Ethiopian rule in the Ogaden. How far such a trend could be sustained was difficult to forecast.

Before leaving this record of the Republic's growing isolation at the bar of African opinion, brief mention must be made of the rôle of Egypt. As the leading Arab state and the African country most heavily involved in Somali affairs, Egypt was obviously placed in a difficult position. This was illustrated by the clumsy attempts made by Radio Cairo to profess support for both the Somali and Kenyan leaders through Arabic and Somali broadcasts on the one hand, and Swahili on the other. When it soon became evident that each side was aware of what was being said to the other this tactic was dropped, and by the time of the Addis Ababa conference Egypt's position was one of uneasy neutrality. No state which aspired to play a leading rôle in Pan-African affairs could afford to commit itself on the Somali side.

Isolation

Although the value of positive statements in favour of the Somali case may be questioned, there is little doubt that the concerted opposition which Somalis had encountered in the three years since independence was heavily damaging. Britain's hand had been conveniently strengthened by her accurate assessment of Pan-African opinion, the indirect effect of which was further illustrated at the futile meeting between Kenyan and Somali representatives held at Rome in August 1963 under British auspices. At these talks, which Britain convened under some criticism at home for her management of the issue and, apparently, in the hope of lessening tension in the N.F.D. itself and between Kenya and the Republic, the leader of the British delegation explained that his government judged their decision not to grant secession to be in accordance with the concensus of African opinion expressed in Addis Ababa. Consequently, proposals by the Somali government that, pending a final solution, the disputed area should be placed either under joint Somali-Kenyan, or United Nations administration, received scant attention and the talks broke down.

Thus the end of 1963 saw the Somali Republic cast in the rôle of the odd-man-out in African affairs, and Kenya launched into independence with, from the Somali point of view, the N.F.D. issue unresolved, or as some British officials seemed to assume, settled by default. Yet, despite this, hitherto the Republic had followed the general Afro-Asian pattern of non-alignment at the United Nations and in her dealings with the two world power blocs. Moreover, within the Pan-Africanist camp, she had generally found herself aligned with that group of African states which included Ethiopia notwithstanding the serious local difficulties of the two neighbouring states. Clearly vital though the Pan-Somali issue was to Somali national sentiments, it could not be allowed to override the Republic's other interests. Since independence these had prospered with generous grants of aid and capital loans from both East and West. Indeed, foreign aid has assumed such proportions by the middle of 1963 that it was possible to launch an ambitious Five Year Development Plan (1963–67) costing £70 million, of which almost half the capital was already available.

This success in attracting such substantial aid might be thought to have vindicated the government's policy of not allowing the Pan-Somali dispute to affect the Republic's general position as an uncommitted state closely associated with Ethiopia within the Afro-Asian camp. Opponents of the S.Y.L. government, however, did not see the matter in this light: and, some at least, were prepared to sacrifice their other interests to a much more definite course of action on the N.F.D. issue. The rupture of diplomatic relations with Britain, conducted in a most civilized manner, had by no means assuaged the deep wound to Somali pride caused by Britain's action. And popular indignation against Britain and her allies in the West found much to feed upon and brood over in the long history of Britain's past conduct of Somali affairs. Accused of not providing sufficiently strong leadership on the N.F.D. issue, and increasingly unpopular for its management of home affairs, the S.Y.L. government searched anxiously for some dramatic action which might restore its popularity and enhance its position before the coming elections.

In these conditions of Somali anger and despair it seemed at first most likely that the Chinese Peoples' Republic, which had already shown considerable interest in Somali affairs and which had no conflicting commitments in Ethiopia, would proffer support. The Prime Minister had already visited China, and also India, in the middle of the year, no doubt with these matters very much in mind, and trade and aid agreements had been signed with both countries. Thus it seemed likely that these negotiations would be followed up by some new and striking manifestation of Chinese help which, in the context of East-West relations, might restore the Mogadishu government's flagging prestige. Most unexpectedly, however, it was not from this quarter but from Russia, that Dr 'Abd ar-Rashid found the means by which he hoped to recapture popular support. In November 1963 it was officially announced that the Republic had refused an offer of Western military assistance valued at almost $£6\frac{1}{2}$ million in favour of Russian military aid to the tune of nearly $£11$ million.

To what extent this move represented a definite change of direction in Russian policy in the Somali dispute remained to be seen. Its local effects, however, were more immediately discernible. In the November municipal elections the government party won 665 of the available 904 seats (74 per cent), while its principal rival the Somali National Congress gained 105 seats. In the elections for the national assembly which followed on 30 March, 1964 – by which time the long train of border incidents with Ethiopia had erupted into open war and the Ogaden was in resurgence – the S.Y.L. position was again strongly maintained, though with a slightly reduced majority (S.Y.L., 69 seats; S.N.C., 22; S.D.U., 15; H.D.M.S., 9; others, 8). These results speak for themselves and show how effectively the League had recovered much of its wide popular support in circumstances which were bound to strengthen the government's position. At the same time, the manner in which the elections were conducted, and the extent to which opposition parties participated in them, reaffirmed the Republic's continuing commitment to the principles of parliamentary democracy. Thus in the conduct of its internal political life as much as in its external nationalist interests, the Somali Republic remained isolated from many of its neighbours.

The final phase of civilian government

The composition of the new government formed after the elections led to prolonged and bitter conflict within the Darold leadership of the S.Y.L. and this, inevitably, had wide repercussions. 'Abd ar-Razaq Husseyn, a politician of considerable personal charisma and courage, replaced 'Abd ar-Rashid as Prime Minister and energetically sought to institute a number of administrative reforms. In the National Assembly the government was severely harassed at every possible opportunity by the ousted premier and his faction. This covert sabotage was facilitated by the Assembly practice of normally voting by secret ballot, thus making it extremely difficult for 'Abd ar-Razaq to control his ill-disciplined party which, following defections from other parties, now held 105 seats.

At the cost of several cabinet reshuffles, 'Abd ar-Razaq and his supporters were able to survive until the Presidential elections of June 1967. President Adan Abdulle 'Isman, who was eligible for re-election, was supported by Premier 'Abd ar-Razaq to whom he was related by marriage. The main rival candidate was the ex-Premier, 'Abd ar-Rashid, who had formed an alliance with the Isaq politician and former leader of the S.N.C., Muhammad Haji Ibrahim Igal (now officially a member of the S.Y.L.). In the event, 'Abd ar-Rashid secured the Presidency and in July summoned his ally Muhammad Haji Ibrahim Igal to form a government. A British-trained northerner had thus assumed the reins of government, and allocated portfolios to ministers representing the main lineage blocs in the normal way. With the continued division of the Darod hegemony in the League, the fragile coalition of Dir, Isaq and Hawiye lost its point and the S.N.C. became virtually redundant as an anti-Darod party. Division along the north–south axis was also difficult to sustain under the joint rule of a southern President and northern Premier. There was thus a general tendency to revert to local lineage rivalry, the encompassing major lineage blocs dissolving, for the time being, into component fractions. This re-emergence of small group factionalism coincided with the growing disillusionment and frustration felt by many of the urban elite at the ineffectiveness of the Pan-Somali struggle.

Taking stock of the general situation on the wider Pan-Somali issue, the new Premier found little cause for comfort. The clandestinely supported Somali guerrilla campaign in Northern Kenya (known to the Kenyans as the *shifta* – i.e. bandits – war), which had developed in the region after Britain's failure to implement the findings of the 1962 Commission, was making little headway at great cost to the local civilian Somali population. In Jibuti matters were even worse. In the referendum, held two months before the Mogadishu presidential election and carefully orchestrated by the French authorities, the inhabitants of the Côte (or at least those permitted to vote there) had again endorsed the continuance of French control, rejecting outright independence. The 'Afars had now indeed seized the political initiative so long enjoyed by the Somalis and had turned the knife in the wound by changing the name of the Côte to the 'French Territory of the 'Afars and 'Ises'.[34] Nothing could more directly reflect the new political complexion in Jibuti.

With so little to show for the bold pursuit of the Somali cause favoured by his predecessors, Muhammad Haji Ibrahim Igal decided to see what might be achieved by more conciliatory diplomacy. Following encouraging exchanges with the Ethiopian delegation at the O.A.U. heads of state meeting at Kinshasa in September, Premier Igal met President Kenyatta at Arusha in Tanzania in October and both sides agreed to the immediate normalization of their relations, to the establishment of peace in the N.F.D. and to further negotiations through the good offices of President Kaunda in the search for a final settlement to the problem. In keeping with these developments, diplomatic relations with Britain (which had given military support to the Kenyans in the 'shifta war') were restored and steps taken to promote a less anti-Western image to balance the impression inevitably conveyed by the Somali Republic's increasing military dependence on the U.S.S.R.

Although Muhammad Haji Ibrahim Igal claimed that his new diplomacy did not make any concessions to Ethiopia or Kenya and indeed represented a new understanding of the Somali point of view, in Addis Ababa and Nairobi it was tempting to interpret the new Somali policy as a capitulation. This view naturally commended itself to the Somali Premier's opponents in Mogadishu, where demonstrators accused him of a 'sell-out'. With the financial resources at its disposal, the government was, however, able to survive these criticisms, securing a cautious balance of support sufficient to carry it into the campaign for the general election held in March 1969.

New electoral regulations were introduced to discourage one-man lineage parties and to encourage national parties. Each constituency was assigned an 'electoral quotient', determined by dividing the number of votes cast by the number of seats available. Only parties polling more votes than this target quotient could gain seats. There was tremendous national interest in the impending contest and political activity on a greater scale than ever before. Many prominent civil servants resigned their posts to stand as candidates. Large sums of money were spent in campaigning; figures of £15,000 being quoted in a number of cases (the national budget at this time was £15 million). The government rallied all its resources and the much respected police commander, General Muhammad Abshir, resigned from his post, refusing to agree that police transport should be employed to carry S.Y.L. voters to the polling stations. There was a great deal of confusion and in some districts riots occurred, resulting in the reported loss of some forty lives. Despite the new electoral provisions, a record number of 1,002 candidates, representing 62 parties, contested the 123 seats. The S.Y.L. won 73 seats, the emasculated S.N.C. 11 and the H.D.M.S. a mere three. The latter result indicated how the Digil and Rahanweyn tribesmen now evidently felt that their interests were better served through the wide national parties than by their own parochial party. As usual, as soon as the National Assembly opened, a large number of members crossed the floor of the house to join the government, hoping to share in the spoils of office. The unedifying stampede of deputies left 'Abd ar-Razaq Haji Husseyn sitting alone as the sole opposition member of the Assembly! In company with the majority of its peers, the Somali Republic had at last become a one-party state.

CHAPTER IX

THE SOMALI REVOLUTION: 1969–76

The military coup

THE ELECTIONS WHICH had brought the S.Y.L. to power with such overwhelming authority had left a bitter legacy of discontent. Although, at constituency level, rival lineage segments had hedged their bets by supporting several candidates under different party banners, many had not succeeded in returning a trusted representative to Mogadishu. Many of the unsuccessful candidates who had invested so heavily in the campaign were powerful, ambitious people and the conduct of the elections encouraged them to bring forward a large number of electoral petitions and complaints to the courts. The government's answer was provided by the Supreme Court which, contrary to previous decisions, now ruled that it was not empowered to judge such issues. This naturally increased the frustration felt by many of those who had not gained a seat in the Assembly. At the same time, although the S.Y.L. monopolized the Assembly, their very numbers greatly exacerbated the normal problems of party discipline. This encouraged Igal's government to rely even more heavily than its predecessors on the funds at its disposal[1]. Opponents and critics outside the Assembly were consequently able to complain even more bitterly of the corruption and nepotism which they considered now prevailed at all levels of government.

This sense of discontent and frustration was by no means limited only to members of the westernized elite. The democratic parliamentary process which had seemed to blend so well with traditional Somali political institutions and had begun with such verve and promise, had turned distinctly sour. The National Assembly was no longer the symbol of free speech and fair play for all citizens. It was now widely regarded cynically as a sordid market-place where, with little concern for the interests of those who had voted for them, deputies traded their votes for personal gain. Deputies were ferried about in sumptuous limousines, bearing the magic registration letters A.N. (*Assemblea Nazionale*) which the inveterate poor of the capital translated with grim humour as *anna nolahay*: 'I'm all right, Jack'. A story popular in Mogadishu epitomizing the gulf between rulers and ruled referred to an incident in which one man riding on another's back and making the motions of driving a vehicle was stopped by a puzzled guard at the entrance to Government Headquarters (*Governo*). 'What do you think you are doing?' challenged the guard. 'Oh', replied the man riding his human mount, 'I noticed that in order to get in here you had to be conducted by a chauffeur.' In the opinion of the more disillusioned critics, democracy had lapsed into commercialized anarchy and strong rule of a new type was urgently required if the country was to be rescued from the morass of poverty, insecurity and inefficiency into which it had sunk.[2] Premier Igal and President 'Abd ar-Rashid seemed supremely unconcerned by these danger signals and their only acknowledgement of them was to adopt a dangerously high-handed and authoritarian style of rule which added to their unpopularity. Rumours of military intervention were rife and, amongst the alienated young elite particularly, there was much discussion of potential candidates to provide the leadership which would be necessary to save the country from its present difficulties. One name canvassed, despite his known reluctance to act unconstitutionally, was that of the former police commander, General Muhammad Abshir.

In the event, the immediate precipitants of the *coup* were entirely unexpected. During the absence on a visit overseas of Prime Minister Igal, on 15 October, 1969, while visiting drought stricken regions in Las Anod District in the north of the Republic, President 'Abd ar-Rashid 'Ali Shirmarke was shot dead by one of his police guards. At this news, the Premier hastened back to Mogadishu to organize the election of a new President upon whom he could rely for support. The Premier's candidate was an old-campaigner and close associate, Haji Muse Boqor. When, at a late-night meeting on 20 October, the party caucus reached agreement to present this nominee as their official candidate, thus virtually ensuring his election as President and Muhammad Haji Ibrahim Igal's re-appointment as Premier, those army officers who had been closely watching developments decided to act.

In the early hours of 21 October the army occupied key points throughout the capital, members of the government and other leading politicians and personalities were placed in detention (or, as in the case of General Muhammad Abshir, under house arrest). The Constitution was suspended, the Supreme Court abolished, the National Assembly closed, political parties declared illegal, and rule by a Supreme Revolutionary Council established. The new regime's aims stressed the elimination of corruption and tribal nepotism and the re-establishment of a just and honourable society in which proper attention would be given to real economic and social betterment for all. In external affairs, existing treaties would be honoured and the Somali unification struggle continued, while further support would be given to liberation movements generally and to the fight against colonialism. In earnest of these intentions and hopes the state was renamed the 'Somali Democratic Republic'. The membership of the Supreme Revolutionary Council (S.R.C.) was announced on 1 November. As had been anticipated, its President turned out to be General Muhammad Siyad Barre (who had succeeded the late General Da'ud as army commander in 1965) assisted by twenty-four other officers from the rank of major-general to captain. Of the two original Vice-Presidents, one was General Jama' 'Ali Korshell, who had succeeded General Muhammad Abshir as police commander and whose presence signalized the acquiescence rather than active participation of the police force in the *coup* as a *fait accompli*. (General Korshell was discredited and arrested in April 1970.)

The presence of a number of maleable captains and the notable omission from the S.R.C. of several younger army colonels who had earlier agitated for a military *coup*, was widely interpreted as indicating General Siyad's determination to remain firmly in command of the new government, a view which later developments – as we shall see – were amply to confirm. Two weeks after seizing power, the S.R.C. announced the formation of the fourteen-member committee of 'Secretaries' with executive rather than ministerial powers, who would be responsible for day-to-day administration. Except for the police Vice-President, General

Jama' 'Ali Korshell, who was charged with responsibility for Internal Affairs, the other members of the Council of Secretaries were young civilian civil servants – technocrats chosen for their ability rather than with an eye to achieving an even representation of the country's traditional clan and lineage divisions. Assisted by its civilian secretaries, the S.R.C. at once embarked on an energetic revitalization of the country's government, economy and social services. The aim, enjoying wide popularity, was to clean out the Augean stables and to restore Somali virtues with a realistic and concerted onslaught on the people's real enemies: poverty, disease and ignorance.

To this end the civilian district and provincial governors were replaced by energetic young army and police officers; vigilant military personnel were posted to ministries to go through the accounts and scrutinize current transactions; embassy staff were recalled for retraining and, where this was judged necessary, replaced by military personnel. Politicians and officials suspected of irregularities were arrested and investigated, pending court proceedings. The new regional and district governors were appointed as 'chairmen' of local Revolutionary Councils which sought to galvanize productive activity. This pervasive emphasis on directing public resources purposefully towards the *real* development so urgently needed in Somalia was reflected in an expansion of the propaganda activities of the Ministry of Information, which was now also responsible for 'Public Guidance'. Immediate practical measures taken included harnessing the energies of some of the large population of unemployed, poverty-stricken urban tribal 'drop-outs', by giving them food and clothing to work in farms and on road construction and other public projects. Members of the public were invited to lodge complaints about the past mismanagement of the country and to make suggestions about future improvements. At the same time, to discourage the interminable blood feuds between lineages which had done so much to undermine national solidarity in the past, the death sentence was introduced to replace the blood compensation (*diya*) paid traditionally between groups.

Scientific Socialism in Somalia

This vigorous effort to correct the errors of the past and place the country's fortunes on a firm footing assumed a more specific ideological orientation on the first anniversary of the *coup* (October 1970), when General Siyad proclaimed that Somalia would henceforth be dedicated to Scientific Socialism. This choice of direction, already foreshadowed in the retrospective transformation of the *coup* into a Revolution (*Ka'an* in Somali) reflected the army's growing dependence on Russian equipment and advisers in contrast to the complementary connexion of the police force with America and the West. It was also natural that the idealistic young intellectuals associated with the new regime should look to the Soviet bloc for inspiration, since the previous civilian governments had on the whole inclined towards the West (despite, or perhaps because of, the Russian military aid agreement of 1963). Scientific Socialism (in Somali literally, 'wealth-sharing based on wisdom' – *hanti-wadaagga 'ilmi ku dhisan*),[3] was now the cornerstone of official policy and closely linked with the ideals of unity or 'togetherness' (*waddajir*), 'self-reliance' (*is ku kalsoonaan*) and 'self-help' (*iskaa wah u qabso*).[4] The announcement of the advent of Scientific Socialism was coupled with a vehement denunciation of tribalism, which as the official slogan succinctly stated 'divides [where] Socialism unites'. The former government-stipended local lineage headmen (*akils*) were replaced by elders with the appealing title of 'peace-seekers' (*nabad-doon*), or at any rate this new designation was officially adopted. The abolition of payment of blood money was likewise confirmed, and those prone to engage in this or other tribalistic actions connected with the traditional lineage and clan organization warned that they risked swingeing fines and prison sentences. As a positive measure against urban tribalism, the government undertook to provide funeral expenses for those who died in towns without relatives available to help them perform these services.

The national campaign (*olol*) or 'crash programme' (*parnaamaaj*) against tribalism culminated in demonstrations later in the year and early in 1971 when effigies representing 'tribalism, corruption, nepotism and misrule' were symbolically burnt or buried in the Republic's main centres. The circumlocutary use of the term 'ex' (ex-clan) tolerated by previous civilian regimes (see above p. 168) was completely outlawed, and the word comrade (*jaalle*: friend, chum) launched into general currency with official blessing to replace the traditional, polite term of address 'cousin' (*ina'adeer*), which was now considered undesirable because of its tribalistic, kinship connotations. Earlier Somali nationalists, both religious and secular, had appealed to the transcendent *brotherhood* of Somalis, uniting those of different clan and lineage. The new stress on *friendship* appealed for co-operation and unity on the basis of an undifferentiated, nationalistic Somali identity, in which traditional divisions were totally annulled.

The development of this official ideology and of other reinforcing divisions became increasingly important to General Siyad's regime as the public enthusiasm which had greeted the *coup* initially gradually diminished. A national cult, owing something to Chinese, North Korean and Nasserite as well as Soviet influences, was gradually created round the Head of State. The new official hagiography presented General Siyad as the 'Victorious Leader' (*Guulwaadde*), dauntlessly leading the nation in its unremiting struggle against its foes. Posters, poems, songs of praise and panegyric speeches soon monotonously proclaimed throughout the country the sublime calling of the heroic 'Father' of the nation, whose 'Mother' was the Revolution. Inspired by Scientific Socialism, this mystical union was depicted as the source of prosperity and success in the nation's struggle forward. Amongst its more precious progeny were the 'Flowers of the Revolution' (as they are officially designated – destitute children, often orphans, who had been gathered from the streets of Mogadishu and other towns into Revolutionary Youth Centres, where they received food, clothes, education and training in the tasks of nation-building). These new recruits to the nation symbolized the ideal new citizen whose dedication to his country was pure and un-tarnished by atavistic kinship allegiances.

Such pithy exhortations as 'less talk and more work' (*haddal yar iyo hawlweyn*), culled from the General's numerous public harangues, figured prominently in the national daily paper (*October Star*) and were collected together in a little blue-and-white (the national colours) pocket manual, which was widely distributed and proudly displayed by zealous officials. Similar prominence was given to the Head of State's sayings in the daily programmes of Radio Somali. In the same vein, the General's public appearances were scenes of carefully orchestrated jubilation where he was greeted with applause and adulation, feted and saluted by his devoted subjects, who often danced before him to Korean choreography. This leadership cult, so alien to the egalitarianism of traditional Somali nomadic culture, contrasted sharply with the disarming humility and man-to-man directness which the Head of State was careful to display in his face-to-face encounters with his comrades and foreign visitors.

The pomp and ceremony surrounding the Head of State's public appearances also served to highlight his own modest private lifestyle and his much publicized edifying concern for the poor and underprivileged. Thus, despite his exaltation as 'Beneficent Leader' (*buono condottorre*, the legend on an official poster), General Siyad managed to retain his popular image as a man of the people.

State control

The employment of this Maoist cult to focus the vital energies of the masses was supplemented by a growing plethora of other agencies of thought control. The Political Office of the President was expanded into a national organization of *apparatcics* staffing 'orientation centres' (*hanuunin*) which were set up in all permanent settlements of any size throughout the country. Members of the public were expected to assemble in these centres on public holidays to study the aims and methods of the Revolution within walls decorated with pictures of the new holy trinity: *jaalle* Markis (Marx), *jaalle* Lenin and *jaalle* Siyad. In their efforts to instill and maintain revolutionary fervour at the local level, presidency officials were aided by members of the people's vigilantes (the *guulwaaddayaal*), or 'Victory Pioneers', an organization established in the summer of 1972 and recruited largely amongst the unemployed. With their bright green unisex uniforms and Orwellian-eye, symbolizing vigilance, these civilian guards were expected to play a leading role in organizing local support (in kind or cash) for development and 'crash programmes'. Women's branches were entrusted with community and family welfare work.

In the capital, Mogadishu, a national top-level orientation centre for the higher public service cadres was established in the former military academy, which was renamed 'Halane' after a young Somali lieutenant who had died while attempting to save his country's colours in the brief outbreak of fighting with Ethiopia in 1964. Intensive in-service training courses there were run in collaboration with staff from the Somali Institute for Development Administration. These positive organs for shaping and sustaining patriotism at the appropriate pitch were reinforced by other agencies which checked deviations from official policy. Prominent amongst these were the National Security Service (N.S.S.) and the National Security Courts which jointly dealt with a wide range of 'political' offences including nepotism and tribalism, as already indicated, as well as with such charges as 'lack of revolutionary zeal' and treason. Members of the National Security Service, under a Sandhurst and K.G.B.-trained commander, enjoyed arbitrary powers of arrest, sometimes following the denunciation of a suspect by his personal enemies. Members of the public services were kept under surveillance and N.S.S. reports played an important part in promotion and demotion.

In monitoring and seeking to control public opinion, considerable use was also made of *agents provocateurs*. Rights of assembly were limited, and persons wishing to visit the homes of foreign nationals or attend foreign embassy parties required to possess official permits. Otherwise, unless they were sufficiently powerful to enjoy immunity from these petty controls, those who fraternized with foreigners were liable to be held for questioning by the N.S.S. These restrictions were justified by reference to the pervading atmosphere of gossip and intrigue which in the uninhibited days of civilian government, so it was argued, facilitated the subversive activities of foreign governments hostile to Somalia. Rumour-mongers (*Afminshar*) were indeed probably the most frequently denounced of all anti-government influences, and spreading malicious gossip against the regime was a charge incurring serious penalties. Although few political prisoners were brutally tortured or died in custody, this oppressive climate was particularly distasteful to the westernized elite and to many of those who had played a prominent part in political life during the previous civilian regimes. Many of the more outspoken who were able to do so fled the country, seeking employment overseas – notably in Arabia, the Gulf States and in Kenya. There was thus a marked 'brain drain' which substantially depleted Somalia's manpower resources, particularly in those fields where there was most need of talent. While some of those who remained faithfully behind pursued successful careers in government service or in business, others were frequently imprisoned and harassed by agents of the security service.

The N.S.S. had become the main agency supplying defendants for trial in the National Security Courts which were presided over by military officers, often with little or no legal training. These courts handed out rough justice, the accused enjoying few of the rights normally accorded in properly constituted courts of law. Sentences tended to be strict and appeals for clemency to the Head of State were apt to receive a cool reception.

While ordinary criminals found guilty of murder were regularly executed by firing squad, there were also several public executions of persons accused of plotting against the state. The most widely publicized occurred in July 1972 when two generals (one a Vice-President) were executed on the charge of attempting to overthrow General Siyad's regime. This response to internal disagreement within the S.R.C. made it indisputably clear that General Siyad's word was law and brooked no defiance or disagreement. If this uncompromising sentence administered a sharp jolt to national feeling, the public execution of ten local religious sheikhs in January 1975 had wider and more serious repercussions, touching a deeper nerve. With twenty-three others who received long prison sentences, the ten executed religious figures were charged with preaching in the mosques against a liberal new law which, contrary to traditional Islam, gave women the same inheritance rights as men. By this action, taken in International Women's Year, the government demonstrated its secular, reformist intentions – but at the cost of raising in an acute form the whole question of the Islamic identity of the Somali people. This is an issue to which we shall return shortly in a more considered discussion of the compatability of Islam and Scientific Socialism.

While the President regularly exhorted his local representatives to act as channels of communication faithfully relaying the ideas and aspirations of his subjects to him, this pervasive apparatus of state control was hardly conducive to an effective dialogue between rulers and ruled. These transactions were thus, inevitably, somewhat one-sided. Policy did change from time to time (and indeed in 1977 dramatically), partly in response to public opinion, but its course was sufficiently erratic to make it difficult for members of the public to be certain at a particular time of the precise boundaries of acceptable opinion. Reticence was clearly the safest policy, and people naturally told those in authority what they thought they wanted to hear.

All this contributed to the seemingly arbitrary nature of the authority exercised by the Supreme Revolutionary Council. Despite its elaborate and heavy-handed character, however, this essentially autocratic pattern of government still touched the nomadic majority of the population relatively lightly. The nomads, indeed, remained as a refractory challenge despite energetic measures designed to bring them more securely into the fold. In 1974, the eight provinces into which the state had previously been divided were reconstituted as fifteen new regions, comprising seventy-eight districts, where necessary renamed to exclude tribal (or clan) names. Emphasis was placed on the settlement (*digmo*) as the basic unit of association and identification in a further effort to extirpate lingering lineage loyalties. And even among the nomads efforts were made to encourage people to regard the orientation centre at a regularly frequented water point as the hub of social and political activities. Marriages, which had traditionally involved rival (and often potentially hostile) lineages, were now to be conducted at a local orientation centre, with its resident community replacing the kin of bride and groom. It would be unrealistic to expect these measures to have made much immediate impact amongst the nomads. There was thus, inevitably, a considerable gap between theory and practice in the political life of the nomadic majority of the population.

Management of the economy

The same might be said with equal force of the application of Scientific Socialism in the management of the state's economy. The nomads with their privately-owned herds of camels, cattle and flocks of sheep and goats remained obdurate exponents of private enterprise, selling surplus livestock to Somali and Arab-owned exporting firms, buying for the Arab and Persian Gulf market. Not all the off-take from the pastoral economy was distributed through private enterprise. A significant proportion found its way to the Russian built state-owned meat canning factory at Kismayu (where there is an American-built port). The marketing and export of skins was controlled nationally through a government agency. The other mainstay of the export economy, the banana crop, was produced largely on privately-owned plantations, some belonging to Arabs and Italians, in the riverine regions of southern Somalia but exported exclusively through a national marketing agency which allocates producers' 'quotas'. All grain produced, again mainly in the better-watered south, from privately-owned and usually very small farms was likewise purchased by the Agricultural Development Corporation and sold at controlled prices through retailers, or distributed through orientation centres. Each farmer was allowed to retain a proportion of his crop for domestic consumption. Regional storage facilities were provided by the government which, through this system of state-controlled marketing, endeavoured to cut out self-seeking middlemen. Partly in order to attract government finance, some farming enterprises formed themselves into agricultural co-operatives or collectives – of which one of the most successful was the traditionally-based religious commune of El Birdale⁵ in the north-west of the Republic. As has been indicated, there were of course also state farms, some employing prison labour, and the state-owned sugar production complex at Jowhar on the Shebelle River. Prior to the unforeseen demands made on resources by the catastrophic 1975 drought, the 1974–8 Five Year Development Plan allocated 30 per cent (£200 million) of the total budget to further agricultural development. Special consideration was to be given to resuscitate moribund state farms and the formation of further co-operative and crash programme farm settlements to absorb unemployed townsmen and surplus population from the nomadic sector of the economy (a matter of critical urgency following the 1975 drought).

While a number of small private companies existed in towns, some in the form of 'co-operatives', the few large industrial concerns (usually the products of foreign aid) were state run (e.g.

the Chinese-built match factory). And in October 1975 the import and distribution of most foreign manufactured goods was nationalized, resulting in periodic shortages. There were still, however, a number of successful entrepreneurs operating large-scale and highly profitable businesses. Taken as a whole, the economy thus remained in practice mixed, although the element of state control had certainly increased appreciably since the introduction of Scientific Socialism.

Socialism and development

It was, however, on its extended national 'crash programmes' that the S.R.C. relied for the most direct implementation of its revolutionary ideals. Amongst the most impressive and ambitious of these were the urban and rural mass literacy campaigns of 1973 and 1975. In 1972 General Siyad's government took the bold and sensible decision of adopting the roman alphabet as the official script for the national language, Somali. The question of whether to choose this script, with its secular implications, or the less suitable Arabic alphabet, favoured by many pro-Arab Somalis, had always proved too delicate for previous governments to resolve effectively. Once the decision had been taken it proved popular, and there is little doubt that the urban literacy campaign of 1973 was highly successful.[6] Officials were sent on crash courses with the inducement that, if they failed their literacy exams, they might lose their jobs. Adult literacy classes, which lacked this sanction, drew large and enthusiastic attendances from the most educationally deprived sections of the urban population.

Following this 'Cultural Revolution' as it was somewhat grandiloquently if characteristically hailed by the Minister of Information and National Guidance, General Isma'il 'Ali Abokor, the aim in 1974 was to extend 'instant literacy' to the nomads. In July 1974, at an estimated cost of £10 million, a huge taskforce of some 30,000 secondary school students and teachers was dispatched into the interior in triumphant truckloads. In parties of eight, with a teacher as leader and with the participation of veterinary and medical personnel, these young pioneers of the new Somalia set forth to teach the nomads to write their own language, hygiene, modern animal husbandry methods, basic civics and the aims of Scientific Socialism. Equipped with blankets, a folding blackboard, and water-bottle, and drawing a daily allowance of two Somali shillings (approximately 15 English new pence), these privileged urban students were to share the fruits of the Revolution with their neglected nomadic comrades, staying as guests with nomadic family groups and teaching their hosts to read and write. The guiding slogan, supplied by the President, was the same as that for the earlier urban mass literacy campaign: 'If you know teach; if you don't learn'. As General Siyad explained in a speech on Women's International Day on 8 March, 1974; 'The Key . . . is to give everybody the opportunity to learn reading and writing. . . . It is imperative that we give our people modern revolutionary education . . . to restructure their social existence. . . . It will be the weapon to eradicate social balkanization and fragmentation into tribes and sects. It will bring about an absolute unity and there will be no room for any negative foreign cultural influences.' The closely linked goals of modernization, nationalism and independence are here all combined; a modern, integrated nation consisting of those who not only 'speak the same language'[7] but who also read and write it.

However carefully planned, this extraordinarily ambitious project was bound to encounter problems in its execution. The unpredictability of nomadic movements and the exigencies of the nomadic life did not make for easily accessible, unencumbered students, even when watering fees were waived at government wells to attract potential pupils. On the other hand some of the young teachers, whose urban upbringing had precluded experience of the nomadic life, found the rigours of the bush far from appealing. In this 'outward-bound' project, therefore, if those nomads who participated in lessons showed that they could quickly master the new script, their teachers often learnt as much as they taught. How the project would have ended if it had been allowed to reach completion as planned remains a matter for conjecture. In the event, the 'Rural Prosperity Campaign' had to be hurriedly renamed the 'Rural Development Campaign' when it was discovered that it had coincided with one of the worst droughts in Somali history.[8] Unlike the government in Addis Ababa during the earlier Ethiopian famine, the Somali government, much to its credit, did not attempt to conceal the extent of the disaster and mobilized all its resources to save the lives of as many as possible of the drought-stricken nomads. A state of emergency was declared, a 'holy-war' proclaimed against the famine, and vigorous appeals made to the international community for famine relief supplies and medical aid. In the worst affected northern and north-eastern regions, the students were quickly marshalled into organizing famine relief camps to accommodate as many as 200,000 destitute nomads at the height of the drought.

If the drought thus transformed the rural development campaign into a massive famine relief operation, its original aims were recovered by converting the famine relief camps into orientation centres. This, of course, was necessarily only a temporary expedient. Many of the nomads in the camps had lost all or most of their livestock, and their future livelihood posed an acutely challenging problem. Here again, however, advantage could be taken of adversity. The government was quick to seize the opportunity of furthering two of its long-term policies: the sedentarization of nomads and detribalization. While a restocking scheme was also inaugurated, most of those in the relief camps were re-established either in newly expanded collectives and state farms along the Shebelle and Juba Rivers in the south, or in coastal fishing communities to supply the Russian-aided fish-canning industry. Although the Somali government had hoped the costs of this vast re-settlement would be met from Arab funds, in the event it was organized by the Russians who provided air and road transport on a massive scale. This sudden re-location of Somali population, involving up-rooting people from their traditional grazing areas and re-settling them amongst unrelated clans and lineages, where they were to change from nomadic herdsmen to sedentary cultivators or fishermen (both occupations traditionally despised by the nomads), was a bold and hazardous undertaking.

While the mixed cultivating population between the Shebelle and Juba Rivers contained many people of northern nomadic origin,[9] such a large and rapid transformation, as General Siyad's speeches at the time acknowledged, risked refuelling traditional clan and tribal rivalries. And, if no major incident occurred, it was difficult to forecast how many of the re-settled nomads would remain in their new locations once good rains restored their traditional grazing areas and enabled them to rebuild their depleted herds and flocks.

This national catastrophe, which was thus quite effectively contained and even taken advantage of, prompted a major reorganization of the government in December 1974. This in turn helped to prepare for the eventual introduction in July 1976 of the much heralded political party, the Somali Socialist Revolutionary Party, and the official replacement of military by civilian rule, a development for which the Russians had long been pressing.

Socialism and traditional constraints: Islam and tribalism

We must now attempt a deeper assessment of the true extent of the transformation achieved by Scientific Socialism of the most pervasive traditional forces; Islam and the clan (or lineage) system. Although there were said to be a few atheists amongst the young Somali Marxist elite, General Siyad repeatedly insisted that his government's commitment to Scientific Socialism was fully compatible with Islam and indeed, as he pointed out with some justice, expressed the essential communal spirit of Islam. As he declared in a speech a few months after seizing power: 'Our Islamic faith teaches us that its inherent values are perennial and continually evolving as people progress. These basic tenets of our religion cannot be interpreted in a static sense, but rather as a dynamic source of inspiration for continuous advancement. . . . To help our brethren and our fellows, we must go beyond the concept of charity and reach the higher and more altruistic concept of co-operation on a national scale. We must strive with enthusiasm and patriotism to attain the highest possible rate of general welfare for all.' Moreover, as General Siyad explained in a speech in 1972, evidently aimed at young secular radicals, 'The founders of Scientific Socialism were not against religion in particular but they exposed and disproved the reactionary elements of religion that dominate [the] sound reasoning of mankind and hence hinder [the] progress of society.'

There was no question, therefore, of the death of God here – whatever conservative Islamic critics inside Somalia or outside it claimed. As President Siyad declared in another speech in 1972:

'As far as socialism is concerned, it is not a heavenly message like Islam but a mere system for regulating the relations between man and his utilization of the means of production in this world. If we decide to regulate our national wealth, it is not against the essence of Islam. God has created man and has given him the faculty of mind to choose between good and bad, between virtue and vice. We have chosen social justice instead of exploitation of man by man and this is how we can practically help the individual Muslim and direct him to [a] virtuous life. However, the reactionaries wanted to create a rift between socialism and Islam because socialism is not to their interest.' In this eclectic fashion the Siyad regime staunchly defended its blend of socialism *and* Islam against conservative criticism of such reformist measures as the introduction of sexual equality in inheritance rights. In effect, in an old and venerable Islamic tradition, the Head of State claimed to understand the Prophet's message better than his critics. The state media, and particularly the radio, developed a subtle synthesis of Islam and Somali socialism, in which Quranic texts and commentaries led naturally to socialist ideals and to their pithy formulation in the Head of State's much-quoted slogans. If a deep tension still existed, and if external as well as internal reservations about the orthodoxy of Siyad's Islam persisted, it was at least a much less implausible interpretation than that implied in Colonel Gadafy's remarkable Libyan confection of Islam and socialism. With the obvious economic advantages and manoeuvreability vis-a-vis the Russians conferred by official membership of the Islamic world, Somalia's formal entry into the Arab League in 1974 did not thus seem surprising or out of character. It did, however, make the Somali government's internal policies and external alignments much more directly susceptible to the powerful scrutiny of the conservative Arab states.

What then of the tension with traditional tribal allegiances? Banned, as we have seen, shortly after the *coup*, officially buried (perhaps with rituals devised by a Soviet ethnographer?), and resurrected from time to time in the President's ominous public warnings, Somali tribalism is plainly a perversely persistent force. Although it was an indictable offence to say so publicly, it was still in terms of the principle of clan representativeness that the S.R.C. was regarded prior to its formal dissolution in 1975 by the majority of Somalis. As the following table shows, the S.R.C. was in its mixed lineage composition in the same tradition as its predecessor civilian cabinets.

Composition of Somali governments*
by major lineage blocs, 1960–75

	1960[a]	1966[b]	1967[c]	1969[d]	1975[e]
Darod	6	6	6	6	10
Hawiye	4	3	4	5	4
Digil and Rahanweyn	2	3	3	2	0
Dir	0	1	1	0	2
Isaq	2	3	4	5	4
	14	16	18	18	20

* Cabinet Ministers only are included here and, after 1969, members of the Supreme Revolutionary Council. The Somali nation as a whole comprises the five major lineage blocs (or 'clan families' as I have called them in previous publications: see Lewis, 1961), whose representation in successive Somali governments is shown in the table.

a. The first administration of Somalia formed after independence in 1960, headed by Premier 'Abd ar-Rashid 'Ali-Shirmarke (Darod). The President and non-executive Head of State was Adan 'Abdulle Isman (Hawiye).

b. Government formed under the leadership of 'Abd ar-Razaq Haji Husseyn (Darod), Adan 'Abdulle Isman remaining President of the Republic.

c. Government formed by Muhammad Haji Ibrahim Igal (Isaq) from the northern (ex-British) regions of the Republic. Dr 'Abd ar-Rashid 'Ali Shirmarke (Darod) had now become President.

d. Second government formed by Muhammad Haji Ibrahim Igal following March 1969 elections, Dr 'Abd ar-Rashid 'Ali Shirmarke remaining President.

e. Supreme Revolutionary Council, as of 1975, following various changes in composition since the military *coup* of October 1969. The Council was officially dissolved in July 1976 with the formation of the Somali Socialist Revolutionary Party. This had a Central Committee of 73 members and a politburo of five (including the three S.R.C. Vice-Presidents and the head of the National Security Service), presided over by the Head of State and Party Secretary General, General Muhammad Siyad Barre.

Within this typical spread of lineage representation, three groups in particular were widely considered to exercise especial prominence. This was reflected in the clandestine code-name

'M.O.D.' given to the regime. M stood for the patrilineage of the President, O for that of his mother, and D for that of his principal son-in-law, head of the National Security Service. The President's own lineage live along the upper reaches of the Juba River near the Ethiopian and Kenyan frontiers. His mother's clan, the Ogaden, occupy the neighbouring and critically sensitive region of that name (Ogaden) in Ethiopia. The President's son-in-law's clan are also of key importance, for they traditionally herd their stock on both sides of the boundary separating the former British and Italian Somalilands and so constitute the bridge linking these two territorial segments of the Somali state. Just as the President sought to modulate the level of Somali nationalism in the Ogaden through his vital maternal links there, and thus control his external relations with Ethiopia, so through this son-in-law's clan he sought to contain friction between the northern and southern parts of the Republic and their respective Anglophone and Italophone colonial traditions. The M.O.D. constellation was thus an apt formula for ruling Somalia, providing the President with a power base which offered external as well as internal security. Its limitations, as we shall see, were intrinsic to the reciprocal character of these relationships which, if they assured the President of faithful support, did so at the price of making him particularly sensitive to the partisan interests of those involved. This added a direct personal flavour to the President's repeated vitriolic attacks on 'tribalism' as an intolerable abomination. As he declared in a menacing address to regional judges: 'Tribalism and nationalism cannot go hand in hand. . . . It is unfortunate that our nation is rather too clannish; if all Somalis are to go to Hell, tribalism will be their vehicle to reach there'. 'Speak for yourself', some of his listeners must have muttered under their breaths.

Although no-one could utter the secret symbol of General Siyad's power openly, the M.O.D. basis of his rule was public knowledge and discussed and criticized in private. With their usual verbal facility, ingenious Somali sophists developed an alternative circumlocution, substituting dates, starting from that of the Glorious Revolution, to represent the major power-holding groups. In this idiom 21 October was used as a synonym for M, 22 October for O and 23 October for D. This new code had the additional advantage of being sufficiently elastic to embrace a wider range of groups and, if necessary, to register changes in their relative power and ranking. The formation of the Somali Socialist Revolutionary Party in June 1976, with its large Supreme Council, composed of seventy-three members, provided a widely representative setting for the M.O.D. power cell.

The Central Committee, presided over by President Siyad as Secretary General of the Party and as Chairman of the Council of Ministers, included all the members of the former S.R.C. with the addition of nineteen others – mainly, but not exclusively, military personnel. Each new member was responsible for a particular area of government. At the same time separate government ministers were also appointed to act in co-ordination with the Political Bureau. Finally the vital Political Bureau consisted, as might have been expected, of the President (no longer styled 'General') and the three Vice-Presidents, Generals Husseyn Kulmiye, Muhammad 'Ali Samatar (army commander), Isma'il 'Ali Abokor (Assistant Secretary General of the Party); and the N.S.S. head, General Ahmad Sulayman 'Abdulle. If this extraordinarily complex apparatus, far more elaborate than any previous civilian administration, included any members capable of seriously challenging the authority of the President it was certainly by accident, and they were well advised to maintain a low profile. Although the number of people and range of interest groups implicitly represented in official policy-making was greatly enlarged, it was clear that the President had every intention of retaining as complete control as ever.

There was no question of his seeking to abandon or seriously modify his own special version of benign, despotic paternalism. What the new structure sought to do was to endow the President's authority with greater legitimacy. Two years after its foundation, the official Party could boast no more than 20,000 members, a figure which hardly suggested massive popular support in the country at large.

Socialism and Siyadism

It would be over-simplistic to characterize this period of Siyad's rule as a phase in which a superstructure of Marxist rhetoric concealed an infrastructure built upon enduring clan and lineage loyalties. The factions vying for influence were not solely based on kinship ties. Doctrinal and ideological differences, Marxist and Islamic, were also significant, as well as competition between exponents of the two rival colonial traditions – the Italian and British. The Head of State treated criticism on these fronts as seriously as on any other, stoutly maintaining that Scientific Socialism was a system of universal applicability, pragmatically adaptable to all conditions – Islamic as well as non-Islamic. As he contemptuously observed in a speech at the Halane National Orientation Centre in 1972, narrow-minded orthodox Marxists missed the point when they said 'that Comrade V. I. Lenin confiscated such and such property after the Great October Revolution, or in [the] 1940s Comrade Mao Tse-Tung did this and that in his country against the reactionary forces. These people are totally ignoring the historical context of the teachings of the great socialist thinkers. They recite quotations from the founders of scientific socialism out of their proper context'. In a different setting the same point was made in much the same spirit by a young Somali Marxist intellectual who concluded a heated private debate with a well-known French Marxist anthropologist with the dismissive declaration: 'I don't need Marx; Marx needs me!'

Nevertheless, if the ideology of class struggle was scarcely very appropriate to local conditions, 'class' could easily be replaced by 'tribe' and the Marxist dialectic blended readily with military jingoism. Waging ceaseless wars against his country's enemies – poverty, disease, ignorance – and launching national campaign after campaign, Siyad was presented as the omnipotent leader in the relentless struggle forward to progress and victory. In such an atmosphere of *Sturm und Drang* there are traditional precedents for Siyad's style of leadership. In the past, however, personal authority of this kind and scale had usually only been successfully wielded by national religious heroes, waging the holy war (*jihad*) against the infidel. The two outstanding examples of this proud tradition in the Somali national consciousness were the famous Islamic champion, Ahmad Gran (1506–43) who conquered and briefly ruled the Christian Ethiopian heartland in the sixteenth century, and the fiery twentieth-century Dervish hero, Sayyid Muhammad 'Abdille Hassan (1864–1920).[10] While the latter was related to President Siyad both maternally and by marriage, the former some Somalis suppose to have been a patrilineal ancestor of the Head of State.

This is the formidable endorsement which President Siyad sought to capture and exploit as he presented himself as the perennial crusader in the endless battle against the nation's foes. The lay and the religious were thus conjoined in a fertile union as the President proclaimed himself the divinely guided saviour of his people. No wonder some Somalis were heard to mutter, under their breaths, that Somali socialism was a religion.

Life in Somalia in the period under review was indeed a battle and one in which every victory was hailed as the achievement of the Great Leader. This atmosphere of perpetual strife was confirmed by such natural calamities as the 1975 famine and by repeated government discoveries of internal 'traitors' and subverters of the Revolution. As the President's speeches incessantly warned, and as the arbitrary arrests and unpredictable rehabilitations of political prisoners confirmed, the state was constantly menaced by internal as well as external adversaries dedicated to the overthrow of Scientific Socialism. Socialism, as the President declared in one of many harangues to the nation,[11] cannot exist without opposition which must be overcome by a ceaseless struggle towards victory. In this dialectical conflict it was President Siyad who identified the enemy and kept the battle tally. Although Lenin, Mao Tse-Tung and the peripatetic Kim Il Sung (to say nothing of Mussolini) all had some influence on the homespun philosophy of development and power constructed by the Siyad regime,[12] local political realities suggest that 'Scientific Siyadism' might be an appropriate description of the Somali experience at this time. Certainly socialism was here a means rather than an end.

CHAPTER X

NATIONALISM, ETHNICITY AND REVOLUTION IN THE HORN OF AFRICA

Somalia's new prominence in international affairs

THE FIRST PHASE of General Siyad's military rule (roughly up to 1974) may be characterized as a period of concentration on internal problems, namely, local development and the consolidation of the regime's authority. The dramatic progress which had been achieved on these fronts encouraged in the second phase of Siyad's government a more extrovert policy with a greater involvement in external affairs – both locally and internationally. Tentative steps had already been made in this direction on a number of occasions, as for instance in 1972 when Somalia successfully mediated in the confrontation between Uganda and Tanzania. But this forward external policy assumed much greater prominence in 1974 when, having joined the Arab League as the only non-Arabic-speaking member state, Somalia also acted as host for the Organization of African Unity. Although the elaborate arrangements involved in providing the necessary facilities (including security) for the official delegations and numerous guests and news reporters posed a serious challenge to local resources in Mogadishu, the country rose to the occasion which proved to be a considerable success. No expense was spared to take this opportunity of promoting the image of Somalia in African, Arab and international eyes as a proudly independent progressive socialist state, with an impressive record of achievements to boast. The O.A.U. meeting was held in June in the sumptuous new People's Palace in Mogadishu, constructed at great cost, and a fleet of Mercedes Benz limousines was acquired for the use of the visiting Heads of State. Although there were naturally those who criticized such extravagant hospitality as a ridiculous waste of scarce resources, many ordinary people were proud of their country's newly found importance. As one young official pointed out, Gross National Pride was sometimes more significant than Gross National Product!

In seeking a more prominent and forceful role in African affairs, the regime stressed how well placed geographically Somalia was to act as a natural mediator between the Islamic world and sub-Saharan Africa. Since the Sudan had previously presented itself in this light, Somalia's bid for the same position brought a new component of rivalry to the hitherto generally close relationship between the two states. Collaborating with Cuba in the training of guerrilla forces for the African Liberation movements, and as O.A.U. Chairman, General Siyad was particularly well placed to participate in the delicate pre-independence negotiations between the Portuguese government and the liberation organizations in Angola and Mozambique. This was in line with the Somali government's general stance of actively supporting independence movements in the struggle against colonialism and imperialism. The all-pervasive African rhetoric on these issues, to which previous civilian governments had paid little attention, and even rather despised, was now given wide local currency on the radio and in the government press, as well as in rather crudely designed posters and slogans. It was also imported into local folkloric theatrical productions where the anti-imperialist struggle became an officially favoured, if unsubtly executed, theme. All this was another index of Somalia's growing involvement in, and commitment to, African issues. As the regime saw it, the masses were at last coming to realize the burning importance of the struggle against the sinister forces of colonialism and neo-colonialism.

It was in this wider African context that General Siyad's regime now turned again to consider the perennial issue of Pan-Somali nationalism. Since their assumption of power in 1969, the military had, of course, frequently acknowledged their abiding commitment to the liberation of those parts of the Somali nation which still languished under foreign rule – the French Territory of the 'Afars and Issas (Jibuti); the Ogaden (Ethiopia); and the north-eastern region of Kenya. But they had hitherto shown a moderation all the more remarkable in a military government in pursuing this aim. The opportunity which the O.A.U. chairmanship provided, and the constraints it imposed, suggested that if this nationalist issue were now to be vigorously revived, the anachronistic persistence of French rule in Jibuti should be the first target. The uncertainty and confusion that began to spread through Ethiopia in 1974 as the ageing Emperor increasingly lost control and was finally overthrown on 12 September by the armed forces, inevitably greatly encouraged Somali hopes of achieving autonomy for the Ogaden. Exciting though this prospect was, for the time being it was considered prudent to watch and wait to see what would happen in Ethiopia while concentrating primarily on Jibuti. This policy, as we shall see, did not exclude making a more encouraging, if still guarded, response to a variety of dissident refugees from Ethiopia, including Ogaden Somalis.

The end of French rule in Jibuti

In Jibuti itself, the elections held in November 1974 proclaimed the strength of 'Afar dominance in the local chamber of deputies where, under the defiant slogan *Union et Progrès dans L'Ensemble français*, 'Ali 'Ariif's 'Afar party won all the seats. The Somali opposition was represented officially by the *Ligue populaire Africaine pour l'Independence* (L.P.A.I.) while the more militant, outlawed *Front de la Côte des Somalis* (F.L.C.S.), with headquarters in Mogadishu, remained underground. This organization made its presence felt by kidnapping the French Ambassador to Somalia in May 1975. His safe release, achieved with the aid of the Mogadishu government, led to some brief improvement in Franco–Somali relations. Certainly Jibuti was receiving an increased amount of attention and publicity. In December, following a meeting between 'Ali 'Ariif and President Giscard d'Estaing, it was announced that the territory would be granted independence, with France retaining a local military base. Predictably, this arrangement was denounced by the pro-independence L.P.A.I. and did little to satisfy those (not all now only Somalis) who were pressing for independence.

The political situation in the Territory was rapidly becoming bewilderingly complex. Although a number of violent clashes between 'Afar and 'Ise tribesmen had occurred earlier in the year, the 'Afar – essentially a loose congeries of groups – were now themselves riven by powerful divisions. 'Ali 'Ariif was losing support in his own community, and the 'Afar as a whole had been thrown into turmoil by the bitter conflict which had recently flared up between the 'Afar leader Sultan 'Ali Mirreh at Asaita in Ethiopia and the new military regime in Addis Ababa. To understand the significance of this development it needs to be appreciated that, for many years, the 'Afar had had in effect two heads: their modern political party leaders in Jibuti; and their more traditional spokesman, Sultan 'Ali Mirreh, who, under Haile Sellasie's system of indirect rule, controlled the strategically and economically important Awash Valley. 'Ali Mirreh's flight to Jibuti, following a bloody engagement with Ethiopian forces, which stormed Asaita and inflicted savage civilian casualties, created a powerful new anti-Ethiopian 'Afar movement which might find a Somali alliance expedient. This anti-Ethiopian faction, which mooted the possibility of an autonomous 'Afar state, soon established the 'Afar Liberation Front, a guerrilla movement which threatened the security of the vital rail link between Addis Ababa and Jibuti.

Meanwhile, within the Territory itself, in February 1976 several F.L.C.S. terrorists hijacked a school bus containing the children of French military personnel and drove it to the Somalia border. The hijackers, who were demanding unconditional independence, were overcome with some loss of life when French forces stormed the bus. Shots were apparently exchanged with Somalia forces across the frontier, provoking angry accusations and denunciations by both parties and leading to a sharp deterioration in relations between Somalia and France. In the ensuing political upheaval in Jibuti the extent of public support (not exclusively Somali) for the banned L.P.A.I., became evident. Premier 'Ali Ariif was deserted by most of his colleagues in the Assembly. In the face of mounting pressure as the pendulum swung back again in favour of the Somalis, he had little option but to resign and was replaced in July by his former Secretary-General 'Abdallah Muhammad Kamil, an 'Afar married to a Somali. This able, young administrator had been chosen by the French authorities as ideally suited to head a new interim coalition government, including representatives of all the main parties, and to steer the territory to independence, which, it was announced in November, would be achieved in the following summer.

In March 1977, talks on the preparations for independence were held in Paris. The leaders of all the 'Afar and Somali parties had been invited, but only those who favoured the coalition government responded. They agreed that a new referendum on the issue of independence would be held in May, as well as elections for an enlarged Chamber of Deputies. The Somali dominated L.P.A.I. and F.L.C.S. and some of 'Ali 'Ariif's former supporters agreed to form the coalition *Rassemblement populaire pour l'Independence* (R.P.I.), presenting a single list of candidates which consisted of 33 'Ise, 30 'Afar and 2 Arabs. Although the 'Afar parties boycotted the combined election and referendum, there was a 77 per cent poll with 99 per cent of the voters favouring independence and the composite list of official candidates: only 10 per cent of those who voted obeyed the 'Afar parties' call to protest by casting blank votes. On 16 May Hassan Guled, chairman of the L.P.A.I. and former deputy in the French National Assembly, was elected President of the Council, heading a government of ten ministers, six of whom belonged to his own party and none to F.L.C.S. Half of the new ministers were 'Afar. Finally, at midnight on 26 June, under the neutral title 'Republic of Jibuti', the territory became independent with the veteran Somali politician, Hassan Guled as its first President and 'Abdallah Muhammad Kamil as Prime Minister. The new infant state became the 49th member of the O.A.U. and the 22nd member of the Arab League. Armed with French guarantees of aid and defence and promises of Arab support, Hassan Guled gave no commitment, one way or the other, on the question of possible union in the future with Somalia and, presumably with Ethiopia in mind, indicated that Jibuti would not become the 'agent' of any East African state and would respond in kind to acts of external aggression. This bold declaration of independence towards each of Jibuti's powerful neighbours (Somalia and Ethiopia) could not, however, conceal the extent to which the future of this tiny, precariously poised enclave depended on its relations with both these states. The intimate character of this dependence had already been poignantly underlined when, a few weeks prior to independence, Somali (and

perhaps also 'Afar) guerrillas had blown up sections of the Jibuti–
Addis Ababa railway, paralysing the line of communications and
trade which was equally important to Ethiopia and to Jibuti. With
its already high rate of unemployment, Jibuti thus achieved
formal political sovereignty with its entire livelihood in jeopardy.
All the indications were, moreover, that the mounting tension
between Ethiopia and Somalia would add further pressures
threatening the territory's fragile identity and the delicate 'Afar–
Somali alliance on which its future security depended. The main
hope for future viability lay in the mutual incompatability of
Ethiopian and Somali ambitions, in external French and Arab
support, and in the complexities of the factional as well as tribal
divisions in the local population.

The Ogaden War (1977–8): Western Somalia or Eastern Ethiopia?

If the immediate precipitants of the 1977 Ogaden War can be
traced to the upsurge of competing regional nationalisms unleashed by the Ethiopian Revolution and the brutal repression
practised by Colonel Mengistu's regime, its ultimate origins take
us back to the beginning of Ethiopian imperialism in the region –
Menelik's conquest of Harar in 1886 and subsequent military
expeditions (equipped with arms supplied from France, Italy and
Tsarist Russia) against the surrounding Somali, 'Afar and Oromo
tribesmen. This extension of Ethiopian dominion, coinciding with
the partition of the Somali coast between France, Britain and Italy
provoked the fierce Dervish struggle which, under the leadership
of the fiery Ogaden Sheikh, Muhammad 'Abdille Hassan, sought
between 1900 and 1920 to regain Somali independence from alien
rule. The first major Dervish attack in March 1900 was, significantly, on the Ethiopian military post at Jigjiga. The full impact
of Ethiopian jurisdiction in this peripheral area only began to be
felt after the British withdrawal in 1947 and 1954 (see above p.
151) prompting a revival of active Ogaden nationalism. As we
have seen, friction between Ethiopia and the newly formed
Somali Republic, exacerbated by armed clashes between the local
Ethiopian authorities and Ogaden tribesmen, flared up into a
brief outbreak of war in 1964. When peace was restored, the
Ogaden insurgents lost momentum and went underground, the

focus of the Pan-Somali struggle veering to the Somali population in Northern Kenya.

Meanwhile, in the adjacent Ethiopian province of Bale, and similarly stimulated by opposition to Amhara rule, a parallel resistance movement developed amongst the Cushitic-speaking Arussi and Oromo peoples who were closely related to the Somalis. A leading figure here was a local Oromo warlord called Wako Guto. Fighting started in 1963 and continued sporadically until 1970, when a massive Ethiopian military operation succeeded in re-establishing Amhara control. Characteristically, the defeated Wako Guto made peace with Haile Selassie and received the title of Dajazmach.[1] In the course of this protracted struggle, many refugees – many but not all Muslim Arussi – sought refuge from their Ethiopian oppressors by escaping across the border into Somalia where, particularly during the efforts of Prime Minister Igal and later President Siyad to maintain good relations with Ethiopia and Kenya, they were something of an embarrassment. Indeed, some of the more militant Oromo leaders were actually imprisoned by the Somali authorities. Similar sanctions were from time to time applied to militant Ogaden Somalis in prominent positions in the Somali government and armed forces when they inopportunely sought to press General Siyad into armed intervention in the Ogaden. By 1975, as disorder spread throughout Ethiopia, and the capacity of the new military rulers to hold the country together was increasingly in question, the attitude of those in power in Somalia was shifting to a more sympathetic response to Ogaden aspirations. Wako Guto was in Mogadishu seeking support and the Western Somali Liberation Front, which included Muslim Oromo, Arussi and Ogaden leaders, could no longer be cold-shouldered by President Siyad if serious domestic upheavals were to be avoided. In 1976 Wako Guto apparently returned to Bale to lead a new and highly successful campaign against the Ethiopian government, this time under the banner of the W.S.L.F.[2] About the same time General Siyad sent emissaries to Addis Ababa to attempt to negotiate with the new military leaders on the question of autonomy for the Ogaden. Despite the common commitment of the Ethiopian and Somali regimes to revolutionary socialism, these overtures proved as unsuccessful as the later attempt in March 1977 by Fidel Castro to manoeuvre General Siyad and Colonel Mengistu into accepting a loose socialist federation, under Soviet patronage, which would allow the Ogaden Somalis an unspecified measure of local autonomy. This effort to apply the Soviet formula for accommodating local nationalism did not go sufficiently far to satisfy Somali aspirations while vastly exceeding Mengistu's concept of acceptable Ethiopian devolution.

By the spring of 1977 Oromo guerrilla forces had succeeded in recovering control of most of the countryside in Bale. In the north the war in Eritrea had reached a critical phase, with the local nationalist forces controlling almost the whole area and pressing hard on the beleaguered and demoralized Ethiopian garrisons in Asmara and Massawa. By this time relations between the new rulers of Ethiopia and President Carter's new administration in Washington had also gravely deteriorated. Ethiopia's traditional superpower protector was withholding military supplies and urging a negotiated settlement with the Eritreans. In April Mengistu's regime retorted by closing U.S. installations (including the Kagnew communications station in Asmara – no doubt less significant to U.S. strategy since the acquisition of Diego Garcia), expelling U.S. personnel, and angrily denouncing the hypocrisy of human rights criticisms, which it was claimed had never been voiced against the Emperor. This move signalled the commencement of a seismic shift in superpower alignments in the Horn of Africa with wide-ranging consequences, the full repercussions of which were difficult to foresee, far less measure.

The immediate effect was Mengistu's visit to Moscow in May which produced a 'solemn declaration' of mutual collaboration and the denunciation of 'imperialist' and 'reactionary' forces which were accused of aggravating tension in north-east Africa. This was clearly not merely rhetoric since, on the eve of Jibuti's independence on 26 June, the new Cuban-trained and Russian-armed peasant army, numbering at least 70,000, was proudly paraded in Addis Ababa. If the Ogaden Somalis were to recover their independence there was clearly not much time left. Having disrupted communications between Jigjiga and Harar and Harar and Diredawa, the W.S.L.F. consequently began to muster its forces for concerted attacks on the Ethiopian garrisons in the Ogaden. By the end of July when the W.S.L.F. claimed to have liberated the strategic centre of Gode, Ethiopia was accusing the Somali Democratic Republic of mounting a full-scale war of aggression and appealing for external help. At the beginning of August a mediatory initiative by the Organisation of African Unity failed when the Ethiopians refused to allow the issue of Somali self-determination to be discussed or to permit W.S.L.F. representation. The shift of Russian patronage to Ethiopia and the lack of sympathy for Ogaden aspirations brought General Siyad to Moscow at the end of the month on what seemingly turned out to be a disappointing and fruitless visit. Breznev, the Party Chairman, had little time to spare for the Somali President who, drawing his own conclusions, set off in September on a series of urgent visits to Arab states; it was later reported that Saudi Arabia had promised Somalia £230 million for armaments, on the understanding that Somalia severed its Russian links. On 7 September, as the fighting in the Ogaden became increasingly fierce, Ethiopia broke off diplomatic relations with Somalia and on the following day a joint Ethiopio-Kenyan statement was issued, condemning Somalia's 'brazen and naked aggression'. Although formally Ethiopia and Kenya were bound by a defence pact aimed at containing Somali irridentism, Kenyan aid in the ensuing conflict was limited to official denunciations of Somali 'aggression' and to allowing Ethiopia to import munitions through Mombasa while denying over-flying rights to air consignments of weapons for Somalia.

Later in September as the massive Russian airlift of M.I.G.s, tanks and heavy weapons to Addis Ababa was reported to have gathered momentum, the W.S.L.F. achieved their greatest triumph: the liberation of Jigjiga, the main Ethiopian military headquarters in the Ogaden. Their opponents – whose morale had been weakened by successive bloody internal army purges – had offered little resistance, the Ethiopian third division retreating, according to some sources mutinously, from their key defensive position on the Marda Pass which commanded the road to Harar. Extensive quantities of largely American equipment were abandoned to the jubilant Somalis as they recovered military control of their country.

Controlling Jigjiga, W.S.L.F. forces swept on towards Harar in pursuit of their ultimate objective of freeing the entire Somali area up to the Awash Valley of Ethiopian domination. This would entail the expulsion of the Ethiopians from areas round Harar with mixed Somali, Oromo (Galla) and 'Afar populations and require defeat of the regrouped Ethiopian forces in Harar and Dire Dawa. As the theatre of conflict grew larger, involving associated ethnic groups, official W.S.L.F. statements as well as those from the Mogadishu government emphasized the close affinity of the Somalis and Arussi and other Oromo in Bale and the Harar area. The terms 'Abo-Somali' and 'Wariya-Somali' (from *abo* in Oromo and *wariya* in Somali, used to attract a person's attention) were coined to emphasise the close affinity between the Somali members of the W.S.L.F. and their Oromo allies; and on these lines, the Somali Abo Liberation Front (S.A.L.F.) was formed as an offshoot of the W.S.L.F.

The break with Russia

Meanwhile, a dramatic distraction occurred in the Somali Republic when, on 18 October, with full Somali collaboration, a West German anti-terrorist squad successfully rescued a hijacked Lufthansa jet at Mogadishu airport. This naturally greatly encouraged Somali hopes of Western sympathy and support for the struggle in the Ogaden. Somali–Soviet relations were strained to breaking point. The only major impediments to a formal rupture were Siyad's concern to avoid the potential destabilization of his regime which an abrupt breach might encourage, and a natural reluctance to terminate his main source of arms supplies before reliable alternative arrangements had been secured. There was also perhaps the hope that Russia might, under appropriate pressures or blandishments, still somehow wring from Mengistu the necessary concessions to Somali nationalism in the Ogaden. No progress in this direction was achieved, however, and on 13 November the predictable breach with Russia was announced in Mogadishu. All naval, air and ground military facilities – including the important communications and submarine missile handling station at Berbera – were withdrawn, the Somali–Soviet treaty of friendship (whose terms Russia had violated by supplying arms to Ethiopia) was renounced, and 6,000 military and civilian personnel and their families given a week to leave the country.

Diplomatic relations with Russia were retained; while with Cuba there was an abrupt and complete severance. This long-anticipated, but still delicate breach with Russia and her satellites received a tumultuous public welcome. In contrast to the Chinese, the Russians had never been popular in Somalia. The long suppressed public antagonism and resentment felt towards Somalia's erstwhile official 'friends' (associated in most people's minds with the more oppressive aspects of Siyad's regime) fanned into hatred by the frenetic climate of the Ogaden War were at last given free rein, bringing a further wave of popularity for the Mogadishu government.

Nationalist sentiments in the Republic, stimulated to an unforeseen degree by Somali literacy, had reached a climax. The fighting in the Ogaden, in which many were directly and all indirectly involved, had become a national obsession. All interest focussed on the progress of the war and the unofficial contribution to the war effort had unquestioned priority over all other activities. All aspects of life in the Republic were affected. In every government department and ministry there were conspicuous absentees away 'on leave', while in the armed forces those from the Ogaden had similarly gone to join their brothers and clansmen in the fight against the Ethiopian usurper. Mother and child care centres were hastily converted into cottage factories for making uniforms. Radio reports of the progress of the war were followed throughout the state with rapt attention; such was the demand for news that it became impossible to find transistor radios and batteries in the shops. This consuming preoccupation with the Ogaden left little time or need for the official cult of the Glorious Leader, President Siyad, which was quietly allowed to subside – at least for the time being.

The Ethiopian reconquest

We must now return to our chronicle of the war. By the end of November the fighting round Harar had become particularly fierce, and reports that Cuban personnel had been evacuated lent substance to W.S.L.F. claims that they were poised to seize control of this ancient Muslim city – or what was left of it after so many devastating attacks. The prospect of a W.S.L.F. breakthrough into Harar seemed all the nearer when the news came that the 'Afar Liberation Front, who with the Oromo Liberation Front were also now waging a guerrilla war against the Ethiopians, had cut the vital road from the port of Assab which, with Massawa and Jibuti out of action, was the sole port of entry for Russian supplies. However, despite these encouraging developments, the massive influx of Russian and Cuban equipment and advisers was evidently beginning to have some effect for, although they claimed to have entered Harar on more than one occasion, the W.S.L.F. were not able to capture the town. The anticipated victory turned into a stalemate, with reported long-range artillery exchanges between the opposing forces. Late in December while General Siyad was in Iran seeking support, Ethiopian war-planes made a limited series of air-strikes on targets in Northern Somalia. Somalia was now desperately seeking a substitute for her former Russian military patronage and trying to convince the United States and Western governments that it was in their interest to exert pressure to halt the menacing Russo-Cuban build-up in Ethiopia. Although prior to the breach with Russia, the American government had implied that it was prepared to supply Somalia with arms, it now appeared that no direct military aid would be forthcoming from this or other Western sources unless Somalia was prepared to cease supporting the Ogaden nationalists and to renounce her Pan-Somali commitments. Somali appeals for support brought angry reactions from Kenya and were consequently treated with great caution by the N.A.T.O. governments. Another important factor which reinforced this very circumspect and unenthusiastic response to Somali requests was the delicacy of the Anglo-American Rhodesian negotiations. The British and American governments were particularly concerned to avoid any step which would alienate O.A.U. opinion and consequently stressed the importance of finding a settlement to the Ethiopia–Somali dispute in the African context. While they were prepared to denounce Russian and Cuban interference in African problems with increasing outspokenness as the prospect of Cuban intervention in Rhodesia became a serious possibility, they firmly declared their adherence to the O.A.U. doctrine of the inviolability of existing frontiers – which the British Foreign Secretary referred to as 'the map of Africa'.

It was a bitter irony to the Somalis that these Western policy statements were construed by the Ethiopians, in official pronouncements, as support for Somalia! In fact, the furthest Western governments appeared prepared to go was to offer the eminently sensible advice that it would be in Somali interests to negotiate from a position of strength, while the W.S.L.F. were still in control of the Ogaden. What those who made these suggestions did not perhaps appreciate was the delicacy of relations between the Siyad government and the various clan elements in the W.S.L.F. There was a natural but mistaken tendency to see the W.S.L.F. as literally a 'front' for Mogadishu when the reality was rather that the initiative came from the Ogadenis.

Somalia was thus by all sides cast in the role of aggressor and little or no attention paid to the claims to self-determination of the Ogaden Somalis. The clandestine rather than open participation of army units from the Somali Republic tended to confirm the view that the Somalis were the aggressors, 'invading Ethiopian territory'. Even Iran, which was prepared to break off diplomatic relations with Kenya on the issue of Somali interests, stated categorically that her support was designed to protect Somalia's borders and not to recast African frontiers. With this only limited support from a handful of Arab states, with no battle-hardened foreign auxiliaries to set against the Yemenis and Cubans, and with Russian equipment smaller in quantity and inferior in quality to that now so abundantly available to Ethiopia, the Somali position was increasingly precarious. In an atmosphere of mounting apprehension in February 1978 Somalia officially entered the war and announced a general mobilization. The long-awaited Russian and Cuban counter-offensive was now properly underway and already claiming some successes. The final putsch occurred at the beginning of March when, after subjecting the 8,000 strong Somali force between Jigjiga and Harar to heavy aerial bombardment, the 10th Ethiopian division supported by an entire Cuban armoured brigade of sixty to seventy tanks bypassed the Marda Pass and attacked Jigjaga from the unexpected direction of the north. Cuban-crewed tanks were also air-lifted behind the Somali lines and Cuban-piloted M.I.G.s supported the attack in which a number of sophisticated new Russian weapons seem to have been deployed. Having evacuated the local civilian population to

Somalia, the Somali defence abandoned Jigjiga to the invaders. A relief brigade thrown into the battle from Somalia, straffed by M.I.G.s, was unable to stem the Ethiopian advance.

After a flurry of international exchanges, on 9 March President Siyad announced that, in response to American requests, Somali forces were being withdrawn from the Ogaden and that Russian and Cuban forces should follow suit, thus in effect conceding victory to the Ethiopians. There was in fact considerable anxiety in Somalia that the Ethiopian advance would not stop at the border but would press on into the Republic. Quantities of arms were thus nervously issued to the civilian population in the north. In the event, as the Russians had promised, the Ethiopian advance halted at the frontier, limiting itself to gradually reimposing Ethiopian rule in the Ogaden. If the fact that the former head of the Russian military mission to Somalia, General Grigory Barislov, had directed this successful operation against them added a bitter piquancy to their defeat, stories were also current amongst the fleeing Somali survivors of the moderating influence exercised by the Russians in the treatment of prisoners. There was, however, no immediate indication that the Russo-Cuban presence was to be withdrawn from the Ogaden, far less from Ethiopia – a proposition which was angrily rejected by Mengistu's government. It soon became clear also that W.S.L.F. guerrilla activity in the Ogaden would continue; indeed only a few weeks after the official Somali withdrawal, and following a presidential visit to China, the Mogadishu government announced that it would not cease supporting the Ogaden liberation movement. This inevitably led to provocative exchanges with Ethiopia and assertions that if Ethiopia's boundaries were not respected there was no reason why Somalia's should be. Time would tell whether this defiant Somali policy was an effort to save face after the terrible Ogaden debacle, or an indication that Somalia had at last found powerful Arab backing (e.g. Iran and Saudi Arabia) prepared to come to the Republic's defence in the event of an Ethiopian attack.

The wider implications of the Ogaden conflict

The Ogaden conflict, as we have seen, prompted an extraordinary *volte-face* in superpower alignments in the Horn of Africa. The

Russians who had, as it were, come in to Somalia with the Ogaden (see above, p. 201), went out with it, an about-turn which testified to the abiding force of local nationalism in the area – a point to which we shall return shortly. The opportunist Russian thrust into the power vacuum created in Ethiopia by the withdrawal of American support from Colonel Mengistu's reign of terror, may initially have seemed advantageous to Western interests. America was no longer involved in sustaining a precariously poised regime which, *soi-disant* socialist as it was, was clearly determined to remain in power by liquidating all opposition in the most savage manner. Russia had taken on a perilous and ultimately arguably thankless task, since it was far from clear whether Ethiopia could be held together, except at a cost in manpower, arms and involvement at which even the U.S.S.R. might baulk. What had not perhaps been foreseen were the lengths to which the Russians and their Cuban allies were in fact prepared to go in shouldering the unenviable burdens of shoring up Mengistu's uncertain authority.

By the summer of 1978, after the reconquest of the Ogaden, the Russo–Cuban directed Ethiopian war-machine had, predictably, transferred its attentions to Eritrea. Here the situation for the Russians and Cubans was much more delicate and potentially damaging than that in the Ogaden. The Eritrean freedom-fighters had previously enjoyed direct Cuban support in their struggle to recover independence for the former Italian colony of Eritrea, federated to Ethiopia in 1952. They had, moreover, a much longer tradition of highly organized resistance to the Ethiopians and had succeeded in recovering control of virtually the whole country except for the beleaguered Ethiopian garrisons in Asmara and the port of Massawa. The mountainous Eritrean terrain was also, unlike the Ogaden, ideally suited to successful guerrilla operations – as previous campaigns had illustrated. A protracted and inevitably exceedingly bloody war, with a high casualty rate on both sides, seemed bound to cause embarrassment to the Cuban image in Africa and might also adversely affect Russian interests in the continent. It would certainly complicate both countries' relations with left-wing and right-wing parties in the Arab world on whose support the Eritreans depended. Any prolonged military action against the Eritreans which excluded the possibility of a negotiated political settlement to their demands for autonomy would also strain the strange marriage of convenience (or 'unholy alliance' as the Somalis denounced it) which had developed in support of Ethiopia in the Ogaden War. Perhaps 'marriage' is too strong a term for the curious *mélange* of Russian (and other East European), Cuban, South Yemeni, Israeli and Libyan support which enabled Mengistu to reimpose Ethiopian rule in the Ogaden. Israel's willingness to supply napalm and military technicians was readily intelligible in terms of her interest in sustaining a powerful Christian presence in the Red Sea as a counterpoise to Arab influence. What the Libyan paymasters would gain from participating in suppressing the Eritrean separatists, particularly the left-wing Muslims whose status in some Middle Eastern eyes approached that of the Palestinian liberation movements, was less self-evident.

Of course it was in the interests of the Ethiopian regime, and in the Ethiopian tradition of foreign policy, to have composite external support. However, their external connexions were now so clearly dominated by the Russians that nothing could disguise the fact that Ethiopia had become a Soviet client state. The long-cherished Tsarist ambition of making Ethiopia a Russian protectorate, prominent at the end of the nineteenth century when Russian arms and advisers had facilitated Menelik's conquests, and romanticized in the Ethiopian origins ascribed to the national poet Pushkin, had at last borne fruit.[3] This happy outcome which in the nineteenth century was to have been achieved within the bosom of the Christian Church was now realized under the successor ideology of communism in circumstances strongly reminiscent of the Soviet Union's own revolutionary experience. For the Cubans, too, the turmoil and bloodshed in Ethiopia had all the hallmarks of an authentic 'on-going' revolution, giving the strongman Mengistu at its head a natural appeal for Fidel Castro in contrast to the paternalistic Somali leader Siyad Barre. The latter was all too reminiscent of Latin American benevolent dictators in an older tradition; and whatever its achievements, the placid Somali Revolution could certainly not match the Ethiopian in turmoil, death and terror.

But if, with this Russian-controlled aid, Mengistu finally succeeded in quelling the Eritreans and restoring and consolidating his authority in the other dissident provinces as well as in the urban centres of Ethiopia, it would also be in the Ethiopian tradition for him to try to dispense with his foreign patrons once they had served his purpose. Whether and when this would happen were speculations which only the future could resolve. Certainly it is in the tradition of the region to repulse foreign intervention as insistently and urgently as it is requested.

The position in the summer of 1978, when our account closes, was unbalanced and shifting. Ethiopia had moved from the American to the Russian camp. Somalia had lost the patronage of one superpower without, in the post-Vietnam era, gaining that of the other. The extent and significance of Arab support was still an uncertain quantity. Communist China, which had consistently championed both the Somalis and the Eritreans, continued to issue powerful condemnations of Russian imperialism. The degree to which China was able and willing to supplement her well-conceived and popular civilian aid projects in Somalia with military support at the level needed had yet to be seen. In the wake of the rift with Russia, the E.E.C. countries had concentrated their efforts on supplying an emergency aid programme to continue projects abandoned by the Russians, and no doubt China would develop her own distinctive contribution (which need not exclude supplying arms to the W.S.L.F. guerrillas). Improbable though it might seem, the possibility of some new Somali accommodation with the Russians was not to be totally excluded as President Siyad took stock of his bewilderingly complex foreign relations.

Local problems

The plethora of external uncertainties competed for attention with the pressing local problems posed by the humiliating defeat in the Ogaden. There were naturally bitter recriminations both on the conduct of the military operations, directed at the end by the President himself, and on Somali foreign policy. The numerous foreign missions undertaken by the President and his representatives had gained no unqualified public support from a powerful source for this new phase in the Pan-Somali struggle which had begun with such verve and promise and closed so disastrously.

There were ample grounds for criticism in this grim postmortem. If the government had spent a minute fraction of its military budget on a professional public relations campaign it might have been easier to convince outsiders of the justice of the Somali case for self-government in the Ogaden. Sustained publicity over the years would have kept the issue alive in the public mind and made it more difficult for foreign governments (such as those of Britain and Italy) to forget their past involvement in the origins of the Somali–Ethiopian dispute. More prominence could thus have been given to the fact that Somalia became independent with an inherited boundary dispute with Ethiopia which much previous Italian and United Nations' effort had failed to solve. The 'map of Africa' in this region was thus far from settled at the time of Somalia's independence.

If, moreover, during the heyday of Somali–Soviet friendship, the regime had prudently continued to cultivate a few friends in the Western bloc it might have been easier to switch sides when the time came. It would also, clearly, have been extremely advantageous to have taken every possible step to have tried to allay the natural (and not unjustified) anxieties of the Kenyans. There was also the issue of the questionable wisdom of pretending not to support the W.S.L.F. and so, in a way, confirming the Ethiopian (and general) impression of the Somalis as aggressive invaders. It was certainly a cardinal error not to have accompanied or prefaced the W.S.L.F. offensive in the Ogaden with a concerted diplomatic offensive presenting the Somali case in the strongest possible terms. Little effort was made even to clarify the objectives and limits of the W.S.L.F. campaign.

The importance of all these neglected factors was strikingly illustrated in the reports in the Western press and on the radio by commentators sympathetic to the Somali case which, during the initial Somali successes, described the W.S.L.F. forces as 'capturing', 'taking' and 'seizing' etc. various 'Ethiopian' centres in the Ogaden. These subtle and quite undeliberate politically-loaded semantics strengthened the impression that the Somalis were the aggressors brazenly invading Ethiopian territory, when in reality it was Somali settlements whose independence was being restored – with help from the armed forces of the Somali Republic. In the euphoria of victory the W.S.L.F. used exactly the same terms in announcing their successes when it would have been more prudent to have spoken of the recovery of Somali sovereignty. The Ministry of Information and National Guidance might have been expected to produce more effective propaganda. But like so many of the other departments of state in Somalia whose performance was critically tested during the conflict, it was directed by people whose appointment seemed to owe more to their loyalty to the Head of State than to their technical skills. The effectiveness of the presentation of the Somali case was also handicapped in unexpected ways. So, for instance, the government's commitment to the eradication of tribalism, as well as the complexities of its relationship with the various clan elements in the W.S.L.F. forces, made it impossible to publish documents demonstrating the local distribution of Somali clans in the Ogaden at the time of Menelik's invasion in the nineteenth century.

The underlying realities here were indeed daunting. The relationship between the 'Ise Somali round Diwe Dawa and the Ogaden was an uneasy one, and there was also a long history of competition over grazing between the Ogaden and Isaq clans to their north. There were even divisions *within* the Ogaden confederation of clans itself, not least between those leading the Ogaden guerrillas and clansmen in prominent positions in the Somali Republic. There was also mistrust and rivalry between the Muslim Oromo supporters of the W.S.L.F. and other Oromo (some Muslim), equally hostile to Mengistu's regime, some of whom supported the Oromo Liberation Front. Other Oromo again (and probably the majority of this large nation) were not directly allied with either of these organizations. The 'Afar, as we have seen, were equally divided into pro- and anti-Ethiopian factions. These numerous divisions greatly reduced the effectiveness of the Western Somali struggle and made relations with the Somali Republic infinitely complicated. And notwithstanding the force of Somali nationalism, there were individuals and groups who found it convenient to be able to move readily across international frontiers and from one state's jurisdiction to another's, rather than unreservedly identifying with the Somali government in Mogadishu. This long legacy of opportunist manipulation of identity and citizenship, reinforcing internal clan divisions, inevitably added to the strains within the W.S.L.F. movement.

In retrospect, with all these problems it was particularly galling to recall how wise it would have been to negotiate from a position of strength – to have, for example, offered Ethiopia secure access to the port of Jibuti in return for independence in the Ogaden. Finally, the conduct of the military operations provided abundant ammunition for criticism and recrimination. There were many occasions on which, with hindsight, it seemed that grave tactical errors had been committed. The sophistication of the Russian- and Cuban-supported enemy tactics had been grossly under-estimated by the over confident and ill-experienced Somali command. It was, apparently, a combination of these factors that led to the tragic mistake of committing a reserve force of Somali regulars to a defeat in which their lack of air covèr guaranteed they would suffer heavy losses.

There was naturally considerable confusion when those who had escaped from the blitzkrieg of Jigjiga arrived at the northern frontier of the Somali Republic. A number of summary military executions were reported to have occurred. According to some accounts, those shot were officers who had refused to obey orders during the final conflict round Jigjiga. Other reports suggested that some of those executed were soldiers who, when ordered to discard their uniforms and return immediately to the Ogaden as W.S.L.F. guerrillas, had threatened mutiny.

The regime also, apparently, considered it prudent to order the majority of those units which had been withdrawn from the Ogaden to station themselves along this northern frontier where they provided a defence against a possible Ethiopian invasion and could not easily spread discontent in the south. These precautions seemed justified since on 9 April an attempted *coup* was made by forces garrisoned in the south. Five hundred rebel soldiers were reported to have died in the ensuing battle with forces loyal to President Siyad, who himself survived unscathed. Several of the rebel leaders – colonels of the Majerteyn clan – escaped to Kenya. How much of the arms distributed among the civilian population in the north had now been successfully recovered remained obscure. Certainly armed dissidence seemed a serious potential hazard.

Thus, while soldiers and civilians accused of complicity in the abortive April *coup* were being tried in Mogadishu in August 1978, there were widespread reports that the Majerteyn clan was holding hostages belonging to the Marehan clan of the President. The Head of State, whose most recent appointments and promotions suggested an increasingly defensive dependence on his own clansmen, was also said to be negotiating clandestinely with Majerteyn clan leaders in an effort to avert a situation which, some local Somali commentators claimed, threatened to lead to widespread tribal war. Perhaps this was an exaggerated view. Certainly, there was much more openly voiced criticism of Siyad's government in Mogadishu in the summer of 1978 than there had been four years previously, before the 1975 drought and 1977 Ogaden War. This seemed less indicative of a deliberate relaxation of previous security measures, although there may have been an element of this, than of an increasing lack of firm central control. Talk of the need for a change of government was, if anything, more rather than less insistent following the unsuccessful Majerteyn attempt to overthrow the regime. There was irritation in some quarters that the attempted *coup* had been so badly mismanaged. And, although the impatience of the numerous Majerteyn clan which had been so powerful in the days of parliamentary rule was understandable, their narrow, parochial initiative alienated members of other groups who shared their feelings of discontent.

In view of these trends it was not surprising that the President's bizarre decision to consign the director-generals of all ministries and government agencies to a five months' stint in the national orientation centre in Mogadishu should be seen by some as a defensive reaction in the wake of the April uprising. If this action brought all the country's top civil servants under close military control, and also promised 'objective' means of promoting some and demoting others, it exacerbated the grave difficulties which were already being experienced in absorbing the massive quantities of foreign aid (mainly from Islamic and Western sources) which, in lieu of military support, were now pouring into the country following the Ogaden War. It was thus clear that the divisive forces unleashed by the defeat would have a pervasive and corrosive influence within Somalia which would tax to the full all Siyad's remarkable powers of endurance. With so many internal as well as external sources of uncertainty and instability, President Siyad's predicament was not enviable. Ironically, the aftermath of the Ogaden conflict thus presented precisely those conditions in which many misinformed commentators believed the war had begun – namely conditions where external aggression seems to offer the best means of recovering waning public support by distracting attention from pressing problems at home.

Retrospect and prospect: nationalism and ideology in Africa

The 1977–8 Ogaden War dramatically underlined the persistent institutional instability which is entrenched in the Horn of Africa by the juxtaposition of two mutually opposed irridentist states: Ethiopia and Somalia. Partly for reasons which we shall shortly examine, Somali irridentism tended to conceal the equally powerful force of Ethiopian expansionism. The former, of course, was more patent and striking. In 1960 Britain and Italy in particular, and the international community in general, had participated in the establishment of a Somali state which excluded three parts of the Somali nation and was consequently incomplete. The new state's constitution and flag committed it to striving to attain independence and statehood for the remaining Somali communities under alien rule. Given the history of foreign involvement in the dismemberment of the Somali nation, including such attempts as the Bevin plan to rectify it, this was not an unreasonable aspiration, particularly in the African world of 1960. Ethiopia's position was very different. After the Second World War, following the Italian fascist conquest, which Britain and her Allies had done little to avert, Ethiopia was most generously treated. The gallant little Emperor who had so appealed to Western sympathies was not only restored on the throne of a liberated Ethiopia but was also given the Ogaden and Eritrea. In this case the short-lived Italian colony of Ethiopia was not merely restored to independence but fortified by the addition of another, historically distinct ex-Italian possession, Eritrea, with the Ogaden (the Ethiopian claims to which we have examined, p. 130) thrown in for good measure. By any standards this was over-compensation! It was also, of course, in the Ethiopian political tradition in the sense that Ethiopia was the last and largest of Africa's traditional conquest kingdoms, a fact obscured by the preoccupation of European Ethiopian specialists with Ethiopia's Semitic languages and

Christian religion. This obsession reinforced the Ethiopian rulers' own predeliction, associated with their confident sense of superiority in comparison with other Africans, stressing their links with Europe and ignoring those with Africa.

To appreciate Ethiopia's inherent expansionist dynamic we need to look at its internal political anatomy.[4] The contrast with Somalia is striking. While the Somali state is based on homogeneous ethnic nationalism, Ethiopia is an unwieldy congeries of different peoples and language-groups, even races, welded loosely together by the domination over the last five centuries of the Semitic-speaking Christian Amhara who have provided both a sturdy highland peasantry and an equestrian aristocracy. The preeminence of the Amharas replacing that earlier enjoyed by the Tigreans of Tigre and Eritrea has coincided with the gradual southwards movement of the capital in an ever-expanding empire. When, in the nineteenth century, Menelik succeeded in establishing the far-flung frontiers of modern Ethiopia the new capital of Addis Ababa in Shoa Province became the hub of the empire. It was left to his successor, Haile Selassie, to establish his authority by consolidating and building on Menelik's foundations. This Haile Selassie did in a masterly fashion, adjusting the old formula of divide and rule, implemented by a subtle combination of direct and indirect rule, to the exigencies of the modern world into which Ethiopia was gradually but inevitably drawn.[5] As with his predecessors, under his aegis, Amhara hegemony was tempered by an implicit melting pot philosophy which offered upward mobility and assimilation to Amhara identity to ambitious members of the other ethnic groups, including the numerically dominant Cushitic-speaking Oromo (or Galla) as long as they adopted the Amharic language and Christian faith. The elasticity of Amhara ethnicity was enhanced by the freedom with which Amharas married non-Amhara women and by the bilateral Amhara kinship system. Amhara rule was thus buttressed by a powerful plinth of Amharized Oromo, while other Oromo remote from power in the distant southern provinces (Arusi, Bali, Sidamo) were treated on their own lands as colonized subjects, open to all the exactions of insatiable Amhara landlords. More remote still were the ethnic cousins of the Oromo, the 'Afar and Ogaden and other Somalis in Harar Province on the very periphery of the empire. The Amhara presence in these regions was, as we have seen, primarily limited to military garrisons, the veritable 'beau-geste' outposts of empire.

The claim to rule this sprawling mosaic of peoples was tradi-tionally validated by demonstrations of force and by new con-quests. Since, as was inevitable, in a conquest state of this kind, the power of the centre over the periphery waxed and waned over the centuries, in some periods the claim to rule was legiti-mated less by fresh conquests than by internal consolidation. But, however the balance lay in any period, Ethiopia incorporated an expansive dynamic which was integral to its political history. Thus, in the recent conflict between Ethiopia and Somalia which we have just surveyed, it was critically important for the Amharized Ethiopian leader Mengistu to demonstrate his authority by con-quering the Ogaden Somalis, and this was all the more crucial in view of his rejection of the ancient Solomonic myth of kingship employed so skilfully by Haile Selassie and earlier rulers to sacralize their power. The subjection of Eritrea, as well as the suppression of internal currents of ethnic nationalism, has the same significance. It would have been more difficult for Mengistu than for Siyad to survive without controlling the Ogaden. Of course, once the Somali offensive had started, Mengistu's victory inevitably detracted from Siyad's authority in Somalia.

These points are, arguably, even more significant given the official dedication of both the Ethiopian and Somali regimes to Scientific Socialism. The fact that Ethiopia now enjoys Russo–Cuban legitimation while China endorses Somalia, which is itself an outcome of rival nationalisms in the Horn of Africa, may give the Somalis a slightly less tarnished socialist image in the inter-national context. But in the local setting, this has not persuaded those Marxist Ethiopians who denounce Mengistu's regime as a 'fascist-*junta*' to give unqualified support for the Somali and Eritrean nationalist causes. Here, as elsewhere, ideology, in prac-tice, is strongly tempered by patriotism.

State and nation in Africa

Stripped of the trappings of modern government and ideology at a more basic level, Ethiopia and Somalia represent two opposing types of traditional African state. In pre-colonial Africa, the political units were either multinational states of the Ethiopian type, or homogeneous ethnic units like the Somalis. Both types were probably equally common. The European partition and its aftermath radically changed this pattern. As is well known, European colonies and protectorates were almost universally haphazard assemblages of tribes and language groups thrown together by the vagaries of conflicting imperial designs. The word 'tribe', it should be noted, had acquired a pejorative and etymologically misleading meaning. Unlike the divisions in the urban Roman state to which it originally referred, it had been applied in Africa to designate speech communities which were ethnocentrically regarded as backward, barbaric, generally uncivilized. This curious development contrasted strikingly with the situation in parts of the Caribbean and Latin America where the word nation was correctly applied to those units of population which in Africa were derogatively designated 'tribes' by Europeans.[6] In any event, what distinguished these colonial artefacts from each other was the identity of the colonizing power and the frontiers defining its jurisdiction. This emphasis on *territorially defined*, polyglot and ethnically heterogenous states tipped the balance in favour of the pre-colonial Ethiopian model, itself reminiscent of the multi-national Habsburg empire. Independence and the post-colonial era saw, inevitably, a further stress placed on frontiers which, as President Nyerere once expostulated, were so ridiculous they must be sacred. Hence the commitment of the Organisation of African Unity to the inviolability of the colonial frontiers and the pronounced frontier fetishism of contemporary African states. Here we may interpolate that, if there is substance in Elie Kedourie's[7] argument that African nationalism is a product of European nationalism, the special circumstances of colonial Africa favoured a pluralist revision of the European nation-state concept of the type associated with modernity and nationalism by Ernest Gellner.[8]

With such powerful structural vested interests involved, it was scarcely surprising that in 1977, as in an earlier decade, there was little African enthusiasm for the Somali cause which threatened to undermine the prevailing Ethiopian pattern of African state. If the principles of self-determination had to be denied to part of the

Somali people this, many argued, was a small price to pay for keeping firmly shut the pandora's box of problems which, if unleashed, would jeopardize the stability of a whole continent – and certainly unseat many African leaders.

Sensitivity on the part of African leaders on this issue perhaps reflected their increasing awareness of the mounting strength of rival ethnic forces in the continent and of the conspicuous absence of any general formula (other than tyranny) with which to accommodate them. In its modern and largely, though not exclusively, urban form, rampant tribalism or ethnicity was as many anthropologists had emphasized[9] partly a response to increased group interaction and competition for scarce resources, rather than a lingering primordial[10] anachronism. This interactionist or strategic perspective, treating ethnicity as an infinitely elastic vehicle for shared economic and/or political interests tended, however, to neglect its subjective appeal as a focus of identity – a point well made recently by A. L. Epstein[11] among others. Moreover, while in Africa, as elsewhere, ethnicity could be manufactured and manipulated as in the case of Idi Amin's synthetic Nubi identity in Uganda, it also had to be recognized that, once formed, national cultures were readily politicized into active nationalism. This, indeed, is the case with Somalia nationalism. As we have seen, this began as a primarily cultural force, no doubt shaped by centuries of interaction with surrounding populations, and with growing contact first with Islam, which it assimilated, and then with Christianity, which it rejected, acquired an increasingly sharp political edge. This book has attempted to chart the course of that politicization. The weakness of this traditional endowment, wryly recognized by modern Somali nationalists, has been its segmentary character – which through modernization and literacy President Siyad's military regime has attempted, not altogether successfully, to overcome.

Nationalism and ethnicity are notoriously reactive and infectious. This is already evident in the Horn of Africa. If Ethiopia is riven by ideological divisions on the left and right, its most powerful schisms and those most menacing to its future are based on a growing sense of ethnic identity and consciousness. The nationalist movements in Eritrea and the Ogaden are merely advanced forms of a general ferment amongst the constituents of the old empire which rejects the implicit Amhara melting-pot philosophy and seeks fulfilment in a multitude of diverse local nationalisms. The potentially most significant of these is the Oromo Liberation Front, representing the nascent nationalism of the largest ethnic group in Ethiopia. With a population of some ten million and a geographical distribution which makes it literally the backbone of the country, this large nation with its many divisions clearly holds the key to the future stability of Ethiopia. Numerically prominent in the armed forces, the Oromo have in the past been used by their Amhara rulers to suppress the subject populations, including their own kinsmen. Intoxicated with the novel force of their new-found nationalism, Oromo Liberation Front militants are today demanding independence first and only then discussion of a form of association in a plural state that would do justice to the 'nationalities problem'. If within Ethiopia and elsewhere in Africa these trends continue, the Somali problem may take on a different complexion. Just as it was wrong in the past to attribute a spurious immutability to Africa's 'traditional tribes', so today it may be equally mistaken to regard the present geo-political map of the continent as fixed for all eternity.

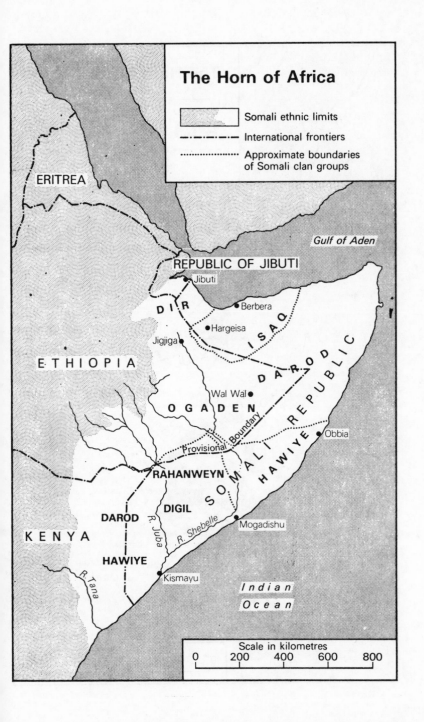

The Horn of Africa

Somali ethnic limits
— ·· — ·· — International frontiers
············ Approximate boundaries
of Somali clan groups

ERITREA

Gulf of Aden

REPUBLIC OF JIBUTI

• Jibuti

D I R

• Berbera

• Hargeisa

ISAQ

Jigjiga •

ETHIOPIA

DAROD

REPUBLIC

• Wal Wal

O G A D E N

Boundary

Provisional

Obbia •

RAHANWEYN

SOMALI

HAWIYE

DIGIL

DAROD

R. Juba

R. Shebelle

Mogadishu

KENYA

HAWIYE

R. Tana

Kismayu

Indian

Ocean

Scale in kilometres
0   200   400   600   800

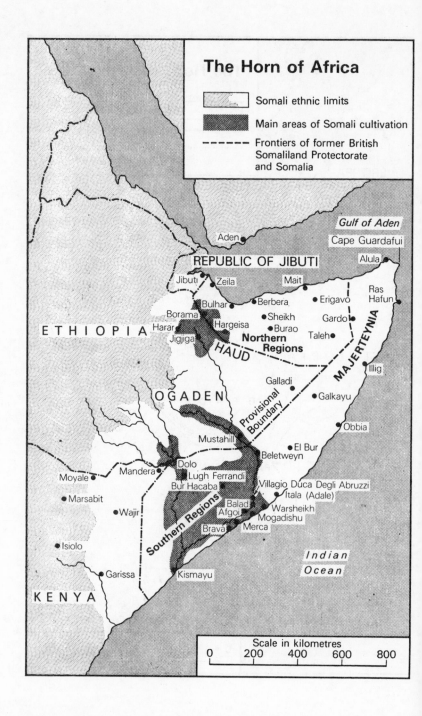

The Horn of Africa

- ☐ Somali ethnic limits
- ■ Main areas of Somali cultivation
- ----- Frontiers of former British Somaliland Protectorate and Somalia

Gulf of Aden

Cape Guardafui

Aden

REPUBLIC OF JIBUTI

Alula

Jibuti

Zeila

Mait

Ras Hafun

Bulhar

Berbera

Erigavo

ETHIOPIA

Borama

Sheikh

Gardo

Harar

Hargeisa

Burao

Taleh

Jigjiga

Northern Regions

MAJERTEYNIA

HAUD

OGADEN

Galladi

Illig

Provisional Boundary

Galkayu

Obbia

Mustahill

El Bur

Beletweyn

Dolo

Moyale

Mandera

Lugh Ferrandi

Villagio Duca Degli Abruzzi

Bur Hacaba

Itala (Adale)

Marsabit

Balad

Warsheikh

Southern Regions

Afgoi

Mogadishu

Wajir

Brava

Merca

Isiolo

Indian Ocean

Garissa

KENYA

Kismayu

Scale in kilometres

0   200   400   600   800

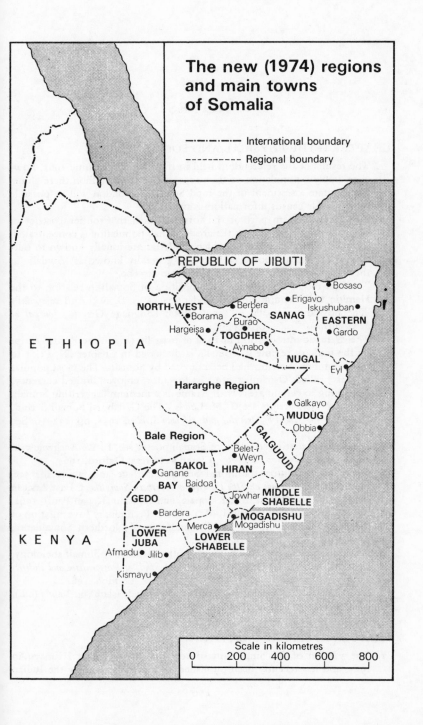

The new (1974) regions
and main towns
of Somalia

International boundary
Regional boundary

REPUBLIC OF JIBUTI

Bosaso

Erigavo
Iskushuban

NORTH-WEST
Borama
Berbera

SANAG

EASTERN

Hargeisa
Burao
Gardo

ETHIOPIA
TOGDHER

Aynabo

NUGAL

Hararghe Region
Eyl

Galkayo
MUDUG

Bale Region
Obbia

Belet-
Weyn

BAKOL
HIRAN
GALGUDUD

Ganane
BAY
Baidoa

GEDO
Jowhar
MIDDLE
SHABELLE

Bardera
MOGADISHU

Merca
Mogadishu

KENYA
LOWER
JUBA
LOWER
SHABELLE

Afmadu
Jilib

Kismayu

Scale in kilometres
0   200   400   600   800

NOTES

CHAPTER I: THE PHYSICAL AND SOCIAL SETTING

1. The results of the referendum held in the Republic in June 1961, however, imply a population of the order of over four million there alone. No accurate assessment of the total Somali population will be possible until reliable census information is available.

2. This is the eastern part of the former Northern Frontier District of Kenya in which the bulk of the area's Somali population is concentrated.

3. This is the Arabic name by which the 'Afar are usually known to outsiders. To Somali, however, they are generally known as 'Awdali. In the Republic of Jibuti they number some 150,000.

4. The best recent discussion of the position of Somali in relation to the Hamitic and Semitic groups of languages is B. W. Andrzejewski's 'The position of Galla in the Cushitic Language Group', *Journal of Semitic Studies*, 1964, pp. 135–8.

5. The dramatic introduction in 1972 of mass literacy in the Roman script by the military regime in Somalia is discussed in Chapter IX. Prior to this a number of scripts had been devised by Somalis. The most popular of these, called 'Osmaniya' after its inventor, enjoyed limited currency, competing in certain areas with Arabic as a medium for writing Somali. On these early scripts see; I. M. Lewis, 'The Gadabursi Somali Script', *Bulletin of the School of Oriental and African Studies*, 1958, pp. 134–56. See also below, p. 115.

6. For a representative selection of Somali poetry see, B. W. Andrzejewski and I. M. Lewis, *Somali Poetry*, Clarendon Press, Oxford, 1964.

7. For fuller details on traditional Somali marriage and family life see, I. M. Lewis, *Marriage and the Family in Northern Somaliland*, East African Institute of Social Research, Kampala, and London (Kegan Paul), 1962.

8. See K. L. G. Goldsmith and I. M. Lewis 'A Preliminary Investigation of the Blood Groups of the "Sab" Bondsmen of Northern Somaliland', *Man*, Vol. LVIII, 1958, pp. 188–90.

9. For a detailed discussion of this and other aspects of Somali sociology, see I. M. Lewis, *A Pastoral Democracy: A Study of Pastoralism and Politics among the Northern Somali of the Horn of Africa*, London, 1961.

10. I. M. Lewis, 'Conformity and Contract in Somali Islam', in Lewis (ed.), *Islam in Tropical Africa*, London, 1966.

CHAPTER II: BEFORE PARTITION

1. One version of this important source was discovered at Kismayu in 1923, and has recently been published with a translation by the Italian

scholar Enrico Cerulli (Cerulli, *Somalia: Scritti vari editi ed inediti*, I, Rome, 1957, pp. 231–357).

2. The main Oromo invasion of Abyssinia from the south-east is documented by contemporary sources, outstanding amongst which is *The History of the Galla*, written by the Abyssinian monk Bahrey, about 1593. On the Galla see, G. W. B. Huntingford, *The Galla of Ethiopia*, London, 1955. H. S. Lewis, *A Galla Monarchy*, Madison, 1965; A. Legesse, *Gada: three approaches to the study of African society*, New York, 1973.

3. The interpretation of Ibn Sa'id's evidence is critically assessed by Cerulli in *Somalia I*, pp. 93–95.

4. In addition to Cerulli, *op. cit.*, for independent numismatic evidence on this dynasty, see G. S. P. Freeman-Grenville, 'Coins from Mogadishu c. 1300 to c. 1700', *Numismatic Chronicle*, 1963, pp. 179–201 and M. H. Yusuf, *Numismatic inscriptions National Museum*, Mogadishu, 1970.

5. According to one legend popular in Ethiopia, Ahmad Gran was the issue of a Coptic priest and a Muslim harlot. A recent writer has more seriously suggested that the *Imam* may have belonged to a section of the Beja tribes.

6. See Shihab ad-Din, ed. and trs., R. Basset, *Futuh al-habasha*, Paris, 1897–1909.

7. These cities are today all in ruins and although a preliminary survey of the majority of them was made by Major Curle in 1940, they have not yet been systematically excavated. A thorough excavation should throw considerable light upon this period. For an excellent recent survey see N. Chittick, 'An Archaeological Reconnaissance in the Horn: The British–Somali Expedition, 1975', *Azania*, 1976, pp. 117–33. The best general history of the wars between the Abyssinian Christians and the Muslims is J. S. Trimingham's *Islam in Ethiopia*, London, 1952.

8. In 1624, Father de Valesco, a Jesuit missionary, visited Pate and Malindi and heard the news of Mogadishu's conquest. There are also other records in Somaliland which refer to this event.

9. This distribution of peoples is corroborated by a Portuguese document of 1625 which describes the caravan route from Mogadishu into Abyssinia.

10. Much light on these further movements has been shed by the studies made by Sir Richard Turnbull while serving in the Northern Province of Kenya. For references to these and the general sequence of movements into Kenya, see, I. M. Lewis, 'The Problem of the Northern Frontier District of Kenya', *Race*, 1963, pp. 48–60. On the expansion of the Somali as a whole see also, I. M. Lewis, 'The Somali Conquest of the Horn of Africa', *Journal of African History*, 1960, pp. 213–30.

11. After his boat foundered, von der Decken was murdered by hostile members of the religious community at Bardera, but some of his companions escaped and managed to reach the coast safely with the expedition's scientific records.

12. The name Galla, which is of obscure origin, is first recorded in the sixteenth century: it is used without always a specific ethnic connotation

in Ethiopia to designate traditionally 'subject' peoples. The Galla call themselves Oromo.

13. Richard Burton, *First Footsteps in East Africa*, Everyman edition, 1943, pp. 288–9.

14. That is, the coastal strip from the mouth of the Juba in the south to Itala in the north, and including the ports of Brava, Merca, and Mogadishu.

15. Guillain estimated that there were about 1,000 weavers in 1847, and that the annual production of cloth amounted to some 37,000 pieces, each three yards long. This was consumed locally and also exported to the Swahili coast and northern Somaliland. Some of it travelled as far as the ports of Arabia, the Persian Gulf, the Red Sea, and Egypt. Cloth was also produced on a smaller scale at Brava and Merca. See C. Guillain, *Documents sur l'histoire, la géographie, et le commerce de l'Afrique Orientale*, 3 vols., Paris, 1856.

CHAPTER III: THE IMPERIAL PARTITION: 1860–97

1. Although the Khedive claimed that the firmans of 1865 and 1866 which conveyed to Egypt the Red Sea ports of Suakin and Massawa also included Zeila and the Somali Coast, this was not the case and the latter cession was provided for in a third firman of 1875. The best account of the Egyptian period is G. Douin, *Histoire du Règne du Khédive Ismail*, Cairo, 1941, Vol. III.

2. Between 1884 and June 1885, however, Italy pressed Britain to agree to an Italian occupation of Zeila and Harar. In June 1885, Lord Granville indicated that notwithstanding the *de jure* sovereignty of Turkey over these, Britain would not oppose an Italian bid. By this time, however, the Italian parliament would not accept an Italian occupation. For an excellent and fully documented analysis of Italian diplomatic manœuvres up to this date see C. Giglio, *L'Italia in Africa: Etiopia-Mar Rosso, 1857–1885*, Rome, 1958.

3. The 'Haber Garhajis' are an alliance of two separate northern Somali clans, the Habat Yunis and 'Idagalle. Eastern clans with whom Britain concluded a protectorate treaty were the Haber Tol Ja'lo; the Warsangeli; and the Majerteyn. The Majerteyn eventually fell within the Italian sphere. The Dulbahante clan to the east of what became the British Somaliland Protectorate was not included in the protectorate treaties.

4. These treaties are conveniently reproduced in *The Somali Peninsula: A New Light on Imperial Motives*, London, 1962. This important official publication by the government of the Somali Republic contains the fullest study which has yet been made of Anglo-Somali relations in this period.

5. L. P. Walsh, *Under the Flag and Somali Coast Stories*, London, n.d., p. 311.

6. Yusuf 'Ali established himself as Sultan of Obbia, the hinterland of

which is occupied by clansmen of both the Hawiye and Majerteyn, about 1870 after a dispute with the hereditary Majerteyn Sultan 'Isman. Earlier, in 1839, a British commercial treaty had been signed with the Majerteyn clan.

7. Menelik had by now officially denounced the Ucciali treaty with Italy and repaid the Italian loan which he had received. Britain, however, in contrast to France, refused to accept Menelik's position, and continued to treat with Italy although it was abundantly clear that the Italians had little control over Abyssinian policy towards the Somali.

8. There were at this time, of course, no Italian administrators in the Ogaden, and apart from the unofficial agreements signed between Ogaden clansmen and Italian explorers, Italy's claims derived from her 'protectorate' over Abyssinia, and thus ultimately depended upon the forays made by Abyssinian forces into this territory.

9. For a thorough account of Russian penetration and interests in Ethiopia at this time see C. Jesman's excellent study, *The Russians in Ethiopia: an essay in futility*, London, 1958.

10. R. Rodd, *Social and Diplomatic Memories, 1894–1901*, 1923, p. 173.

11. The post at Biyo Kaboba consisted 'of a fragile block-house built of loose stones and thatched with straw, . . . it is garrisoned by seven men . . . a nondescript and ragged riff-raff of Somali and Sudanese – no Abyssinians amongst them . . . those poor devils, who receive no pay . . . only live on passing caravans. . . .' (Count Gleichen, the Intelligence Officer with Rodd's party, *With the Mission to Menelik, 1897*, London, 1898, p. 27.) Alola, another place where a temporary Abyssinian post had been opened within British territory, was found to be deserted in 1897. Thus the Abyssinian encroachments were mere tokens, but the effect of this rather nominal Abyssinian pressure was to make Britain realize that her Somali territory was more extensive than was really necessary for her purposes.

12. This important point is also reflected in Rodd's dispatches to London, see *The Somali Peninsula*, pp. 55–58.

13. Rodd, *Social and Diplomatic Memoirs, 1894–1901*, p. 187.

14. A discussion of the interest of Russia in the triangular contest between France, Italy, and Britain, in the Red Sea coast and hinterland would be out of place here. But it is significant to record that Russia was involved as an intermediary in the peace negotiations between Italy and Ethiopia after the battle of Adowa.

CHAPTER IV: THE DERVISH FIGHT FOR FREEDOM: 1900–20

1. For further information on Islam in Somaliland see, I. M. Lewis, *A Pastoral Democracy*, London, 1961, pp. 213–28; E. Cerulli, *Somalia, scritti vari editi ed inediti*, Rome, 1957; B. G. Martin, *Muslim Brotherhoods in 19th century Africa*, Cambridge, 1976.

2. In the 1890s the settlement at Hargeisa consisted of a few hundred huts surrounded by a high fence enclosing roughly a square mile of sorghum

gardens. In this centre the poor and destitute, and cripples, used to collec
to receive succour and support. Sheikh Maddar's reputation extended
far into the Ogaden and he had contacts with the leaders of most of the
surrounding Somali clans. In 1893, the Sheikh helped to save Lord
Delamere's life after he had been mauled by a lion in the course of a
hunting expedition in the interior. In return, Delamere gave Sheikh
Maddar an imposing stone house which he had had constructed near
the settlement. Sheikh Maddar's tomb in Hargeisa is regularly visited
by those in search of blessing and is the scene of an annual ceremony of
remembrance. The fullest descriptions of the settlement in Sheikh
Maddar's lifetime are those given by H. G. C. Swayne, *Seventeen Trips
through Somaliland and a Visit to Abyssinia*, London, 1903.

3. This date, and much of the material relating to the Sayyid's personal
life and the Dervish movement, are based upon family records in the
possession of his son, Sheikh 'Abd ar-Rahman Sheikh Muhammad, and
his brother, Sheikh Hassan Sheikh 'Abdille. I have also made extensive
use of information collected from a number of surviving members of
the Sayyid's close associates, and from accounts of the period by the
present head of the Salihiya Order in Somaliland, Sheikh 'Isman Sheikh
'Umar, and the Dulbahante historian Haji Nur 'Ise. The first authori-
tative study of the Dervishes by a Somali historian is Aw Jama 'Umar
'Ise's *Taariikhdii Daraawiishta*, Mogadishu, 1976. This work comple-
ments the same scholar's brilliant compilation of the Sayyid's poems,
Diiwaanka Gabayada Sayid Maxamad Abdulle Xassan Mogadishu, 1974.

4. *Catha edulis* which grows in Ethiopia. The succulent green leaves when
fresh have stimulant properties similar to those of the benzedrine family
of drugs. They are often chewed by Sheikhs of the Qadiriya Order to
keep themselves awake during night services.

5. See Swayne, *op. cit.*, pp. 6, 7, 128, etc.

6. Quoted from D. Jardine, *The Mad Mullah of Somaliland*, London, 1923,
p. 43.

7. The fullest and most detailed account by an official who was Chief
Secretary to the Somaliland government during part of the period, is
Jardine's book referred to above. For the initial phase see also the
British government's official record, *Correspondence relating to the rising
of the Mullah Mohammad Abdulla in Somaliland and consequent military
operations, 1899–1902*, London, 1903. For particular periods and aspects
of the British operations, and on the part played by Ethiopia, the fol-
lowing are also worth consulting: M. McNeill, *In Pursuit of the Mad
Mullah*, London, 1902; J. W. Jennings, *With the Abyssinians in Somaliland*,
London, 1905; and for the contribution made by the King's African
Rifles regiment, H. Moyse-Bartlett, *The History of the King's African
Rifles*, London, 1956. The standard Italian record of the *jihad*, with
particular reference to its effects in Somalia, is, F. S. Caroselli, *Ferro e
Fuoco in Somalia*, Rome, 1931.

8. For the terms of this and the Illig treaty see, *The Somali Peninsula, cit.*,
pp. 118–22. (These, and all other treaties up to 1908, relating to the

Horn of Africa, are of course to be found in E. Hertslet, *Map of Africa by Treaty*, 3 vols., London, 1909 – 3rd edition.)

9. For an unusual account of conditions in the British Protectorate at this time see, F. Swayne, *A Woman's Pleasure Trip to Somaliland*, London. 1907.

10. A translation of this letter is given by Jardine, *op. cit.*, pp. 184–5.

11. For the full text and translation of this and other poems by Sayyid Muhammad see, B. W. Andrzejewski and I. M. Lewis, *Somali Poetry*, Oxford, 1964. Of Corfield and the camel constabulary which he raised, a sympathetic account is given by H. F. Prevost Battersby, *Richard Corfield of Somaliland*, London, 1914.

12. Quoted from Jardine, *op. cit.*, p. 249. The Sayyid's correspondence with the British Commissioner was conducted in Arabic. His poetic messages, however, were generally in Somali.

13. H. G. C. Swayne, *op. cit.*, p. 117.

14. The continuation of slavery under the Company's rule of the Benadir caused a scandal and led to an Italian commission of inquiry directed by Gustavo Chiese and Ernesto Travelli. The Commission's revealing findings were published in 1904, as, *Le Questioni del Benadir* (Milan), and fully support the charges which were made against the Company accusing it of negligence. Nor was the Italian government blameless. For an accessible though decidedly anti-Italian account of the position see, E. S. Pankhurst, *Ex-Italian Somaliland*, London, 1951, pp. 38–83.

15. At this time very few Somali were recruited into the Italian forces engaged in the work of 'pacification' – for obvious reasons. There were, however, a few Somali askaris mainly from the north. Later the Italians drew heavily upon their Somali subjects to staff their police and military units, the qualities of the northern nomadic Somali, in particular, being frequently eulogized in Italian reports during the fascist period as the outstanding representatives of this 'race of warriors'.

16. T. Carletti, *I Problemi del Benadir*, Viterbo, 1912, p. 270.

17. For a brilliantly vivid record of Ferrandi's years at Lugh see his, *Lugh. Emporio commerciale sul Giuba*, Rome, 1903, one of the few classics which have been written on Somalia.

18. For the full terms of the treaty see *The Somali Peninsula*, *cit.*, pp. 107–10. Apart from political objectives, the treaty laid down the commercial and economic aims and spheres of interest of the three powers in this area of Africa. These included: for France an extension of the Jibuti railway from Dire Dawa to Addis Ababa (under a French company with British, Italian, and Ethiopian representatives); for Britain (and Egypt) control of the Tana and Blue Nile waters; and for Italy the possibility of a link across Ethiopia between her two colonies of Eritrea and Somalia.

19. The Italian Foreign Minister at that time, Tommaso Tittoni, explained to the Italian parliament that the treaty reserved for Italy 'the share which is due to us and is necessary to assure the future of the two colonies' (Eritrea and Somalia). For the official edition of the Minister's speeches see, Baron Quaranta, *Italy's Foreign and Colonial Policy: Speeches of Senator Tommaso Tittoni,* London, 1914.

20. As officially reported by C. Riveri, Governor of Somalia from 1916–20, quoted in G. Corni, *Somalia Italiana*, Vol. ii, Milan, 1937, pp. 21–22.

CHAPTER V: SOMALI UNIFICATION: THE ITALIAN EAST AFRICAN EMPIRE

1. For further details see Carletti's record of his governorship, *I Problemi del Benadir*, Viterbo, 1912, pp. 187 ff.
2. For Cesare Maria De Vecchi de Val Cismon's own account of his period of administration see his *Orizzonti d'Impero: Cinque Anni in Somalia*, Milan, 1935.
3. An admirably comprehensive study of the S.A.I.S. enterprise and of the Duke of the Abruzzi's part therein is given by C. Maino, in her *La Somalia e L'Opera della Duca degli Abruzzi*, Rome, 1959.
4. For fuller information on the detailed terms of these regulations and contracts the reader is referred to G. Corni (ed.), *Somalia Italiana*, Milan, 1937, Vol. ii, pp. 412–18; and to P. Barile, *Colonizzazione fascista nella Somalia Meridionale*, Rome, 1935, pp. 179–81.
5. A useful discussion of the problem of labour scarcity, on which there is an extensive literature in Italian, is given by M. Karp, *The Economics of Trusteeship in Somalia*, Boston, 1960, pp. 104–10, and 117 ff.
6. Typical comments are to be found in Barile, *op. cit.*, pp. 149 ff.
7. For full details of the structure and growth of the police and military forces in Somalia during the period, see Corni, *op. cit.*, pp. 185–236.
8. Rivalry between the Marehan and Awlihan clans in this region assumed serious dimensions about 1910 when a British post was opened at Serenleh. From this base attempts were made in 1912 to bring the Marehan under effective administrative control. Further friction, however, led to the mounting of an expedition of the King's African Rifles between 1913 and 1914. Tension between the two clans appears to have been fanned by the activities of 'Abd ar-Rahman Mursal, a prominent headman of the Awlihan employed as an agent by the British authorities. He seems to have been a rather unhappy choice, for in 1915 after making an official visit to Nairobi, he returned to the area to broadcast the news that the country between Wajir and Serenle had been placed under his authority. This encouraged the Awlihan to provoke their enemies the Marehan and in the resulting tension to rebuff all attempts at mediation on the part of the Administration. In 1916, after a savage Awlihan attack on the Marehan, matters came to a head and 'Abd ar-Rahman Mursal was warned that unless camels looted in the raid were returned he would be dismissed from government service and imprisoned. He was not, however, to be intimidated and contrived a daring attack on Serenle post in which the local British official was killed along with the majority of his guard. With the arms and ammunition which had been seized, Serenle remained in the hands of the Awlihan until the Italian Resident at Bardera, on the opposite side of the Juba, crossed the river with his askaris and drove the Awlihan out.

Thereafter, although no British punitive expedition could be dispatched until 1917, 'Abd ar-Rahman's following began to dwindle so that when the expedition did arrive they were able to break the Awlihan resistance without difficulty. The majority of the clan's firearms were captured and the stupendously heavy fine of 25,000 camels imposed. As well as this, most of the clan's leading elders were arrested and imprisoned.

Thus although the disarmament of the clansmen of this turbulent region was by no means complete, some respect for the administering authority had been instilled by 1924, when the treaty of London was signed providing for the transfer of Jubaland to Italy. In the interval between the announcement of this new fate, and its actual execution, the clans, who were given no opportunity of expressing their views, split up into anti-Italian and anti-British factions. Delicate handling of the situation was required to prevent an outbreak of violence. This short record may serve to give some impression of the general conditions in Jubaland at the time.

9. D. Jardine, *The Mad Mullah of Somaliland*, London, 1923, pp. 316–18.
10. For fuller information on cultivation in this part of the Protectorate, see I. M. Lewis, *A Pastoral Democracy*, London, 1961, pp. 90–127.
11. For details of the record of events over this period see the official annuals, *Colonial Reports: Somaliland*. An impressionistic and lively account of the work of a District Commissioner at the time is provided by H. Rayne's *Sun, Sand and Somalis: Leaves from the Notebook of a District Commissioner in British Somaliland*, London, 1921. For another interesting record of the conditions and atmosphere of the period see, M. Perham, *Major Dane's Garden*, London, 1926. For discussion of the Protectorate's needs and potentialities by a Governor of the time see, H. B. Kittermaster, 'The Development of the Somali', *Journal of the African Society*, 31, 1932, pp. 234–44.
12. See above, Chapter III, pp. 55–6.
13. See H. M. Clifford, 'British Somaliland–Ethiopian Boundary', *Geographical Journal*, 97, 1936, pp. 289–307. And for the Italian version of the events of Walwal the account by the Banda commander Major Roberto Cimmaruta, *Ual-Ual*, Milan, 1936.
14. Corni, *op. cit.*, pp. 34–37.
15. Corni again provides some of the details, others are drawn from local Somali sources. See also S. Pankhurst, *Ex-Italian Somaliland*, London, 1951, pp. 99–103, for an account from the Ethiopian viewpoint.
16. Cf. also M. Perham's excellent general work, *The Government of Ethiopia*, London, 1948, pp. 336–8.
17. See Chapter IV, p. 88.
18. For a discussion of these from the Ethiopian side see again, Pankhurst, *op. cit.*, pp. 99–111, and A. de la Pradelle (who represented Ethiopia in the attempt at arbitration with Italy), *Le Conflict Italo-Ethiopien*, Paris, 1936. For an English assessment of Britain's part, see C. Hollis, *Italy in Africa*, London, 1941, pp. 141–203. See also E. M. Robertson, *Mussolini as Empire-Builder, Europe and Africa, 1932–36*, London, 1977.

19. The part played by anti-Ethiopian Ogaden clansmen is enthusiastically described by H. de Monfried, *Les Guerriers de L'Ogaden*, Paris, 1936.

20. See, for example, R. R. de Marco, 'The Italianisation of African Natives', in *Government Native Education in the Colonies, 1890–1937*, New York, 1943. See also R. L. Hess, *Italian Colonialism in Somalia*, Chicago, 1966.

21. T. Carletti, *I Problemi del Benadir*, Viterbo, 1912, pp. 274.

22. See M. Pirone's very useful outline history of Somalia, *Appunti di Storia dell'Africa, II, Somalia*, Rome, 1961, pp. 140–1.

23. On the rise of Somali nationalist parties generally see, I. M. Lewis, *A Pastoral Democracy*, London, 1961, pp. 266–96; and 'Modern Political Movements in Somaliland', *Africa*, 1958, pp. 244–61; 344–63.

24. These matters are discussed more fully in, I. M. Lewis, 'The Gadabursi Somali Script', *Bulletin of the School of Oriental and African Studies*, 1958, xxi, pp. 134–56. See also below, p. 216.

CHAPTER VI: THE RESTORATION OF COLONIAL FRONTIERS
1940–50

1. For the official British account of the Italian collapse in Somalia and the Allied occupation see George Steer, *The Abyssinian Campaigns. The Official Story of the Conquest of Italian East Africa*, London, 1942. For an Italian version of the circumstances of the Italian defeat see, R. di Lauro, *Come Abbiamo Diffeso L'Impero*, Rome, 1949.

2. For details of this treaty see, *The Somali Peninsula, cit.*, pp. 122–5.

3. Conditions in Somalia at this time and shortly after the Italian collapse are graphically described in *The First to be Freed*, a pamphlet prepared by the Ministry of Information and published by H.M. Stationery Office, London, 1944. For a more detailed study of events under the British Military Administration up to 1947, see Lord Rennell of Rodd, *British Military Administration of Occupied Territories in Africa, 1941–47*, London, 1948. Also of considerable interest in conveying the atmosphere in the British Protectorate immediately after its recapture is Gordon Waterfield's *Morning Will Come*, London, 1945. For a vivid, impressionistic, and semi-autobiographic record of the British Military Administration and the life and activities of its police and administrative officials see, Douglas Collins, *A Tear for Somalia*, London, 1961. A more sophisticated glimpse of the period is contained in Gerald Hanley's novel, *The Consul at Sunset*, London, 1951.

4. Rennell of Rodd, *cit.*, p. 153.

5. This and other information here is based chiefly upon material drawn from the official reports of the British Military Administration.

6. See the official communiqué issued by the Administration, summarized in E. S. Pankhurst, *cit.*, pp. 224–5.

7. 'Abdillahi 'Ise (of Mudugh Province, born in 1922) had in 1938 been employed as a clerical official in the Italian Administration. In 1941 he resigned his post to set up in business. Joining the S.Y.L. in 1945 he was elected to the League's central committee in 1947, and after acting

as the principal S.Y.L. spokesman to the Four Power Commission in 1948, served as a representative at the United Nations from 1949–52.

8. Both these men are Catholics, and in Mr Mariano's case his adherence to Christianity has not prevented his playing an important rôle in Somali politics.

9. See Four Power Commission of investigation for the former Italian Colonies, *Report on Somaliland*, Vol. ii, London, 1948. This report has not been fully released to the public in this country but can be consulted at the library of the Foreign Office. As well as containing its record of the submissions made in Somalia by the various parties and interest-groups, the report is useful in including material on the changes effected in all spheres during British military rule. Large parts of the report are published in E. S. Pankhurst's *Ex-Italian Somaliland*, pp. 222 ff. See also the article by the British member of the Commission, F. E. Stafford, 'The ex-Italian Colonies', *International Affairs*, Vol. xxv, January, 1949, pp. 47–55.

10. 'Abd ar-Rashid 'Ali Shirmarke (of Majerteyn Province, born 1917) served as a clerical official in both the Italian and British Administrations, was Secretary of the S.Y.L. from 1948–51, and a member of its central committee.

11. For an account of the U.N. debates see Pankhurst, *op. cit.*, pp. 260–9, 298–354. See also B. Rivlin, *The United Nations and the Italian Colonies*, New York, 1950; and G. H. Becker, *The Disposition of the Italian Colonies*, Annemasse, 1952. The future of Somalia was complicated by the general issue of the other ex-Italian territories, but especially by that of Eritrea to which Ethiopia advanced strong claims (see Pankhurst, *cit.*, and the same author's *Eritrea on the Eve*, London, 1952; and for a less partisan point of view, G. K. N. Trevaskis, *Eritrea: a colony in transition, 1941–52*, London, 1960). Briefly, the Bevin–Sforza compromise had proposed that Libya should be placed under U.N. trusteeship for ten years; Cyrenaica should be administered by Britain; Tripolitania by Italy; that Eritrea should be divided between Ethiopia and the British Sudan; and that Somalia should remain indefinitely under Italian trusteeship. This plan, however, foundered on several counts, and it was only at the Fourth Session of the United Nations Assembly that a further compromise proposal was accepted placing Somalia under Italian administration and U.N. trusteeship for a period of ten years. Significant provisos were attached to ensure that the U.N. should exercise a large measure of overriding control.

12. The claims made to the contrary by the Ethiopian government and by such distinguished supporters of Ethiopia as Miss Sylvia Pankhurst are generally unfounded, as of course is also the pretension that the Ogaden formerly formed part of the 'ancient Ethiopian empire'. As has been seen, Ethiopia's claims to the region were originally established by infiltration and conquest in the late nineteenth and early twentieth centuries, and only acquired some status in international law in the 1897 and 1908 Italo-Ethiopian agreements. There were, of course, pro-Ethio-

pian Somali elements in the Ogaden, Somali attachments and attitudes towards external influences being always partly influenced by internal factional divisions and the exigencies of the local Somali political scene. A somewhat parallel situation existed in Somalia in the final phase of British rule, when the division in attitudes towards a return of Italian control between the S.Y.L. and H.D.M.S. was partly a product of internal differences between the supporters of the two groups.

13. D. Collins, *A Tear for Somalia*, 1961, pp. 170, 177.

14. See above, pp. 59–61.

15. Influenced by security assessments in the Northern Frontier Province of Kenya rather than in Somalia, the S.Y.L. was initially regarded by the Protectorate authorities as dangerously leftish, if not Communist-inspired. This mistaken characterization took several years to live down. Hence, although not subject to a total proscription, the League was certainly not encouraged in its early efforts to attract adherents in British Somaliland.

16. See H. Deschamps, *et all.*, *Côte des Somalis, Réunion-Inde*, Paris, 1948, and *Notes et Etudes documentaires, Le Côte français des Somalis*, 29th April, 1961.

17. For an interesting expression of French views on recent Somali questions see, R. Lamy, 'Le destin des Somalis', in *Cahiers de l'Afrique et l'Asie. Mer Rouge-Afrique Orientale*, Paris, 1959, pp. 163–212.

CHAPTER VII: FROM TRUSTEESHIP TO INDEPENDENCE
1950–60

1. No extensive study of the important rôle of the U.N. in Somalia has yet been published. For some valuable comments, however, see A. A. Castagno, 'Somalia', *International Conciliation*, New York, March, 1959, pp. 395–400.

2. After 1954 the Administration jointly with UNESCO opened three centres for fundamental education in the south of Somalia. Two, at Dinsor and Villabruzzi, were amongst part-cultivating clans, while the third, at Afmadu, was concerned only with fully nomadic groups. It proved the least successful and was discontinued after two years of operation.

3. On the development of education generally, in Somalia particularly, and also in British Somaliland, see A. A. Castagno, 'The Somali Republic', in H. Kitchen (ed.), *The Educated African*, London and New York, 1962.

4. See, A.F.I.S., *Plans de Développement Economique de la Somalie, Années 1954–1960*, Rome, 1954; and G. F. Malagodi, *Linee Programmatiche per lo sviluppo economico e sociale della Somalia*, Rome, 1953. The Seven Year Development Plan is critically discussed in M. Karp, *The Economics of Trusteeship in Somalia*, Boston, 1960.

5. See Karp, *op. cit.*, pp. 87–104.

6. On these two parties, the first of which eventually became incorporated in the Liberal Party, see, I. M. Lewis, *A Pastoral Democracy*, London, 1961, pp. 283–90.

7. Progress throughout the trusteeship period in Somalia is excellently documented in the Administration's annual reports, *Rapport du gouvernement italien a l'Assemblée generale des Nations Unies sur L'Administration de tutelle de la Somalie*, Rome, Ministry of Foreign Affairs. For further details on the position up to 1958, see also I. M. Lewis, *Modern Political Movements in Somaliland*, International African Institute Memorandum XXX, London, 1958, and Castagno, *cit.*, 1959. For an extremely detailed report of the procedural aspects of the 1956 elections see, A.F.I.S., *Le Prime Elezioni Politiche in Somalia*, Mogadishu, 1957.

8. For an original and very personal view of conditions in the Protectorate at this time by the wife of the engineer in charge of this scheme see, M. Laurence, *The Prophet's Camel Bell*, London, 1963.

9. For fuller discussion of the social implications of the new Local Authorities see, I. M. Lewis, *cit.*, 1961, pp. 200–3.

10. The Emperor's address is recorded in a brochure in Amharic, Arabic, and English, published by the Ethiopian Press and Information Department, 1956.

11. For further information see, Lewis, *cit.*, 1958, pp. 346–9.

12. See, *Report of the Commission of Enquiry into Unofficial Representation on the Legislative Council*, Government of the Somaliland Protectorate, Hargeisa, 1958.

13. A Commissioner for Somalization was appointed and in April 1959 his report was being studied by the government. In July of that year an Advisory Public Service Board was created to select candidates for overseas scholarships; to recommend the selection of civil servants for promotion; to advise on entry conditions to the public service and to deal with other related matters. The Board, which was chaired by the Attorney-General, consisted of two other official members and two independent Somali members.

14. See G. A. Costanzo, *Problemi costituzionali della Somalia nella preparazione all' independenza*, Milan, 1962.

15. See above, p. 152.

16. In March 1957, the government had brought out a Somali news-sheet ('The Somali Messenger', *Wargeyska Somaliyed*) written in Somali transcribed in a simple but accurate Roman script. But popular reaction was so unfavourable that after two editions this was withdrawn.

17. See *Report of the United Nations Advisory Council for the Trust Territory of Somaliland under Italian Administration* (1 April, 1958, to 31 March, 1959), document T.1444, 1959, pp. 24–31.

18. See *Report of the Somaliland Constitutional Conference held in London in May 1960*, Cmnd. 1044, London, 1960.

19. This body, still essentially advisory, had replaced the former Protectorate Advisory Council and constituted a sort of Upper House.

20. For the British agreements see, *Agreements and Exchanges of Letters between the Government of the United Kingdom and the Government of Somaliland in connexion with the Attainment of Independence by Somaliland*, Cmnd. 1101, London, 1960; and for the Italian, *L'Amministrazione fiduciaria della*

Somalia e i Rapporti dell'Italia con la Repubblica Somala, Rome, Ministry of Foreign Affairs, 1961, pp. 127–206. This report also contains a summary account of the entire trusteeship period.

CHAPTER VIII: THE PROBLEMS OF INDEPENDENCE

1. See Lewis, *A Pastoral Democracy, cit.*, pp. 266–96; and 'Problems in the development of modern leadership and loyalties in the British Somaliland Protectorate and U.N. Trusteeship Territory of Somalia', *Civilisations*, 1960, pp. 49–62.

2. Thus in the Protectorate in 1957 the legislative council asked the government to institute an inquiry into the abolition of the tribal system. An inquiry was consequently begun, but at the time of independence had not resulted in any conclusive action being taken. Similarly, the S.Y.L. government formed in Somalia after the March 1959 elections, set up a tribunal to study the problem of tribalism and to consider how traditional tribal ties could best be adapted to the needs of a modern state.

3. See S. Santiapichi, *Appunti di Diritto penale della Somalia*, Istitut. Universario della Somalia, Rome, 1961; P. Contini, *The Somali Republic, an experiment in Legal Integration,* London, 1969; M. R. Ganzglass, *The Penal Code of the Somali Democratic Republic,* New Brunswick, 1971.

4. In October 1960 a committee under the chairmanship of Mr Muse H. I. Galal, the distinguished authority on Somali poetry, was set up to recommend the most suitable script for the mother-tongue. The Committee's recommendations favoured the use of a Roman orthography, but no decision was taken by the government of the Republic at the time.

5. The fact that only some 100,000 persons voted out of the north's estimated population of 650,000, suggests that at least half the electorate boycotted the referendum. All adult men and women were entitled to vote, women voting for the first time in the north's history.

6. The Prime Minister's statement of policy is fully reported in *The Somali News*, 25 August, 1961.

7. For further information on this disaster and the measures taken to combat its effects, see *Rehabilitation programme drawn up by the Committee set up by His Excellency the Prime Minister to recommend measures essential to repair damages caused by the flood,* Somali Republic: Ministry of Information, Mogadishu, 1962.

8. For a report of the judicial proceedings, see *The Somali News*, February 1963. The lieutenants fought bravely against the Ethiopians in the spring of 1964.

9. A national civil service establishment commission was set up at the end of 1962 to regulate appointments and promotions, on the former British Protectorate pattern.

10. Late in the summer a general re-posting of all District and Provincial Commissioners took place.

11. The tax on petrol in the north was raised to the rate currently applied in the south, causing petrol prices in the north to double. At the same

time the tax on diesel fuel was reduced and also import duties on alcohol and cigarettes to bring the northern prices into line with those in the south. These latter measures were expected to offset the increases in petrol prices. Unfortunately, however, for reasons which are difficult to understand, the government failed to realize that almost all motor vehicles in the north use petrol and not diesel oil. Northerners found little comfort in the reductions in alcohol and cigarette prices which they regarded in the circumstances as derisory.

12. Sheikh Mahamud Muhammad Farah (Ogaden) who had occupied this office as a compromise candidate for the two previous years. Sheikh Mahamud was Minister of Justice in the 1959 S.Y.L. government.

13. A number of articles on this theme urging the need for strong government appeared in the government newspaper. See *The Somali News*, 21 and 28 December 1962.

14. The Bill received the support of 72 members of the Assembly, ten members opposed it, and one member abstained: other members had apparently left the Assembly in protest. The new law which consisted of 78 articles provided, *inter alia*, for tighter control of public meetings and associations and empowered the Supreme Court to suspend or dissolve political parties which violated the provisions of the Republic's constitution. To what extent the opposition's criticisms were justified can only be judged from the way in which this legislation was applied. Certainly, in the past some opposition groups had abused the democratic privileges of the Republic to an extent dangerous to public security.

15. As noted above, however, women in the north had participated in the national referendum on the Republic's constitution.

16. *The Somali Peninsula: a new light on imperial motives,* London, 1962, p. vi.

17. Article VI, section 4, of the Constitution read: 'The Somali Republic shall promote, by legal and peaceful means, the union of Somali territories and encourage solidarity among the peoples of the world, and in particular among African and Islamic peoples.'

18. See *A Pastoral Democracy, cit.* pp. 303–4.

19. For details see, *The Somali News*, 8 December, 1958.

20. For further information on events in the *Côte,* see S. Touval, *Somali Nationalism*, Cambridge, Massachusetts, 1963, pp. 123–31; and *Notes et Etudes Documentaires: La Côte Française des Somalis,* La Documentation française, Paris, 1961, No. 2,774.

21. For a short summary of these fruitless negotiations and references to the relevant U.N. documents, see A. A. Castagno, 'Somalia', *International Conciliation*, No. 522, New York, 1959, pp. 386–91; and for a statement of the Ethiopian point of view, *The Ethio-Somalia Frontier Problem,* Ministry of Information, Imperial Ethiopian Government, Addis Ababa, 1961. See also, A. A. Castagno, 'Somali Republic' in J. S. Coleman and C. G. Rosberg (eds.), *Political Parties and National Integration in Tropical Africa*, Berkeley, 1964, pp. 512–59.

22. The Ethiopian government on its part at first announced that after the Protectorate had become independent, the northern clans' grazing rights

in the Haud would be cancelled. Later, however, a few days prior to independence, a further Ethiopian statement assured the Somali government of the Protectorate that the grazing rights would continue as long as the 1897 boundary was recognized by Somalis. Since the formation of the Republic both sides have in practice respected the existing frontier, although this uneasy situation has led to a train of incidents. See *The Danot Incidents*, a pamphlet published by the Ministry of the Interior, Somali Republic, Mogadishu, 1961. For a discussion of some of the legal aspects, see D. J. Latham Brown, 'The Ethiopia–Somaliland Frontier Dispute', *International and Comparative Law Quarterly*, 1956, pp. 245–65; and 'Recent Developments in the Ethiopia–Somaliland Dispute', *ibid*, 1961, pp. 167–78.

23. Movement into and out of the District was restricted under the Outlying Districts Ordinance, 1902, and the Special Districts (Administration) Ordinance, 1934. A form of control over movement between towns in the District, not far short of the South African 'pass system', was also applied.

24. See *Report of the Kenya Constitutional Conference*, 1962, Cmnd. 1700. London, 1962, p. 11.

25. See *A People in Isolation: a call by political parties of the Northern Frontier District of Kenya for Union with the Somali Republic*, London, 1962. This pamphlet sets out the Somali case for the three principal secessionist parties – The Northern Province Peoples' Progressive Party, the Northern Frontier Democratic Party, and The Northern Province Peoples' National Union.

26. For a full report see *The Somali News*, 23 March, 1962.

27. This speech was delivered at a state banquet held in honour of Jomo Kenyatta on 28 July, 1962. For further information on these visits see *The Somali Republic and African Unity*, an illustrated commemorative brochure published by the Somali Republic, Mogadishu, 1962.

28. *Kenya: Report of the Northern Frontier District Commission*, Cmnd. 1900, London, 1962.

29. *Kenya: Report of the Regional Boundaries Commission*, Cmnd. 1899, 1962.

30. See the excellent and full description of the negotiations between the Republic and Britain contained in J. Drysdale's valuable study *The Somali Dispute*, London and New York, 1964. For further information on the issue see also I. M. Lewis, 'The Problem of the Northern Frontier District of Kenya', *Race*, 1963, pp. 48–60.

31. Speech of 28 July, 1962. The President made these points more explicit in a further speech on 16 August, during Ronald Ngala's visit to Mogadishu. Referring to democratic practice in the Republic on that occasion, President Adan said he regretted that many other African states, 'because of the intolerances that are inevitable among a heterogeneous populace' had had to resort, for the sake of cohesion to a single-party system of government. 'Others forbid politics altogether', he added. See *The Somali Republic and African Unity, cit.*; and I. M. Lewis, 'Pan-Africanism and Pan-Somalism', *The Journal of Modern African Studies*, 1963, pp. 147–61.

32. See Dennis Austin, 'The Ghana–Togo Frontier', *The Journal of Modern African Studies*, 1963, pp. 139–45.
33. The full text of this speech is given in *The Somali News*, 31 May, 1963. For a convenient summary of the main events in the Republic up to December 1963 see; Somali Government *Government Activities from Independence until Today (1st July 1960–31st December 1963)*, Mogadishu, 1964.
34. See I. M. Lewis, 'Developments in the Somali Dispute', *African Affairs*, 1967, pp. 104–12; V. Thompson and R. Adloff, *Djibouti and the Horn of Africa*, California, 1968; P. Oberlé, '*Afars et Somalis: les dossiers de Djibouti*, Paris, 1971.

CHAPTER IX: THE SOMALI REVOLUTION 1969–76

1. An official statement made after the military coup of 1969 alleged that Premier Igal had expended £500,000 in public funds in payments to members of the Assembly between January and October, 1969.
2. For a vivid evocation of the corrosive atmosphere in the capital, Mogadishu, see Nuruddin Farah's novel, *The Naked Needle*, 1974.
3. This term was originally devised long before 1969 by members of the BBC Somali programme to refer to socialism and communism in Europe and the Middle East.
4. This expression was in circulation in the mid-1950s in the then British Somaliland Protectorate, where the expatriate administrators strongly encouraged self-help schemes for school construction, farming and other development projects.
5. For a sympathetic Russian account of this enterprise written during the heyday of the Somali–Soviet *entente*, see P. Kuprijanov, 'Somalian Village: Social and Economic Transformations', *3rd International Congress of Africanists*, Addis Ababa, 1973.
6. For a detailed account see B. W. Andrzejewski, 'The Introduction of a National Orthography for Somali', *African Language Studies*, 1974, pp. 199–203; and 'Five Years of Written Somali: A Report on Progress and Projects' *Bulletin of African Studies: Notes and News* (supplement to *Africa*), 1977. See also O. O. Mohamed, *From Written Somali to a Rural Development Campaign*, Mogadishu, 1975.
7. This is one of the few concise definitions of nationalism generally preferred by political scientists, see e.g. K. Minogue, *Nationalism*, London, 1967, p. 154.
8. See I. M. Lewis (ed.) *Abaar: the Somali Drought*, London, 1975 and Somalia, Directorate of Planning and Co-ordination, *Revised Programme of Assistance Required to the Drought Stricken Areas of Somalia*, Mogadishu, 1975.
9. See I. M. Lewis, 'From Nomadism to Cultivation: the Expansion of Political Solidarity in southern Somalia' in M. Douglas and P. Kaberry (eds.), *Man in Africa*, London, 1969: 'The Dynamics of Nomadism: Prospects for Sedentarization and Social Change' in T. Monod (ed.), *Pastoralism in Tropical Africa*. London, 1975.

10. See Chapter IV, pp. 63–91.
11. These and other speeches are reproduced in *My Country and My People: Selected speeches of Jaalle Major-General Mohammad Siyad Barre*, Mogadishu, 1974.
12. For fuller discussion of these issues see A. Wolczyk, 'Il "socialismo" Somala; un industria per il potere', *Concretezza*, Rome, January, 1972, pp. 23–6; L. Pestalozza, *Somalia, Cronaca della Rivoluzione*, Bari,1973; B. Davidson 'Somalia: Towards Socialism', *Race and Class*, 1975, pp. 19–38; I. M. Lewis, 'Kim Il Sung in Somalia; The end of tribalism?', in P. Cohen and W. Shack (eds.), *The Politics of Office*, Oxford, 1979.

CHAPTER X: NATIONALISM, ETHNICITY AND REVOLUTION IN THE HORN OF AFRICA

1. P. Gilkes, *The Dying Lion*, London, 1975.
2. In 1977 the Ethiopian military government claimed to have discovered documentary proof of a concerted Somali campaign designed to spread civil insurrection throughout south-eastern Ethiopia. The alleged Somali plot was referred to by the title 'War Clouds in the Horn of Africa', by a strange coincidence the title of T. J. Farer's Carnegie monograph, *War Clouds in the Horn of Africa: a crisis for Detente*, New York, 1976. This interesting study examined the implications for the superpowers of conflict between Ethiopia and Somalia over the Ogaden on the assumption that Ethiopia was still supported by the U.S.A. and Somalia by the U.S.S.R. For a partisan Ethiopian view of the problem, couched in the new Marxist–Leninist language, see M. Wolde Mariam, *Somalia: the problem child of Africa*, Addis Ababa, 1977. See also C. Legum and B. Lee, *Conflict in the Horn of Africa*, London, 1977.
3. See C. Jesman, *The Russians in Ethiopia: an Essay in Futility*, London, 1958.
4. Cf. J. Markakis, *Ethiopia: Anatomy of a Traditional Polity*, Oxford, 1975.
5. For an unusually well-informed analysis of this period see, C. Clapham, *Haile-Selassie's Government*, London, 1969. J. Markakis and N. Ayele, *Class and Revolution in Ethiopia*, Nottingham, 1978, supplies a critical analysis of Mengistu's regime.
6. So for instance in the syncretic Haitian religion of Voodoo and in Umbanda in Brazil, the gods or spirits were divided into different 'nations' including those of such African nationality as 'Yoruba', 'Ibo'.
7. See E. Kedourie (ed. and introd.), *Nationalism in Asia and Africa*, London, 1971.
8. E. Gellner, 'Scale and Nation', *Philosophy of the Social Sciences*, 3, 1973, pp. 1–17.
9. See e.g. F. Barth (ed.), *Ethnic Groups and Boundaries*, Boston, 1969; A. Cohen (ed. and introd.) *Urban Ethnicity*, London, 1974, and *Two-Dimensional Man*, London, 1974.
10. See e.g. C. Geertz (ed.), *Old Societies and New States*, Glencoe, 1963; L. Mair, *New Nations*, London, 1963.
11. A. L. Epstein, *Ethos and Identity*, London, 1978.

INDEX

Somali and Arabic proper names are indexed as they appear in the text, eg. 'Abdi Hassan Boni appears under A. When the name is commonly prefaced with an honorific, it is indexed accordingly, eg. Sheikh Isma'il Sheikh Isaq appears under S. Other names are indexed according to surname initial letters.

'Abdallah Muhammad, Harar ruler, 50

'Abdi Hassan Boni, Deputy Premier, 164

'Abdi Nur Muhammad, Minister of General Affairs, 160

'Abdillahi 'Ise, first Premier of Somalia, 127, 128, 146, 156, 157, 158, 164

'Abd al-Qadir Sekhawe Din, Somali religious leader, 121

'Abd ar-Rashid 'Ali Shirmarke, Secretary of SYL, 128; criticises SYL leadership, 161; head of Republican Government 164; 173; 179; 188; 193; President, 202; assassinated, 206, 221

'Abd ar-Razaq Haji Husseyn, 161; Minister of Interior, 164; Premier 202; 204, 221

'Abdullah Muhammed Kamil, first Premier of Jibuti, 230

Abruzzi, Duke of the, 93, 95

Abyssinia (see also under Ethiopia), war with (13th and 14th centuries), 25–7; arms trade with, 50–1; relations with Italians, 50–62; negotiations with British, 56–62; treaties and boundary agreements with Italy, 62, 88, 89; campaigns against Dervishes, 70–90; peace with Dervishes, 72–4; relations with Italy, position in Somaliland, 87–90; relations with France, 91

Adal, (Ifat) Muslim Emirate, 25–7

Adale, (Itala), 52

Adan 'Abdulle 'Isman, 158; provisional President of Republic, 164; President, 172, 176; loses Presidential election, 202, 221

Aden, 1, 39–40, 114

Administration, Europeans in, 7; Italian system of, 98, 111, 112; in British Protectorate, 106; in French Somaliland, 136; Somalization of, 141, 144, 154–5; Integration, 170, 174

Adowa, battle of, 53, 56, 110

'Afar (Danakil), people, 4, 47, 49, 136, 180, 181, 228

Afgoi, slave market, 87; 94; mission school at, 97

Agriculture, general, 2, 3; nomadic, 7–9; cultivation and crops, 12–15; Italian methods of, 92–6; in British Protectorate, 102; services expanded, 133; Agricultural Bank, 142; 'Tug Wajale Scheme', 175

Agricultural Development Corporation, 215

Ahmad Diini, Vice-President French Somaliland Council, 181

Ahmad Ibrahim al-Ghazi (Gran), 25–7, 81, 224

Ahmad Sulayman 'Abdulle, General, 223

Ahmadiya, Muslim brotherhood, 64, 65

Ajuran, clan, 24, 28, 33, 108

Akil, headman, 43, 105, 149

'Ali Adan Lord, Kenyan Somali leader, 186

'Ali 'Ariif, Jibuti 'Afar leader, 228, 229

'Ali Gerad Jama', Minister of Education, 164

Anglo-Ethiopian Boundary Commission, 61, 106

Anglo-Ethiopian Agreement (1942), 116

Anglo-Italo-French Agreement (1906), 88, 109

Anglo-Italian Protocols, 55, 88; agreements (1907), 73, 89

Anglo-Italian Boundary Commission and agreement (1930–1), 106, 107

273

Anglo-Italian Agreement (1925), 109
Anglo-Somali treaties, 46, 47, 60
Antonelli, Italian Count, 54
Anzilotti, Dr Enrico, Italian administrator, 146
Arabic, 5, 115, 158
Arab League, 220, 226, 230
Arabs, 5, 20–1, 87, 100, 137, 145, 180
Asian, community in Somaliland, 7, 21, 145
Assab, port of, 41, 44 ~

Bananas, export of, 4, 96, 143, 165
Bantu, 5; Somalized, 7; displacement of by Somalis, 19; labour for Italians, 95; 123
Bardera, town, 3, 29, 88, 97
Barislov, Grigory, 239
Beletweyn, district, 87, 109
Benadir, province, 6, 51–3, 74, 90
Benadir Company, 53
Berbera, 2, 21, 27, 35, 35–6, 42–5, 48, 132, 150, 163, 193, 175
Beja, tribe, 4, 27
Bevin, Ernest, British Foreign Secretary, 124, 128, 137, 247
Bimal, clan, 86, 98, 118
Borama, district, 102, 106
Boran Galla, tribe, 4, 31, 191
Brava, 6; 22, 38, 39, 51, 97
British (Britain, British Government), arrival of, 30; blockade Somali coast, 33, 36; Protectorate of Mombasa, 37; treaty with Majerteyn Sultanate, 38; on Somali coast, 40–2; action after Egyptian withdrawal, 45; Anglo-Somali treaties, 46, 60; Agents on Somali coast, 47; protest, 55; mission to Abyssinia, 56; negotiations with Abyssinia, 57–62; dispute with Ras Makonnen, 57, 59; 61; 'most favoured nation' agreement with Abyssinia, 59; war with Dervishes and Sayyid Muhammad, 70–84; Anglo-Italian agreement (1907), 73; review situation in Somaliland, start new policy, 75, 76; raise Camel Constabulary, ·77; peace delegation to Dervishes, 79, 80; cede Jubaland and Kismayu to Italians, 98; progress in Protectorate, 101–107; redefinition of Protectorate boundaries with Somalis, 107; Second

World War campaigns, agreement with Ethiopia, 116, 117; military administration of Somalia and Ogaden, 117–31 (see also under British Military Administration); proposals for union of Somali peoples, 124; proposals abandoned, 128; British Somaliland Protectorate reformed, 131; development programme in Protectorate 132, 133; establish Protectorate Advisory Council, 134, 150; expand education, 149; develop local government, 149, 150; final hand-over of Haud and Reserved Areas to Ethiopia, new agreement with Ethiopia, 150; mission to Addis Ababa, 152; new Legislative Council (elected members), 153; new constitution 161; independence ؍ negotiations with Somali leaders 162, 163; independence announced, 164; influence of British tradition on new Republic, 169; attitude to pan-Somalism in Kenya, 185; discuss future of Kenyan Northern Frontier Districts at Kenya Constitutional Conference, 186; Commission of Enquiry on NFD problems, 187, 191–92; announce NFD to remain with Kenya, 192; strained relations with Somali Republic, ambassador withdrawn, 193; diplomatic relations restored, 203; refuses military aid, 237
BBC, Middle Eastern Service relay station, Berbera, 163, 193
British Military Administration, establishment in Somalia and Ogaden, 116, 117; labour problems, 118; repatriation of Italians, 118; reorganization of police force, Somalia Gendarmerie, 118, 119; education under, 119, 120; attitude of Somalis to, 120, 121; Italian propaganda against, 125, 126; Four Power Commission arrives, rioting in Mogadishu, 126; Somalia becomes Italian trusteeship territory, 128; Ogaden transferred to Ethiopean rule, 130; administration ends, 131
Bulhar, port, occupied by Egyptians, 43; 103
Burao, town, 77, 103, 114, 133, 149

Burton, Sir Richard, 33, 34, 36

Camel Constabulary, 77, 132
Carletti, Tommaso, Italian Governor of Somalia, 87, 92, 112
Castro, Fidel, 232–3, 241
Chinese Peoples' Republic, 200, 210, 216, 224, 225, 242, 249
Christianity (Christians), 25–7, 67, 69, 81, 97, 178
Colonial Development and Welfare grants, 132
Corni, Guido, Italian Governor, 97, 108
Cotton, weaving, 38; export of, 100
Council of Secretaries, 207, 208
Cuba, 227, 233, 236, 237–9, 240, 241

Dakkar, capital of Kings of Adal, 25
Danakil ('Afar), people, 4, 27, 47, 49, 136
Darod, clan-family, 6, 12, 22, 23, 26; 29, 30, 122, 146, 147, 157, 158, 159–61, 168, 170
Da'ud, General, Commandant of National Army, 174, 207
Dervishes, 69, 70–91, 87
Diya system, 11, 208, 209
Digil, tribe, 5, 7, 12, 13, 123, 125, 146, 156, 160, 204
Dir, 'Samale' clan family, 6, 12, 23, 24, 153, 158
Dulbahante, clan, 6, 70, 71, 76, 150

Education, 97; 102; 115; 133, 148, 149, 136, 140, 148, 149, 218–19
Egypt (see also United Arab Republic), 41–3, 45, 46, 141, 165, 173, 199
Erigavo, district, 21, 23, 133
Eritrea, 233, 240, 247–9
Ethiopia (see also under Abyssinia), boundaries of defined, 62; boundaries with British Protectorate, 107; friction with Italians in Ogaden, 'Walwal Incident', 108–10; war and treaty with Italians, 109, 110; liberated from Italians, 116; asks for return of Ogaden and Reserved Areas, Ogaden transferred from British administration, 129–31; assumes full control in Haud and Reserved Areas, 150, 151; United Nations boundary commission, 182, 183; opposition to pan-Somalism,

182–3; relations with Somali Republic, 181, 185, 201, 203, 227–8, 231–41; coup and revolution, 228, 231, 232; expels Americans, 233; Russian support, 234, 237–44; nature of state, 247–52

Filonardi, Vincenzo, Italian consul and commercial venturer, 51–3
Finance (and economics), 100, 101, 104, 104, 142, 143, 144, 165, 173, 176; 200, 201
Five Year Development Plan (1974–8), 215
Four Power Commission, 125, 126, 127, 128
France, 54, 91, 181, 228, 229, 230–1
French Somaliland (see also under Jibuti), 1–3, 23, 49, 91; 116, 136–8, 179, 180–1, 203, 227–30

Gadabursi, clan, 23, 43, 54, 56, 106
Galawdewos, Abyssinian Emperor, 27
Galkayu, town, 28, 99
Galla, see under Oromo
Garissa, town, 5; Kenyan Somali district, 183, 186, 191
Genale, 93, 117
Genealogy, use of among Somalis, 10, 104, 168
Germany, 78, 173, 236
Gogle, Italian rural constabulary, 98, 119

Habar Awal, clan, 35, 46, 54
Habar Tol Ja 'lo (Isaq) clan, 46, 69, 150, 153
Habar Yunis (Isaq) clan, 35, 46, 49, 135
Haile Selassie, Emperor of Ethiopia, 152, 182, 185, 228, 229, 232, 247–9
Haji 'Abdallah Sheheri, 75
Haji Farah 'Omar, 114
Haji Muhammad Husseyn, 121, 127, 159, 175
Haji Muse Boqor, 206
Hamitic peoples, 4; early history of, 18–21
Haq ad-Din, Sultan of Ifat, 25
Harar, province of Abyssinia, 1, 2, 23, 44, 45, 48, 49, 65; 129, 130, 236–7
Hargeisa, town, 2, 59, 132, 102, 135, 150, 175

Hassan Guled, first President of Republic of Jibuti, 180, 230
Haud, the, region of Somaliland and Abyssinia, 2, 3, 6, 56, 59, 129, 131, 150, 151
Hawiye, clan family, 6, 12, 24, 125, 147, 158
Health Services, 95, 97, 132, 136
Her, form of political contract, 10
Hiran, province, 6
Hunter, Major, Br. Consul, 45, 46
Husseyn Kulmiye, General, 223

Ibn Sa'id, early Arab geographer, 24
Ifat, early Muslim state, 25
Illalos, tribal constabulary, 68; 98; 105
Iran, 237, 238, 240
Isaq, clan, 23, 24, 83, 106, 129, 135, 170, 178
'Ise (Dir) clan, 46, 49, 54, 55, 56, 130, 136
Islam, 5, 16, 27, 20–3, 25–7, 63, 64, 83, 100, 105, 133, 156, 213, 219–20, 224
Isma'il 'Ali Abokor, General, 216, 223
Isma'il Jabarti, Sheikh, 22
'Isman Yusuf Kenadid, 115
Israel, 241
Italo-Ethiopian peace treaty, 62
Italy (Italians, Italian Government), interests in Somaliland, 41, 44, 45, 50, 51, 53–62; struggle with Dervishes, 70–91; Anglo-Italian agreement(1907), 73; assume limited responsibility for Sayyid Muhammad, 74; purchase Benadir coast from Sultan of Zanzibar, 74; colonial policy, 85; operations against Dervishes, create auxiliary force, 86; pacify coastal areas, extend administration, 87; relations with Ethiopia, definition of influence in Somaliland, 87–90; policy and progress of colonization, 92–101; redefinition of boundaries with British Protectorate, 107; forward policy in Ogaden, 108, 109; 'Walwal Incident', 109, 110; war with Ethiopia, 109, 110; conditions in Somalia after Ethiopian war, 110–12; Second World War campaigns, 116; position of Italians under British Military Administration, 117, 118; attempt to create a pro-Italian front in Somalia, 125; clash with SYL, 126, 127; UN

trusteeship agreement, 139; dispute with SYL, 140; seven-year development plan, 142; Somali independence, 164; post independence relations, 171, 173

Jama' 'Abdullahi Qalib, 164
Jama' 'Ali Korshell, General, 207, 208
Jibuti, capital of French Somaliland, 2, 49, 59, 71, 116, 136, 181; Republic, 230–1
Jigjiga, 71, 89, 102, 106, 108, 116, 129–30; 231, 234, 238–9, 245
John of Tigre, Abyssinian King, 46, 50
Juba, river, 3, 5; Italian colonies, 92
Jubaland, 19, 51, 98

Kadis, muslim magistrates, 100, 105, 133, 156
Kenya, Somali population of, 1, 183, 184; border with Somali Republic, 5; frontier with Abyssinia, 89; Somali Youth League active in, 122; SYL banned, 184; Northern Provinces Peoples' Party formed, moves for Somali unification, 186; Kenya Constitutional Conference, 186; British Commission to Northern Frontier Districts, 187, 191, 192; Kenyan leaders visit Somali Republic, 189, 190; British Government announces decision on NFD, 192, 199; Somali unification issue, 203, 207; as refuge, 213, 245; attitude to Ogaden War 234, 237
Kenyatta, Jomo, 189, 190, 196, 197, 203
King's African Rifles, 127
Kirsch, Emil, 78
Kisymayu, 3, 97, 98, 175

Language, 5, 6, 171, 216
Law, 100, 105, 133, 134, 156, 170, 212–13
League of Nations, 110
Lennox-Boyd, Mr Alan, 161
Libya, 220, 241
Lij Yasu, Emperor of Abyssinia, 78
Lugh, town of, 57, 87, 88, 89

Macleod, Mr Iain, 163
Macmillan, Mr Harold, 185, 192
Mahamud 'Ali Shirre, 74
Mahamud Harbi, 180, 181

Mahdi, 48, 50
Majerteyn, province, 6, 38, 87, 96, 99, 121, 125, 161, 245–6
Mandera, Kenyan Somali district, 183, 186
Mariano, Michael, 127, 151, 162
Maudling, Mr Reginald, 187
Menelik, Abyssinian King, 46, 50, 54; 55, 58, 72, 202, 231, 244, 248
Mengistu, Colonel, Ethiopian Head of State, 231, 233, 235, 239–41, 244, 249
Merca, district, 6, 22, 24, 51, 52, 86
Mogadishu, capital of Somalia, 4, 22, 24, 28, 37, 51, 52, 86, 97, 126, 172, 174, 188
Moyale, Kenyan Somali district, 186, 191
Mudugh, province, 6
Muhammad 'Abdi Nur, 160
Muhammad Haji Ibrahim Igal, 154, 164, 176, 202, 203, 206–7, 221
Muhammad Abshir, General, 204, 206, 207
Muhammad 'Ali Samatar, General, 223
Muhammad Siyad Barre, President of Somalia, 207, 209, 210–11, 213, 216–18, 219–20, 221–2, 223–4, 224–5, 226–8, 232–4, 235–6, 239, 242, 245–6, 249
Mustahil, 108, 109
Muzaffar dynasty, 24, 28

National Assembly of the Republic 164, 165, 172, 173, 176, 177, 201, 202, 204, 205–6, 207
Nationalism, Somali, influence of Islam on, 16; modern Somali start of, 113, 114; effect of Second World War, 116; clubs and societies after Second World War, 121; use of 'Osmaniya' script, 123; Somaliland National League founded, 134; feeling in 1949, 138; protests against transfer of Haud to Ethiopia, formation of National United Front, campaign for return of Haud, 151–8; in Somalia, 140–8, 155–60; and tribalism, 166–9, 221–2, and Scientific Socialism, 209–13, 219–20, 224–5; literacy campaign, 216; Somali unification, 157–8, 161–2, 178–83, 202–3, 227, 233, 236, 242, 247
National Security Courts, 212, 213
National Security Service, 212, 213
Nkrumah, Dr., 197, 198

Nomads, 3, 7–12, 102, 214, 216–17, 217–19

Obbia, Sultanate of, 73, 87, 99
Ogaden, plain of, 3; region of, Somali clans move into, 24; claimed by Abyssinia, 51; Italian sphere of influence, 56; Sayyid Muhammad returns to, 71; 80; Italian policy in, 108, 109; returned to Ethiopian control, 130, 131; and Somali unification, 179, 196, 197, 198, 201, 227, 228; Ogaden War, 1977, 213–41; position of Ogaden clan in Ethiopia, 248–9
Oman, 37, 38
'Omar Samatar, 100, 108, 109
Orma, Galla clan, 184
Organisation of African Unity, 203, 226–8, 234, 237, 250
Oromo, people, 4, 12, 19–24, 27–30, 31–2, 184, 191, 232, 233, 235, 237, 244, 248, 252
Osmaniya script, 115, 123, 216

Pan-Africanism, 195–9
Persians, 7; arrival of, 21, 22
Plague, bubonic, 94; of locusts, 102; 133
Pokomo, tribe, 184, 191
Political Parties (see also Somali Youth Club, Somali Youth League). Christian Democrats (Italian) 121; Greater Somalia League, formed, 158; contests election, 159; Hawiye Youth League, 147; Hizbia Dastur Mustaqil Somali, 156; Hizbia Digil-Mirifle Somali (originally Patriotic Benefit Union), 123; evidence to Four Power Commission, 127; seats in Legislative Assembly, 146; Member assassinated, 147, 148; Isaqiya Association, 134; Liberal Party, 159; Marehan Union, 146; National Pan-Somali Movement, 155; National United Front, campaign for return of Haud to British Administration, 151–3; Progressive Majerteyn League, splinter from S.Y.L., 125; 'Somalia Conference', 127; Somali Democratic Party, 146; Somali Democratic Union, attempts amalgamation of G.S.I. S.N.L. U.S.P.

and H.D.M.S., 175; Somaliland National League, 134, 150–5, 162, 164; Somali National Congress, 176; United Somali Party, 154, 162, 164; S.N.C. decline, 202; parties abolished, 207; Somali Socialist Revolutionary Party, 219; in French Somaliland: *Ligue populaire Africaine pour l'Independence,* 228–9; *Front de la Côte des Somalis,* 228–30; *Rassemblement populaire pour l'Independence,* 230

Population, of Somaliland, 1–4, 6, 7
Portuguese, 21, 26
Protectorate Advisory Council, 134

Qabradare, 152, 181
Qadiriya, Muslim Order, 64, 65, 79, 84, 85
Quran, 15, 65, 220

Rahanweyn, tribe, 5, 7, 12, 13, 123, 125, 147, 159
Railways, 59, 91, 91, 96, 229, 231
Ras Makonnen, 50, 56–9
Rendille, tribe, 184
Reserved Areas, 124, 131
Ribi (Wa-Ribi), 19
Robecchi-Bricchetti, Italian explorer, 52
Rodd, Rennell, 56–61

Sa'd ad-Din, Sultan of Ifat, 25
Sab (Digil and Rahanweyn), 6, 14, 15
Sab, hunters and metal workers, 60, 156
Saho, tribe, 4
Salihiya, Muslim Order, 66
Salisbury, Lord, 42, 61
Salole, Aden Somali family, 127
Sandys, Duncan, 192
Sapeto, Guiseppe, 41
Saudi Arabia, 213, 234, 239
Sayyid Muhammad 'Abdille Hassan, 52, 53, 65–8, 70, 71, 72–4, 75, 78, 79, 80–4, 224, 231
Sayyid Muhammad al-Barr, 33
Sayyid Muhammad Salih, Muslim teacher at Mecca, 66, 75; 84
Scientific Socialism, 209, 210, 213, 214–16, 219–20, 223–5
Senusi, Muslim Order, 48
Shebelle, valley and river, 3, 6; Italian colonies along, 92, 93
Sheikhs, as holy men, 15

Sheikh 'Abdallah Sheikh Muhammad, 123
Sheikh 'Abd ar-Rahman Seyla 'i, 64
Sheikh 'Ali Jumaleh, 172, 176
Sheikh 'Ali Maye Durogba, 86
Sheikh Maddar, 65, 66, 132
Sheikh Uways Muhammad, of Brava, 86
Sheikh Isma'il Sheikh Isaq, 79, 80
Shidle, tribe, 7, 94
Shihab ad-Din, 26
Shirmarke 'Ali Salih, Somali Haji, 33, 34, 35, 36
Slaves, former, 7, 19; objections to abolition, 86
Societa Agricola Italo-Somala, 93, 94; 117; 143
Somali Abo Liberation Front, 235
Somali National Society, 114
Somali Officials Union, 114
Somali-Orma (Galla) agreement, 31
Somali Republic, internal politics: formed, 164; constitutional referendum, 172; military coup fails, 173; discontent in north, 175; ministerial investigation, 176; municipal and national elections (1964), 201; presidential elections (1967), 202; national election (1969), 204; military *coup,* 206; Supreme Revolutionary Council established, 207; Somali Socialist Revolutionary Party established, 219; external relations: with Britain, 183–95, 203, 237; with Chinese People's Republic, 200, 242, 244; with Cuba, 227, 236; with Ethiopia, 183, 185, 201, 203, 227–8, 231–41; with Kenya, 227, 234, 237, 243; with other African countries, 196, 226–7, 237, 250–2; with USSR, 142, 171, 175, 201, 203, 233–6; with Arab world, 234, 238, 239, 242; with the West, 200, 237, 243; isolation of, 199, 243, 250–2.
Somali Youth Club – Somali Youth League, 121, 122, 123, 125, 126, 127, 129–31, 134, 135, 140, 146, 147, 150–4, 159, 160, 161, 177, 201, 204–5
Somalis, 1; general, 4–7; religion, culture and social institutions, 7–12, 15–16; first migrations of, 22–4; effects of expansion of, 32; position of under Italians, 110–12

Sorghum, 2–4, 12; 102
Sorrentino, Giorgio, 53
Speke, Lieutenant, 36
Sultans, 9, 10
Sultan 'Abd ar-Rahman 'Ali 'Ise, 98
Sultan Ahmad Abu Bakr, 98
Sultan 'Ali Mirreh, Ethiopian 'Afar leader, 229, 230
Sultan Yusuf 'Ali Kenadid, of Obbia, 51, 73, 99
Sufi and Sufism, 63
Supreme Revolutionary Council, 207, 213–14, 216, 220–2, 223

Tajura, 45
Tana, river, 5, 31, 184; lake, 109
Tittoni, Tommaso, Italian Minister, 74
Tol system, 10
Trade Unions, 114
'Tribalism', 166–9, 221–2
Turks, 26, 27, 78

Ucciali, Treaty of, 45, 56
United Arab Republic (see also Egypt), 142, 160, 165, 173, 199
United Nations, 128, 129, 130, 139, 140, 144, 162, 165, 167, 182
USSR, 128, 142, 171, 175, 201, 203, 209, 218, 219, 233–7, 240
USA, 128, 142, 175, 234, 237, 240
Usted 'Isman Muhammad Husseyn, 147, 148

Vecchi, De, Italian Governor, 95, 96, 99
Victory Pioneers, 211
Villagio duca degli Abruzzi (Jowhar), 93, 95, 96, 97, 117

Wajir, Kenyan Somali District, 30, 183, 186
Wako Gutu, Oromo resistance leader, 232
Walsh, L. Prendergast, British Vice-Consul, 47, 48
Wälashma', Muslim dynasty, 25
Walwal, 62, 90, 101, 107–10
Warsangeli, 'Darod' clan family, 6, 73, 74, 135
Warsheikh, port of, 51
Water, 9, 96, 104, 149, 172
Welfare scheme, 132
Western Somali Liberation Front, 232–7, 242–3, 244
Wingate, General Sir Reginald, Governor-General of Sudan, 75
Women, 8, 158, 178
World Bank Mission, 143, 114

Yasin Haji 'Isman Shirmarke, 121
Yemen, South, 238, 241
Yeshaq, Abyssinian Negus, 25

Zanj, people, 19–22, 24, 29
Zanzibar, 19, 37–9, 51, 52, 74
Zeila, port, of, 21, 25, 33, 34, 42, 49, 91, 103, 124, 133